Purich's Aboriginal Issues Series

ABORIGINAL SELF-GOVERNMENT IN CANADA

CURRENT TRENDS AND ISSUES

Edited by John H. Hylton

Purich Publishing
Saskatoon, Saskatchewan
Canada

PUBLISHER'S NOTE

Aboriginal self-government is a reality in Canada. This book outlines what has already occurred to make it operational and major issues that have yet to be addressed. The book arises out of a happy series of coincidences. Shortly after I decided to leave my position as director of the University of Saskatchewan Native Law Centre, I had occasion to speak to John Hylton regarding other business. I told him I was going into publishing and over coffee we discussed the need for more published work that would deal with the practicalities that have to be faced as self-government becomes operational. This book arises from that discussion. I am proud to offer it to readers as I believe it fills an important gap in explaining the complex issues that need to be addressed.

This is the third in our Aboriginal Issues Series, a series whose goal is to help foster understanding of the aspirations of Aboriginal Peoples. The first two titles were *Indigenous Peoples of the World: An Introduction to the Past, Present, and Future* and *The Cypress Hills: The Land and Its People.*

In addition, readers who want to do further reading on the subject of self-government and justice for First Nations' Peoples should look at our title *Continuing Poundmaker and Riel's Quest: Presentations Made at a Conference on Aboriginal Peoples and Justice.* Co-published with the University of Saskatchewan College of Law and based on a conference sponsored by the College, this book deals with all aspects of Aboriginal Peoples and justice. Topics covered include Aboriginal viewpoints of justice, how treaties give First Nations their own justice systems, how self-government can be financed and coexist with existing governments, problems with circuit courts, why cultural awareness programs for justice workers have failed, what police forces are doing to serve Aboriginal Peoples, and more. Over half the fifty contributors were Aboriginal political leaders, lawyers, judges, and professors.

DONALD PURICH, PUBLISHER

Continuing Poundmaker and Riel's Quest, 1994, 464 pages $39.00
The Cypress Hills, 1994, 136 pages, includes maps and photographs $16.50
Indigenous Peoples of the World, 1993, 80 pages, includes maps $15.50
Law, Agriculture and the Farm Crisis, 1992, 160 pages $23.00
All titles include indexes.

Mail orders: add $3.00 shipping & handling for the first title and 50¢ for each additional title. Canadian orders, unless exempt, must also add 7% GST (our registration # 133216069) to the total order.

Purich Publishing
Box 23032, Market Mall Postal Outlet
Saskatoon, SK, Canada, S7J 5H3
Facsimile: (306) 373–5315; telephone: (306) 373–5311

ACKNOWLEDGMENTS

This project required many helpers. I am grateful to the Royal Commission on Aboriginal Peoples for sowing the seeds for this volume. After attending a symposium to discuss the Commission's research program in 1992, I was persuaded that there was a need to make available the type of practical materials that have been gathered together in this volume. This event also served as a vivid reminder of the extensive expertise on self-government that is now available across the country.

Perhaps more than anything, it was the desire to bring about a collaboration between experts from many different fields, all of whom had an interest in self-government, that motivated me to take on this project. Without the participation of the contributors to this volume, this project would never have advanced past the idea stage.

I would also like to acknowledge the extraordinary assistance that I received from the publisher. Don Purich's extensive background in the field allowed him to be much more than a publisher. His advice throughout the project was very much appreciated.

I am grateful to the staff and volunteers of the Canadian Mental Health Association. They assisted me during a time when there were also many other priorities.

Finally, I owe a debt of thanks to my family—Janet, Sara, Annie, and my parents—for their support throughout this project.

94 95 96 97 5 4 3 2 1

Purich Publishing
P.O. Box 23032, Market Mall Postal Outlet
Saskatoon, SK Canada S7J 5H3

Canadian Cataloguing in Publication Data

Main entry under title:

Aboriginal self-government in Canada
    (Purich's aboriginal issues series)
    includes bibliographical references and index.
    ISBN 1–895830–04–4

1. Native peoples - Canada - Politics and government.*
2. Native peoples - Canada - Government relations.*
I. Hylton, John H., 1950– II. Series.

E92.A26 1994   323.1'197071c94–920219–3

Editing, design, and layout by Jane McHughen Publishing Services, Saskatoon

Cover design by Next Communications Inc., Saskatoon

Printed in Canada by Kromar Printing, Winnipeg

Printed on acid-free paper

CONTENTS

PART I. ABORIGINAL SELF-GOVERNMENT
AN INTRODUCTION

PART II. TRENDS IN THE IMPLEMENTATION
OF SELF-GOVERNMENT

PART III. ISSUES AND DEBATES

PART IV. FUTURE PROSPECTS

FOREWORD

ELIJAH HARPER

The treatment of Aboriginal people in this country by successive federal governments has been a national disgrace; however, the events of June 1990 changed forever the relationship between the Aboriginal Peoples and the governments of this country. After more than a century of being marginalized, Aboriginal people united and forced the federal government to take notice of the Aboriginal reality in Canada.

As a participant in the failed constitutional conferences on Aboriginal issues ending just weeks before the Meech Lake Accord was signed in June of 1987, I witnessed firsthand how little significance was given to our legitimate demands. It was not surprising to me, or to many other Aboriginal leaders, that we were entirely left out of the Meech Lake Accord. Aboriginal Peoples were not even considered one of the founding partners of the constitutional package.

The three years after the Accord was signed were years in which our concerns were once again shuffled to the side, when they were acknowledged at all. When we collectively spoke against the ratification of the Accord in June 1990, we were speaking out not just against the details of that package. We were also speaking about the unsatisfactory relations with Canadian governments that we had tolerated for more than a hundred and thirty years.

In that one month, Aboriginal people became a force to be reckoned with in this country. Canadians finally discovered that the Aboriginal Peoples of this country are living in third-world conditions. For many, the discovery was shocking. They also learned that Aboriginal Peoples have many strong and capable leaders—Ovide Mercredi, Phil Fontaine, Billy Diamond, and many others.

Since Meech Lake, there has been an explosion of commissions, studies, inquiries, and books on the conditions facing Aboriginal people in this country. This book is part of that important process. Unlike most, however, it is a landmark, in that distinguished contributors have each brought forward constructive suggestions for putting Aboriginal self-government into place.

The post-confederation history of Aboriginal Peoples in Canada has not been a glorious one. Aboriginal Peoples were denied their religion and forced into residential schools. They saw their land and resources forcibly taken away. Discrimination was openly practiced for decades. The tragic results were evident to anyone who cared to look, but few bothered. We were relegated to being second-class citizens in our own country. Until 1960, Aboriginal Canadians were not even allowed to vote.

Gradually the residential schools were phased out, and the federal government began giving up some minor control over our lives. However, the fact remains that, even now, the Aboriginal Peoples are under the control of the Department of Indian Affairs, unable to make many decisions. But the current system has now been discredited by virtually everyone.

The Department of Indian Affairs has been a massive failure. It has not resulted in the assimilation of the Aboriginal Peoples, nor has it resulted in our becoming a part of the mainstream society. Instead of working with the Aboriginal Peoples, it has acted as an agent of the federal government, attempting to assimilate and control the Aboriginal Peoples.

Until June of 1990, Aboriginal self-government was an unknown concept in this country. In the past three years, however, support has risen dramatically right across the country. There will be no going back on our legitimate demands for self-government. Never before has there been a greater opportunity to move ahead with implementing Aboriginal self-government.

For hundreds of years Aboriginal Peoples in the area now known as Canada were sovereign and self-sufficient. We are now poised to once again take charge of our lives and destiny.

INTRODUCTION

John H. Hylton, Human Justice and Public Policy Advisor and Canadian Mental Health Association

In the wake of the "no" vote in the October 1992 national referendum, pundits called for a moratorium on attempts to reform the Canadian Constitution. They argued that the Constitution could not be reformed in the current political climate and, besides, governments should be addressing other pressing priorities, notably the economy. In large measure, the pundits got what they asked for.

While there can be little doubt that the citizens of Canada have enjoyed a respite from what had become endless wrangling over the Constitution, the hidden dangers of this de facto moratorium have not been widely recognized. At stake is a desperately needed new deal for Canada's Aboriginal Peoples.

At this writing, nearly two years have elapsed since the referendum on the Constitution. Notwithstanding the establishment of a royal commission on Aboriginal Peoples, formed in 1991, more recent Aboriginal policy initiatives by the federal Liberal government, and the possibility that the constitutional debate will have to be reopened to deal with emerging separatist sentiments in Quebec, there is a real danger that the Aboriginal Peoples will, once again, see attempts to relegate their issues to a place of obscurity on the national agenda. How ironic, since for all the controversy surrounding the Charlottetown Accord, there was political will and strong public support for the proposals relating to the Aboriginal Peoples.

Although the current institutional arrangements affecting the Aboriginal Peoples in this country are costly to maintain, they have not worked very well. Nor are they likely to work in the future. Moreover, the status quo is continuing to breed frustration among the Aboriginal Peoples. This is particularly directed at Canadian governments and Canadian political leaders, but it also dramatically affects the way Aboriginal people think about Canada.

Ignoring the problems or tinkering with solutions, approaches that have characterized Canadian Aboriginal policy for the past one hundred years, cannot possibly bring about the wholesale changes that are needed to recognize the legitimate aspirations of the Aboriginal Peoples to govern their own affairs. On the contrary, these approaches can only breed further contempt.

We live in times when pride in Canada and in its national institutions is being eroded. The many threats to national unity include the emergence of regionalism, cutbacks in funding for long-cherished government programs, widespread unemployment, cynicism about the political leadership of the country, and the apparent inability of governments to work effectively together to confront the pressing problems facing the nation. As a result of these and other trends, there is uncertainty about the future. In this environment, Canada cannot afford continuing conflict with its First Peoples.

There is a better way. It involves the development of parallel social, economic, cultural, and political institutions run by and for the benefit of the Aboriginal Peoples, in other words, self-government. All the available evidence suggests this approach would be far more effective than past and current policies, and it need not be more expensive. Therefore, the implementation of Aboriginal self-government must be a national public policy priority. It should be pursued, both through the constitutional process when it again becomes available and also within the existing constitutional framework.

Although a strong commitment will be needed on the part of all the stakeholders to bring about an effective and just partnership with the Aboriginal Peoples, this book attests to the fact that many exciting programs have already been implemented. Many others are in various stages of initiation. This progress is a testament to the power of goodwill, and to the creativity of both Aboriginal and non-Aboriginal leaders. It is also a testament to the determination of ordinary people who, every day, work in countless ways to open a new chapter in the relations between Canada and the Aboriginal Peoples.

Self-government has been the subject of considerable interest in Canada, particularly over the past decade. Beyond the constitutional process, an extensive literature has emerged (for example, Canada, House of Commons 1983; Little Bear 1984; Boldt et al. 1985; Morse 1985; Bartlett 1986; Long et al. 1988), and the volume of studies on the subject continues to grow (for example, Cassidy and Bish 1989; Hawkes 1989; Cassidy 1991; Hamilton and Sinclair 1991; Boldt 1993; Smith 1993). Moreover, formal research and policy development programs on self-government have now been established within national and provincial Aboriginal organizations, at several universities, and elsewhere. As a result of these developments, there has been much discussion about the meaning of self-government in Canada, and about whether or not self-government is a good idea.

This book is not about defining self-government. Nor is it intended to provide a definitive analysis of the merits of self-government. Rather, it proceeds from a recognition that self-government is already an emerging reality in Canada, and that the momentum to develop new self-governing institutions is building month by month. Therefore, it seeks to provide a practical guide for students and practitioners who are interested in designing and implementing self-government initiatives.

My objective in selecting materials for this volume was to provide a holistic, interdisciplinary perspective on self-government. Therefore, I included contributions from individuals with quite different perspectives on self-government—Aboriginal leaders, government officials, academics, policy analysts, practitioners, and others. In addition, while I relied on the knowledge and experience of Aboriginal experts familiar with traditional Aboriginal beliefs and practices, I also invited contributions from Aboriginal and non-Aboriginal experts grounded in many different disciplines— medicine, law, criminology, social work, sociology, anthropology, geography, psychology, and public administration. By combining these varying perspectives with an analysis of emerging self-government practices in a number of different fields, my hope was to foster an appreciation of the current "state of the art."

This book had a second important objective, however. By demonstrating how self-government is already working, and by pointing out the opportunities that lie ahead, I hope that this volume will help to convince some skeptics that Aboriginal self-government is a public policy option well worth adopting, not only because it is what the Aboriginal Peoples want, but because recognizing the inherent right of Aboriginal Peoples to govern their own affairs also holds great promise for Canada.

* * * * *

The three chapters in part I of this volume are introductory in nature. They are intended to provide a framework for the discussion of self-government trends and issues that is presented in parts II and III. The focus is not on defining self-government. Rather, these chapters point out why self-government is important and necessary in Canada.

In chapter 1, Associate Chief Justice Murray Sinclair, of the Provincial Court of Manitoba, uses an analysis of the justice system to point out that Aboriginal and non-Aboriginal peoples have fundamentally different world views. He demonstrates how it is both ineffective and inappropriate for Euro-Canadian world views, and the systems based on them, to be imposed on the Aboriginal Peoples. Rather, he suggests that the Aboriginal Peoples must be allowed and empowered to "do" for themselves.

In chapter 2, Canada's sad tradition of "doing for" the Aboriginal

Peoples is discussed with particular reference to the social policy sector. In a review of the literature, I catalogue the many failures of the paternalistic approach. A number of evaluations of programs designed and run by and for the Aboriginal Peoples are also discussed. From this analysis, I conclude that self-governing programs show great potential for improving both the efficiency and the effectiveness of social programs for the Aboriginal Peoples.

Chapter 3 provides an international perspective. Professor John Ekstedt, a criminologist from Simon Fraser University, shares his views on the development of self-governing institutions in a number of other countries, particularly Australia. He points out that Indigenous Peoples in many parts of the world, like the Aboriginal Peoples in Canada, are struggling for self-determination. He suggests that Canadian public policy ought to be informed by the experiences in these other countries.

The five chapters in part II describe recent trends in the implementation of Aboriginal self-government in Canada. These chapters detail the rich diversity of self-governing arrangements that have emerged in Canada, particularly over the past decade.

In chapter 4, Professors John O'Neil and Brian Postl of the University of Manitoba examine the implications of Aboriginal self-government for the health and well-being of the Aboriginal Peoples. They point out that the Aboriginal Peoples have experienced an excessive burden of illness, and that the high rates of disease that are still present in many Aboriginal communities are related to long-standing problematic relations between the Aboriginal Peoples and Canada's health care systems. Against this backdrop, a number of Aboriginal initiatives that have had a positive effect on Aboriginal health are discussed. In the long term, the authors believe self-government will result in improved community well-being because it will support the healing process in Aboriginal communities, and foster more culturally appropriate and effective health care and prevention programs.

Education is the focus of chapter 5. Eber Hampton and Steven Wolfson of the Saskatchewan Indian Federated College examine a number of different models for the provision of post-secondary education for the Aboriginal Peoples of Canada. They argue that there are important differences between "education for assimilation" and "education for self-determination." While Canadian approaches to Aboriginal education have been based on a desire to assimilate the Aboriginal Peoples, the authors argue that Canada can meet its obligations to the Aboriginal Peoples by supporting an independent Aboriginal post-secondary education system.

The focus of chapter 6 is on the criminal justice system. Citing extensive field work in Quebec and the Yukon, Carol La Prairie of the federal Department of Justice outlines problems with current approaches to the delivery of justice services in Aboriginal communities, and outlines a number of proposals for developing more effective and appropriate services. A major portion of her analysis outlines the challenges that will face Aboriginal communities as they exercise self-government in the justice field.

In chapter 7, an existing government program—Pathways to Success—is described and analyzed by Tina Eberts of Human Resources Development Canada. Pathways is a training and employment initiative that puts significant decision-making authority into the hands of Aboriginal Peoples. While Aboriginal decision-making is restricted to administrative matters within a program that is centrally defined by the federal government, Pathways provides a useful example of the kind of reform efforts that can be undertaken within existing government legislation and mandates.

Together, the chapters in part II indicate that considerable progress is already being made toward the implementation of Aboriginal self-government in Canada. While the progress is not even in all parts of the country, or in all sectors, the fact remains that Aboriginal Peoples in Canada are increasingly self-governing.

A number of common themes introduced in part I are reinforced in the discussions about the emerging practice of self-government in part II:

1. The importance of a "bottom-up," community-based approach to designing programs;
2. The problems of implementing programs in a "top-down" manner, especially when the programs are not based on Aboriginal values and belief systems;
3. The importance of adapting programs to local community circumstances so that they are not simply transplanted from other communities, even other Aboriginal communities;
4. The value of examining how traditional Aboriginal practices and customs can be adapted to meet contemporary realities in Aboriginal communities;
5. The danger that existing approaches that have not worked very well in the dominant society will simply be replicated in Aboriginal communities, especially if the time and resources available for planning are restricted;
6. The importance of integrative, holistic approaches to meet individual and community needs—approaches that break down the artificial

barriers that exist in current programs that are often narrowly conceived; and

7. The need to invest in and develop human and other capital in Aboriginal communities so that the capacity of Aboriginal communities to be self-governing can be enhanced.

Although there has been considerable progress in implementing Aboriginal self-government in Canada, there are many important issues that have not yet been fully resolved. A number of these issues are discussed in part III.

In chapter 8, Allan Maslove and Carolyn Dittburner of the School of Public Administration at Carleton University discuss the financing of Aboriginal self-government. Drawing on an examination of existing self-government agreements, they present various options for transferring funds from Canadian governments to Aboriginal communities, as well as some of the opportunities available to Aboriginal communities to "self-finance." Finally, the authors discuss the implications for community-based governments of taking on greater responsibilities for financial administration. The authors conclude that financing arrangements consistent with the principles of self-determination are important for ensuring the success of self-government.

In chapter 9, Professor Evelyn Peters of Queen's University discusses the geographies of self-government. The spatial arrangements embodied in self-government agreements, Peters argues, affect public perceptions of the Aboriginal Peoples, the maintenance of Aboriginal cultures, and the administrative efficiency of Aboriginal governments. Peters finds, however, that spatial issues have been largely ignored, and she appeals for more research on spatial questions that is grounded in Aboriginal perspectives and beliefs.

The focus in chapter 10 is on the implications of Aboriginal self-government for Aboriginal women. Professor Margaret Jackson of Simon Fraser University reviews recent legal history, as well as the positions taken by Aboriginal women on a variety of self-government issues. She points out that, at this stage in the process of implementing self-government, many Aboriginal women are uncertain what a return to traditional forms of Aboriginal governance will mean for the rights of Aboriginal women. For this reason, leaders in the Aboriginal women's movement advocate different paths and different paces of reform. An analysis of possible future policy directions is also presented.

In chapter 11, Clem Chartier, a nationally and internationally recognized Métis leader, discusses the implications of Aboriginal self-government for the Métis Nation. He catalogues the long history of challenges that have faced the Métis, discusses the positions taken by the Métis in constitutional negotiations, and analyzes possible future directions for Métis self-government in Canada. He points out that while the Métis have faced many obstacles, there is a strong resolve within the Métis Nation to proceed with reforms based on the right to self-determination.

In the final chapter of part III, J. W. Berry and M. Wells of the Psychology Department at Queen's University discuss public attitudes toward Aboriginal Peoples and Aboriginal self-government. They argue that these attitudes are important because they can facilitate or inhibit the progress toward self-government. The authors conclude that while there are many factors to be considered in the movement toward self-government, both Aboriginal and non-Aboriginal leaders should not forget the importance of informing the attitudes of the larger society.

In the concluding chapter, I discuss future prospects for Aboriginal self-government in Canada. While a number of current trends suggest that a new era in Canada's relations with the Aboriginal Peoples may be on the horizon, the analysis also points out that there are significant barriers standing in the way of self-government. Nonetheless, the momentum toward self-government is significant. Therefore, it appears likely that self-governing arrangements will continue to develop, although not at the same pace or in the same way in every part of the country.

Aboriginal self-government should be the public policy choice for Canada. Recognition and support of self-government would go a long way to addressing many historical injustices. In addition, the available evidence suggests that it would result in improved relations between the Aboriginal Peoples and the Canadian state, and make more efficient and effective use of scarce resources for social support and economic development. Therefore, self-government deserves the support of Canadians, not only because it is respectful of Aboriginal rights, but also because it is good for Canada.

REFERENCES

Bartlett, Richard H. 1986. *Subjugation, self-management and self-government of Aboriginal lands and resources in Canada.* Kingston: Queen's University, Institute of Intergovernmental Relations.

Boldt, Menno. 1993. *Surviving as Indians: The challenge of self-government.* Toronto: University of Toronto Press.

Boldt, Menno, J. Anthony Long, and Leroy Little Bear, eds. 1985. *The quest for justice: Aboriginal Peoples and Aboriginal rights.* Toronto: University of Toronto Press.

Canada, House of Commons. 1983. *Indian self-government in Canada*. Ottawa: Minister of Supply and Services Canada.

Cassidy, Frank, ed. 1991. *Aboriginal self-determination*. Lantzville, BC, and Halifax: Oolichan Books and the Institute for Research on Public Policy.

Cassidy, Frank, and Robert L. Bish. 1989. *Indian government: Its meaning in practice*. Lantzville, BC, and Halifax: Oolichan Books and the Institute for Research on Public Policy.

Hamilton, A. C., and M. Sinclair. 1991. *Report of the Aboriginal justice inquiry of Manitoba*. Winnipeg: Government of Manitoba.

Hawkes, David, ed. 1989. *Aboriginal Peoples and government responsibility: Exploring federal and provincial roles*. Ottawa: Carleton University Press.

Little Bear, Leroy, Menno Boldt, and J. Anthony Long, eds. 1984. *Pathways to self-determination: Canadian Indians and the Canadian state*. Toronto: University of Toronto Press.

Little Bear, Leroy, Menno Boldt, and J. Anthony Long, eds. 1988. *Governments in conflict? Provinces and Indian nations in Canada*. Toronto: University of Toronto Press.

Morse, Bradford W., ed. 1985. *Aboriginal Peoples and the law: Indians, Metis and Inuit rights in Canada*. Ottawa: Carleton University Press.

Smith, Dan. 1993. *The seventh fire: The struggle for Aboriginal self government*. Toronto: Key Porter.

PART I

ABORIGINAL SELF-GOVERNMENT: AN INTRODUCTION

CHAPTER 1

ABORIGINAL PEOPLES AND EURO-CANADIANS: TWO WORLD VIEWS[1]

MURRAY SINCLAIR, PROVINCIAL COURT OF MANITOBA

Early in the 1970s, I had the privilege of attending one of the first national conferences of attorneys-general of Canada that addressed Aboriginal justice issues. Since that time there have been many other conferences, as well as studies, task forces, royal commissions, and public inquiries, on the subject. As a result, the fact that the enforcement and administration of law in this country have an adverse impact on Aboriginal people has become well known.[2] It is now clear that Aboriginal people are involuntarily drawn into the criminal justice system in larger numbers than their proportion in the population warrants.

This truth about the criminal justice system holds for many other systems in our society—the child protection system, the welfare system, the juvenile justice system, the unemployment system, the drug and alcohol treatment system, among others. Regrettably, Aboriginal people seem to be overrepresented in all of these.

While the reasons for Aboriginal overrepresentation are important, they are not the main focus of this chapter. Those reasons have already been the subject of much deliberation and are reviewed in several other chapters in this volume. Rather, this chapter addresses an often neglected and misunderstood dimension of the relations between Aboriginal Peoples and Euro-Canadians: the issue of culture. Cultural differences, and the conflicts to which they give rise, are inherent in the systems that are supposedly assisting Aboriginal Peoples. An understanding of these conflicts must form the basis for a new direction in relations with the Aboriginal Peoples of Canada.

In this chapter, I address the question of whether Aboriginal Peoples are being justly treated in current systems and suggest that, given the opportunity, Aboriginal societies would do things very differently. I hope to show that current approaches are based on cultural beliefs and perspectives that are foreign to Aboriginal Peoples, and that the imposition of such approaches can result in treatment that is unfair, unjust, or inappropriate.

19

While most of the examples I use to illustrate key points are drawn from the justice system, I believe much of what I have to say applies to the other systems I have mentioned as well. Indeed, I believe the perspective I outline here can be applied to any attempts to meet the needs and respect the rights of Aboriginal Peoples in Canada.

THE CURRENT STATE OF AFFAIRS

It is important to understand how our current state of affairs came about, and why it is likely to continue. In the case of the justice system, almost all the studies referred to earlier have come to similar conclusions:

1. The adverse impact of the administration of justice on Aboriginal Peoples has come about because of misdirected and inappropriate government approaches to the use and enforcement of law throughout the history of our country; and
2. There has been a clear unwillingness on the part of Aboriginal people to participate in the justice system in the same way as non-Aboriginal people.

The Commission of Inquiry in Manitoba, of which I was co-commissioner with Associate Chief Justice Hamilton of Manitoba's Court of Queen's Bench, reached several conclusions about this issue:

1. Aboriginal people are often overcharged (that is, they are charged with more and/or more serious offenses than appear warranted);
2. Aboriginal people are less likely than non-Aboriginal people to plea bargain, or to benefit from a negotiated plea;
3. Aboriginal people are less likely than non-Aboriginal people to contest their charges;
4. Aboriginal people are often unrepresented or underrepresented in court. They are usually unable to afford their own counsel. In addition, however, they are also more often charged with summary conviction offenses. For resource reasons, our legal aid plans are unwilling or unable to provide or pay for legal assistance in these cases;
5. Even when they do have counsel, Aboriginal accused see their lawyers less often than non-Aboriginal accused and for shorter periods of time;
6. Aboriginal people are more likely than non-Aboriginal people to plead guilty, even in instances when they are not guilty, or when they do not believe they are guilty;
7. Aboriginal people are more likely than non-Aboriginal people to be

incarcerated upon conviction (although on average, they receive shorter sentences); and

8. Aboriginal people are more likely than non-Aboriginal people to leave the legal process without understanding what has happened to them and, therefore, without respect for the system.

There is an interesting twist to Aboriginal overinvolvement in the criminal justice and child welfare systems. Aboriginal people are underrepresented in the civil and family law systems. Those who are critical of a tendency in our society to be overly litigious may say this is not a problem. Although I agree we must all be concerned about a society where we try to pass laws to deal with every social or political question, or where we see it as the function of the courts to provide solutions to a myriad of issues, there is, nevertheless, an important message in the statistics. Given the choice, Aboriginal people do not engage the Canadian justice system.

The unwillingness of Aboriginal people to voluntarily engage the available institutions of society designed to resolve serious problems has a number of consequences. It is, for example, a sure sign that many problems are going unresolved. Certainly all the recent studies into conditions in Aboriginal communities suggest that there are a multitude of problems that cry out for resolution.

What lies behind this reluctance to use Euro-Canadian institutions? The reasons are multifaceted; however, two may be mentioned here. Aboriginal people have had a long and often bitter relationship with the Euro-Canadian justice system, and they have come to question whether it is just, fair, or effective. Thus, they do not see it as a resource in the way non-Aboriginal people often do. In addition, for reasons that will be discussed more fully below, Aboriginal people tend to seek non-adversarial methods of resolving their problems. Going to court to resolve a dispute just does not fit into Aboriginal thinking. The very premises upon which the system is based do not accord with Aboriginal values and culture.

I must emphasize again that the justice system is by no means unique in this regard. I believe that the same pattern of involvement and non-involvement is evident in many other systems, and that the reasons for these patterns are virtually identical.

ARE WE ASKING THE RIGHT QUESTIONS?

Many times I have heard non-Aboriginal people ask: "What is it about Aboriginal people that causes them to behave like that?" Such a question clearly suggests that "the problem" lies with the Aboriginal person or community. Almost inevitably, that type of question leads to the conclusion that the Aboriginal person or community must change to fit in better with the standards of conduct that are expected in Euro-Canadian society.

Consistent with the way the question has been asked, almost all past efforts at addressing Aboriginal–Euro-Canadian relations have centered on changing Aboriginal people and not on changing the policies and programs of the Euro-Canadian state. In the justice system, for example, reforms have centered on informing or educating Aboriginal people about the justice system, on finding ways to help them access current programs, or on finding ways to help them find their way through the system. Establishing and funding Aboriginal court worker and Aboriginal paralegal programs, printing more or better information kits with an Aboriginal focus, making more or better audio- and videotapes in Aboriginal languages about how courts and laws work, establishing Aboriginal law student programs, hiring more court staff with the ability to speak Aboriginal languages, and appointing more Aboriginal judges, all find their justification in this type of thinking.

There has been no attempt at fundamental reform of current systems. Why not? Perhaps it is because the non-Aboriginal people who are in control of Euro-Canadian systems do not see the problem as lying within these systems. The time is long overdue, however, when we have to begin to question whether at least some of the problem lies in the way that we currently "do business." Perhaps it is time that questions about patterns of Aboriginal involvement and non-involvement in these systems be restated. Maybe we should be asking: What is it about current approaches that Aboriginal people find so alienating? And maybe those of us working in these systems should ask ourselves: What can be done to change current approaches so that they are perceived by Aboriginal people to be more relevant to their values and circumstances?

DIFFERENCES AND SIMILARITIES

The starting point for an analysis of current relations between Aboriginal people and the systems of the dominant society will be difficult for those raised on the liberal ideals of "civil rights" and "equality." This starting point requires an acceptance that being Aboriginal and being non-Aboriginal involve being different. It requires a recognition that Aboriginal belief systems, world views, and life philosophies are so fundamentally different from those of the dominant Euro-Canadian society that they are inherently in conflict. It requires an acknowledgment that Aboriginal cultures are still a vibrant force in many Aboriginal communities, that they have withstood all attempts at extinguishment, and that their influence will not only continue unabated, but likely will grow in the future.

I do not wish to suggest that all Aboriginal Peoples adhere to a single life philosophy, religious belief, or moral code. They do not.[3] There have always been dissenting and non-conformist individuals and groups within Aboriginal societies, as there have been in all other known societies. Nor do I wish to suggest that all the beliefs and values of Aboriginal Peoples are in conflict with those of other groups. This is certainly not the case. There are areas of thought and belief that are substantially shared by both Aboriginal people and Euro-Canadians. Nevertheless, the differences that do exist are important. So much so, that many Euro-Canadian institutions are incompatible with the moral and ethical value systems of Aboriginal Canadians.

At a fundamental level, the differences between Aboriginal and Western traditions are rooted in the perception of one's relationship with the Creator. I am not a biblical scholar, but as I have come to understand the Judeo-Christian tradition, human beings occupy a position just below God and the angels, but above all other earthly creation. Christian belief holds that God created people last, on the sixth day, as the culmination of creation, and gave them dominion over the earth. According to Genesis, God said: "Let us make man in our image and likeness to rule the fish in the sea, the birds of heaven, the cattle, all wild animals on earth, and all reptiles that crawl upon the earth." People were told to "fill the earth and subdue it, rule over the fish in the sea, the birds of heaven, and every living thing that moves upon the earth."

In sharp contrast, the Aboriginal world view holds that human beings are the least powerful and least important element in creation. They cannot influence events, and are disrespectful and unrealistic if they try. Human interests are not to be placed above those of any other part of creation. Regarding the relative hierarchy and importance of beings in creation, therefore, Aboriginal and Western traditions are diametrically opposed.

It goes without saying that one's world view provides the basis for customs, thoughts, and behavior. Each person's understanding of humanity's place in creation, and the behavior appropriate to that place, pervades and shapes all aspects of his or her life. To understand that idea, I ask you to think for a moment about how Canadians learn what it means to be Canadian. In much the same way, one must try to appreciate that there are many ways that an Aboriginal person learns about what it means to be Aboriginal.

Appropriate conduct in Aboriginal societies was assured through the transmission of values—the teaching of proper thought and behavior— from one generation to the next. Moral, ethical, and juridical principles were taught by example. Individuals who lived in accordance with tribal principles were esteemed and honored as living role models. In addition, examples of proper conduct were drawn from the lives of people no longer living, and from fictitious heroes and heroines who were considered worth emulating.

The elders in a tribe were the vital link with the past. They not only played an important role in the teaching of correct conduct to younger generations, but they were repositories of knowledge about how to behave suitably and honorably in every situation. Their personal memories of the recent past, and the information about the more distant past that they had gleaned from their own teachers, were the basis for the unwritten code of conduct for Aboriginal people. The memories and wisdom of the elders constituted the precedents for Aboriginal customary law and the means for interpreting customary law in a manner suitable to particular circumstances. Aboriginal elders are still revered in many communities for their role in these areas.

When I was growing up, at the direction of my Catholic grandmother, I attended the Catholic church and public schools. Many people of my generation, and of my parents' generation, did so because that was the law, and had been the law since as early as the nineteenth century. With the repeal of prohibitions on expressions of Native culture in the 1950s, however, more and more of us were exposed, some for the first time, to the teachings of traditional elders. These elders were able to explain why our parents and grandparents, even though they may have adopted aspects of Christian beliefs, still viewed things differently from other members of Canadian society.

Through attendance at traditional gatherings such as sun dances, feasts, giveaways, namings, weddings, fastings, and Midewiwin lodge meetings, we were able to learn from our elders about the underlying values and approaches of our tribe. We were taught, among other things, that the values of the people are taught not only in direct ways, such as through the correcting of children, but also in more subtle ways, such as through language itself.

Elders have taught me about the seven traditional values of my people—bravery, honesty, humility, love, respect, truth, and wisdom. Later, I came to understand that the core cultural beliefs of other Aboriginal Peoples bear close resemblance to these basic values. Among the Dakota people, for example, values include conformity with the group and harmony within it, taking responsibility for the here-and-now, the development of the ability to make personal decisions, control over emotions, reverence for nature even while using it, and constant awareness of the Creator. The four great virtues taught in their sun dance are bravery, generosity, fortitude, and integrity. Similarly, Apache beliefs and values have been stated as respect for the autonomy of the individual, non-interference, desire for harmony in interpersonal relations, respect for individual freedom, cooperation, and sharing. The basic values of the Cheyenne people include respect for the spirit world, desire for harmony and well-being in interpersonal relationships, desire for harmony and balance with nature, bravery and mastery of self, generosity, sharing and cooperation, individual freedom and autonomy consistent with cooperation and collective well-being, and humility and respect in all relationships.

Most Aboriginal societies value the interrelated principles of individual autonomy and freedom, so long as their exercise is consistent with the preservation of relationships and community harmony. Other values include respect for other human (and non-human) beings, reluctance to criticize or interfere with others, and avoidance of confrontation. As will be discussed more fully below, when the dominant society's justice system is applied to Aboriginal individuals and communities, many of its principles are clearly at odds with the life philosophies that govern the behavior of Aboriginal people.

None of the values referred to above would be found unacceptable or inappropriate by Canadian society. Indeed, the same or similar values exist within most of the world's cultural traditions. However, Euro-Canadian society has developed conventions that allow these ethical and moral values to be separated, at least temporarily, from everyday life. Aboriginal North American cultures have not done so. For example, a member of the dominant society can plead not guilty to a charge for which he or she is, in fact, responsible. In the Western tradition, the plea is not seen as dishonest, rather, it is understood as a conventional response to an accusation and is based on the doctrine that people are innocent until proven guilty. It is justified by the principle that a person should not be required to incriminate him- or herself, and on the practice of requiring the prosecution to prove guilt beyond a reasonable doubt in open court. In Aboriginal cultures, however, to deny a true allegation is seen as dishonest. Such a denial would be a repudiation of a fundamental, highly valued, though silent, standard of behavior.

WHAT IS JUSTICE?

Differences in Aboriginal and Euro-Canadian world views pervade every aspect of life and living. These world views are not theoretical constructs that have no application in everyday life. On the contrary, they are the basis for what is valued in life, and for beliefs about how life goals are attained. Differences in world views, therefore, cannot be separated from ideas about "truth," "law," or "justice." In this section, the importance of world views is illustrated by comparing and contrasting Aboriginal and Euro-Canadian ideas about "justice"—what it is and how it is attained.

1. THE MEANING OF JUSTICE

The concept of justice itself is perceived differently in Aboriginal and Euro-Canadian traditions. In the dominant society, deviant behavior that potentially or actually harms society, individuals, or perpetrators is considered a wrong that must be controlled by interdiction, enforcement, and correction. It must be punished and deterred. It is believed that the punishment of the deviant will exact conformity to socially acceptable forms of behavior, and protect other members of society.

The Canadian justice system frequently deals with people who misbehave by removing them from society for a period of time. It is widely accepted that after completion of the sentence, the offender has "paid the price" and should then be seen as having atoned to society for what he or she has done. The principle of restitution to the victim, and the idea of reconciliation between the offender and the community, do not mark the manner in which the accused is dealt with at any point in the process. While these notions may be referred to, they are not accorded much importance. Institutionalized support for victims is rarely and only minimally offered. Restitution is ordered generally as a form of financial compensation, and usually only if the offender has financial resources.

Nor is rehabilitation a primary aim when dealing with an offender in the Canadian justice system, with the possible exception of very young offenders. It is only one of several factors that judges take into account in sentencing, and it is often undermined by the fact that there is a considerable lack of public support for it. Thus, retribution is often the primary thrust of action taken against those who offend against public standards of conduct.

In Aboriginal societies, the meaning of justice and the methods of attaining it have always been quite different. Justice involves restoring peace and equilibrium to the community through reconciling the accused with his or her own conscience and with the individual or family that has been wronged. Aboriginal cultures approach problems of deviance and non-conformity in a non-judgmental manner, and with a strong preference for non-interference, reconciliation, and restitution. The principle of non-interference is consistent with the importance Aboriginal cultures accord to the autonomy and freedom of the individual, and it is based on the desire to avoid relationship-destroying confrontations. Historically, in exceptional circumstances where behavior was dangerous to the collective, smaller populations and larger areas of uninhabited land made it possible for non-conformists to leave the community, either voluntarily or under pressure from the community.[4]

Thus, there is a fundamental difference between Aboriginal and Euro-Canadian approaches to justice. It is a difference that raises important questions about the many ways that the present justice system tries to deal with Aboriginal people in the resolution of their conflicts, in the reconciliation of accused with their communities, and in maintaining community harmony and good order.

The very important implications of these differences can best be illustrated with several examples centering on Aboriginal and Euro-Canadian approaches to "truth," methods of determining truth, sentencing, guilt and innocence, and remorse.

2. THE CONCEPT OF "TRUTH"

"Truth" is one of the foundations of the Euro-Canadian justice system. But Aboriginal people have a very different concept of truth from most Canadians. As the least important creature in the universe, an Aboriginal person is unwilling or unable to insist that his or her version of events is the complete and only true version. On the contrary, the Aboriginal world view holds that truth is relative, and always incomplete. When taken literally, therefore, the standard courtroom oath—to tell the truth, the whole truth, and nothing but the truth—is illogical and meaningless, not only to Aboriginal people, but, from the Aboriginal perspective, to all people.

The Aboriginal perspective requires the individual to speak the truth as he or she understands it, and not to dispute the validity of other versions of the same event or issue. This perspective holds that no one can claim to know the whole truth of any situation completely, and every witness can perceive an event, or understand its significance, differently. Therefore, it is unusual for an Aboriginal witness to assert that another witness is lying or has his or her facts wrong.

Our justice system frowns upon an individual who appears uncertain about his or her evidence. Failing to assert the superiority of one's own evidence over that of another is often seen as uncertainty. Given the Aboriginal world view, where truth is relative, it can readily be seen that it is virtually impossible for an Aboriginal witness to comply with the strictures of the court in the matter of truth-telling.

Accusation and criticism (giving adverse testimony), which are required in the Canadian justice system, are antagonistic to an Aboriginal value system that makes every effort to avoid criticism and confrontation. As Ross (1993) has pointed out, refusal or reluctance to testify, or when testifying, to give anything but the barest and most emotionless recital of events, appears to be the result of deeply rooted cultural behavior in which giving testimony face to face with the accused is simply wrong. In Aboriginal traditions, every effort seems to be made to avoid such direct confrontation. In Aboriginal societies, it may be ethically wrong to say hostile, critical, implicitly angry things about someone in their presence. Yet, this is precisely what our adversarial justice system requires.

Ross (1993) points out that criticism of others is at odds with the highly esteemed Aboriginal values of non-interference, individual autonomy, and individual freedom. Therefore, the idea that guilt and innocence can be decided on the basis of argument is incompatible with a firmly rooted belief system based on honesty, integrity, and prohibitions against lying.

In a system where one's credibility is largely determined by how well one's testimony "stands up" to cross-examination, the Aboriginal view of the relativity of "truth" can give the erroneous impression that the witness is changing his or her testimony. In reality, the Aboriginal witness may be recognizing that another view of the events, no matter how far-fetched or different from his or her own reality, may be valid.

3. METHODS OF DETERMINING "TRUTH"

Because the very concept of "truth" is different in Aboriginal and Western traditions, the methods for determining truth also differ. The Euro-Canadian approach to truth-determination has the following characteristics:

1. The accused has the right to remain silent;
2. The accused's silence cannot be held against him or her;
3. The accused is invariably discouraged by counsel from testifying;
4. Only the victim, or a small number of people, are called to testify;
5. The questions to be responded to are carefully chosen by adversarial counsel;
6. Questions can be asked in ways that dictate their answers; and
7. Certain topics, including very important information about the accused, the accuser, or their families, is deemed "inadmissible" or irrelevant.

In Aboriginal societies, truth-determination proceeds from a belief in the inherent decency and wisdom of each individual. This means that any person might have useful opinions on any given subject and, if he or she wishes to express them, that person should be listened to respectfully. Aboriginal methods of dispute-resolution, therefore, often allow for any person to volunteer an opinion or make a comment. The truth of an incident would be arrived at through hearing many descriptions of the event. Because it is impossible to arrive at "the whole truth," Aboriginal traditions rely on the belief that more of the truth can be determined when everyone is free to contribute information. In such a system, the silence of an accused in the face of a mounting consensus as to what occurred is taken as an acknowledgment that the consensus is correct.

4. SENTENCING

Differences are also evident in the Aboriginal and Euro-Canadian approaches to sentencing. Justice in Aboriginal societies is relationship-centered. As such, approaches to sentencing take into account the consequences of a particular disposition on other individuals and on the community, as well as on the offender. Justice is achieved only when harmony is restored to the community. Therefore, others who have been (or might be) affected by the offense, particularly the victim, have to be considered. In addition, those dependent on the accused, for example, spouses, children, grandparents, grandchildren, aunties, uncles, or cousins, must also be involved, and the impact of the disposition on them must also be considered. Care has to be taken that actions to deal with the offender and the offense do not bring hardship to those individuals.

At the center of the Aboriginal approach is the desire for reparation or restitution. The victim, the community, and the offender must be restored to balance, and a return to harmonious relations must be the result. Generally, this approach calls for the person who has been wronged, whether bereaved or impoverished, to receive some form of restitution. In the Ojibway concept of order, for example, when a person is wronged, it is understood that the wrongdoer must restore order and repair the disharmony of the community by undoing the wrong that has been done, usually by compensating the person wronged. This concept of order makes the individual responsible for the maintenance of harmony within society.

Sentencing the offender to incarceration, or worse still placing him or her on probation without first addressing the issue of reconciliation, would, in the eyes of many Aboriginal communities, be tantamount to completely relieving the offender of any responsibility for repairing the wrong that had been done. These types of dispositions are viewed as an abdication of responsibility and as totally exonerating the wrongdoer. But such is "justice" in the Western sense, at least from the Aboriginal perspective.

This is not to say that punishment of an individual never occurs in Aboriginal traditions. But punishment is likely to occur only if an accused has repeatedly failed to work with the community to restore peace and harmony, and to rehabilitate him- or herself. In contrast, punishment is entrenched in Western criminal justice systems. Retribution is almost always demanded, even if not always given, and it is usually an important basis for determining most dispositions. As Ross (1993) has pointed out, however, retribution as an end in itself, or as an aim of society, is a meaningless notion in an Aboriginal value system that emphasizes reconciliation and restitution.

5. GUILT AND INNOCENCE

In Western approaches, guilt and innocence are decided on the sole basis of the evidence that is considered admissible in court. In turn, what is considered admissible in court is determined by the application of sometimes archaic rules of evidence, and on the basis of the arguments that take place between legal representatives. When an accusation has been made against an individual, legal counsel representing the plaintiff and the defendant confront one another before an impartial judge or jury. Witnesses are called to testify for or against the accused, that is, to criticize the actions of either the accused or another.

The fundamental thrust of the Euro-Canadian justice system is the guilt-determination process. The principle of fairness in determining whether the accused is actually guilty of the crime alleged is fundamental to what judges and courts do. This arises, one may surmise, because Western criminal justice systems developed from a society where wrongdoers were regularly placed in stocks and chains, flogged, whipped, drawn and quartered, or even put to death. All of this took place in public, and for any one of a large number of offenses. In such circumstances, it is understandable that there would be a preoccupation with ensuring that only those who were "truly guilty" of the charges brought against them were subjected to punishment. Thus, the adage: Better a guilty person go free than an innocent one be convicted.

The concepts of guilt and innocence have no equivalent in most Aboriginal societies, and, therefore, there are no equivalent words. In Aboriginal cultures, the guilt of the accused is secondary. The main issue that arises immediately upon an allegation of wrongdoing is that something is wrong and it has to be fixed. If the accused, when confronted, admits the allegation, then the focus of the community's effort is on what needs to be done to repair the damage caused by the misdeed. If the accused denies the allegation, there is still a problem, and the relationship between the parties must still be repaired.

Because determining the truth in Aboriginal traditions is not usually a prelude to punishment, those accused of wrongdoing are more likely to admit to having done something wrong. Perhaps this is one of the reasons why so many Aboriginal people plead guilty in court. Aboriginal individuals who, in fact, have committed the deed with which they are charged are often reluctant or unable to plead "not guilty." To them, such a plea would be a denial of the truth and, therefore, contrary to a basic tenet of their life philosophy. Thus, to deny an allegation that is "known" by all to be true, and to take refuge in the "white man's court," is damaging both to the individual and to the cultural traditions of Aboriginal communities.

6. REMORSE

A final example of the incompatibility of Aboriginal and Western belief systems has to do with remorse. Lawyers, judges, juries, and the public at large expect that those accused of wrongdoing will display remorse. Moreover, offenders are supposed to express a desire for rehabilitation. However, because Aboriginal traditions call for courage in the face of adversity and the fortitude to accept, without protest, what comes to them, Aboriginal accused may react contrary to these expectations. Many years of cultural and social oppression, combined with the high value placed on controlled emotions in the presence of strangers and authority figures, can result in an accused's conduct appearing inappropriate to the plea.

In acknowledging their powerlessness before the Creator, Aboriginal children are often taught to affirm their dependence upon the Creator and upon all of creation. They learn to wait patiently and quietly, in a respectful manner, to receive the mercy of the Creator. Many cultural traditions and ceremonies are imbued with this philosophy. This attitude can easily be carried over into Aboriginal behavior within the justice system. For example, one of the researchers for the Aboriginal Justice Inquiry in Manitoba told us that in his effort to honor those pleading his case, he tries hard to agree to their requests, to give answers that please, and not to argue or appear adversarial. Judges and juries can, therefore, easily misinterpret the words, demeanor, and body language of the Aboriginal individuals that appear before them.

CONCLUSION

The incompatibility between Aboriginal thought and the processes of the Canadian justice system is profound. The Canadian justice system, like other justice systems in the European tradition, is based on the concepts of adversarialism, accusation, confrontation, guilt, argument, criticism, and retribution. These concepts, however, are not in keeping with Aboriginal value systems. Indeed, they are antagonistic to the high value Aboriginal traditions place on harmony and peaceful coexistence among all living beings.

To require a people to act in ways contrary to their most basic beliefs may infringe upon their rights and may result in discriminatory treatment. Witnesses who do not testify directly or who "change their story," complainants who are not vociferous, and accused who show little emotion may find that their actions are misinterpreted by a justice system founded on different cultural beliefs and associated expectations. Responses induced by different cultural traditions can easily be wrongly interpreted—as a failure to tell the truth, as a sign of guilt, as a failure to show remorse, or even as contempt for the court. Hearings that are less than fair and inappropriate sentencing are all too often the result.

Clearly it is time to do something about this state of affairs. Not only must we undertake reforms to existing systems to change the way we "do business" where Aboriginal people are concerned, but we must also undertake reforms that allow and empower Aboriginal people to administer justice for themselves based on their values and beliefs. Moreover, a similar approach needs to be adopted with respect to many other systems as well.

NOTES

1   This paper formed the basis for a presentation to an Aboriginal justice conference that explored the roles and relationships of federal, provincial, and Aboriginal governments. See Gosse, Henderson, and Carter (1994).

2   See, for example, Horn and Griffiths (1989), Royal Commission on the Donald Marshall Junior Prosecution (1989), Hamilton and Sinclair (1991), Task Force on the Criminal Justice System (1991), and Palys (1993). More recently, the Royal Commission on Aboriginal Peoples (1993) has also focused attention on these issues.

3   Of necessity, the discussion is based on generalizations that cannot capture the nuances of the many different Aboriginal cultures in Canada. I believe, however, that these generalizations are neither inappropriate nor unfair. In addition, I want to speak from my own experience and personal knowledge.

4   Some might think that banishment and incarceration have the same objective. However, there is an underlying value of punishment attached to the principle of incarceration that is not associated with the concept of banishment. It is true that during either a period of incarceration or banishment, the accused is prevented from repeating offenses in the community and, at some point, may be allowed back into the community. However, reconciliation and atonement are integral to Aboriginal banishment practices, whereas they are not values fundamental to incarceration.

REFERENCES

Gosse, Richard, James Youngblood Henderson, and Roger Carter, eds. 1994. *Continuing Poundmaker and Riel's quest.* Saskatoon, SK: Purich.

Hamilton, A. C., and M. Sinclair. 1991. *Report of the Aboriginal justice inquiry of Manitoba.* Winnipeg: Government of Manitoba.

Horn, Charles, and Curt T. Griffiths. 1989. *Native North Americans: Crime, conflict, and criminal justice.* 4th ed. Burnaby, BC: The Northern Justice Society.

Palys, Ted S. 1993. *Aboriginal rights, Aboriginal justice, and Aboriginal self-determination: An annotated bibliography.* Burnaby, BC: Simon Fraser University.

Ross, Rupert. 1993. *Dancing with a ghost: Exploring Indian reality.* Markham, ON: Octopus.

Royal Commission on Aboriginal Peoples. 1993. *Aboriginal peoples and the justice system.* Ottawa: Royal Commission on Aboriginal Peoples.

Royal Commission on the Donald Marshall Junior Prosecution. 1989. *Digest of findings and recommendations.* Halifax: Royal Commission on the Donald Marshall Junior Prosecution.

Task Force on the Criminal Justice System. 1991. *Justice on trial: Report of the task force on the criminal justice system and its impact on the Indian and Metis people of Alberta.* Edmonton, AB: Task Force on the Criminal Justice System.

CHAPTER 2

THE CASE FOR ABORIGINAL SELF-GOVERNMENT: A SOCIAL POLICY PERSPECTIVE[1]

JOHN H. HYLTON, HUMAN JUSTICE AND PUBLIC POLICY ADVISOR AND CANADIAN MENTAL HEALTH ASSOCIATION

Many arguments have been advanced in support of Aboriginal self-government. Aboriginal Peoples have made a strong case that they have an inherent right to govern themselves, that this right can be traced to the common law, that it has never been given up, and, consequently, that it remains in effect today. Professor Ekstedt, in a subsequent chapter in this volume, provides another viewpoint. He points out that self-determination and self-government are not issues unique to Canada but, rather, are being actively pursued by Indigenous Peoples in countries throughout the world. In this chapter, I advance an argument in favor of self-government from still another perspective—a practical one.

Let us suppose there was no legal justification for self-government, and that the Aboriginal Peoples in Canada were alone among Indigenous Peoples in seeking to have their rights recognized. Would this mean that self-government had no validity in Canada? I think not. I believe a strong case for self-government can be made based on the results of our country's long and tragic record of "doing for" and "doing to" Aboriginal Peoples.

This chapter makes the case for Aboriginal self-government from the perspective of social policy and human services. It is beyond the scope of this chapter to provide a comprehensive review of the research literature, since such a review could occupy several volumes;[2] however, the chapter does seek to provide a broad overview of the current state of the research literature. While some references have been provided, they are by no means comprehensive. Rather, they are intended to illustrate the types of research studies that have been completed.

I believe the conclusion of the analysis is inescapable. Existing social programs that have been imposed on Aboriginal Peoples by the governments of the dominant society have failed the Aboriginal Peoples and the Canadians who have supported them. Programs run by the Aboriginal

Peoples for themselves, on the other hand, have generally proved to be both more effective and no more costly. Therefore, Canadian public policy ought to support the movement toward Aboriginal self-government.

THE FAILURE OF CANADIAN SOCIAL PROGRAMS

The social policy sector encompasses a wide array of human service programs—health, justice, education, and social service programs to name a few—that are intended to ameliorate social problems such as poverty, unemployment, family disintegration, child abuse, suicide, crime, juvenile delinquency, substance abuse, illiteracy, inadequate child care, and poor housing. There are a number of reasons why the social policy sector needs to be considered when examining the case for self-government:

1. Aboriginal people in Canada are disproportionately affected by the problems that social programs are intended to address;
2. Social programs have a dramatic impact on the quality of life of Aboriginal people in Canada;
3. In delivering social programs, the state exercises broad powers that frequently interfere with the most fundamental rights and freedoms of Aboriginal people;
4. Social programs are very costly to deliver. The "social envelope" represents the largest group of expenditures in the federal budget. At the provincial level, social spending typically makes up about two-thirds of government expenditures;
5. Both Aboriginal and non-Aboriginal Canadians are unhappy and frustrated with the current approach to the delivery of social programs;
6. For the Aboriginal Peoples, their involvement in designing and delivering social programs goes to the heart of their concept of "self-government";
7. There is substantial evidence that more effective and efficient options are available for the delivery of social programs; and
8. The current approach to the delivery of social programs in Canada is well entrenched. Because of a complex web of financial and jurisdictional arrangements, fundamental changes will not occur without a dedicated effort.

Over the past several decades, there have been literally thousands of studies conducted in Canada to answer questions about Aboriginal people and social policy issues. Some questions have been posed so frequently that a considerable body of literature is now available. Some of the more common types of research questions, and the results they have produced, are described below.

1. WHAT IS THE INCIDENCE OF SOCIAL PROBLEMS AMONG ABORIGINAL PEOPLE? HOW DOES THE INCIDENCE RATE COMPARE WITH THAT FOR THE NON-ABORIGINAL POPULATION?

These types of question are among the most common in the literature. They have inspired numerous studies. These studies typically set out to document the extent of social problems among Aboriginal people. Results may be expressed in quantitative or qualitative terms.

Quantitative studies often focus on incidence rates and then compare these rates with the corresponding rates for non-Aboriginals. These analyses often become quite complex. They may take into consideration a number of social, economic, geographic, cultural, historical, and other variables in an attempt to uncover correlates and causes (for numerous examples, see Havemann et al. 1985).

Qualitative studies, on the other hand, usually focus on the subjective experience of Aboriginal persons and communities as they struggle to overcome numerous social problems and to find a place in Canadian society (for example, Cardinal 1969; Dosman 1972; Nagler 1973; Frideres 1974; Ryan 1978; Krotz 1980; Ponting and Gibbins 1980). There has been particular interest in documenting the unhappy life of Aboriginal people when they migrate from Aboriginal communities to Canadian urban centers.

From these studies, we now know that Aboriginal Canadians disproportionately experience virtually every type of social problem imaginable. Furthermore, because of numerous replications of similar studies, we are often able to make statements about the extent of the disproportion. We also know a good deal about the social, demographic, and economic correlates of social problems.

From these quantitative and qualitative studies, it can be said with a good deal of certainty that, relative to non-Aboriginal Canadians, Aboriginal people commit more crimes and delinquencies, experience more mental and physical health problems, experience more family problems, and disproportionately abuse alcohol and drugs. Furthermore, we know that Aboriginal people have a shorter life expectancy, a higher rate of infant mortality, and a higher rate of suicide. We also know that Aboriginal people have lower incomes, less formal education, higher rates of welfare dependency, and higher rates of unemployment. Moreover, we know that Aboriginal people are disproportionately poor, and they experience all the problems associated with poverty—poor nutrition, poor housing, inadequate child care, and the like.

Regrettably, these types of studies often end up "blaming the victim," because they do not provide a context for understanding why rates are disproportionate.

2. WHAT ARE THE PARTICIPATION RATES OF ABORIGINAL PEOPLE IN VARIOUS SOCIAL PROGRAMS? HOW DO THE PARTICIPATION RATES DIFFER FROM THE CORRESPONDING NON-ABORIGINAL RATES?

While this question is similar to the earlier question, answers to this question are usually based on an analysis of caseload information collected by social agencies and government social programs. These studies typically disaggregate the caseload statistics to show the number of Aboriginal and non-Aboriginal clients who have received a type of service. Often these statistics are compared with the composition of the general population to calculate participation rates. These rates are then often used to determine the extent to which the Aboriginal people are overrepresented in various social programs.

A considerable body of knowledge now exists that describes comparative participation rates for Aboriginal people in many different types of programs. These studies consistently show that, relative to the non-Aboriginal population, Aboriginal people are overrepresented in adult correctional programs, hospitals, mental health care facilities, alcohol and drug abuse programs, programs for young offenders, family service programs, income security programs, social housing programs, programs for the unemployed, programs for neglected and abused children, and family violence programs (for example, Hawthorn 1966; Hull 1987; Department of Indian Affairs 1989). About the only instance where overrepresentation does not seem to occur, is when Aboriginal people do not have access to the particular program being studied.

As with the earlier studies, these analyses often do not discuss the historical antecedents that have lead to disproportionate participation rates. Therefore, they may inadvertently "blame the victim."

3. WHAT ARE THE SOCIAL, DEMOGRAPHIC, AND OTHER CHARACTERISTICS OF ABORIGINAL PEOPLE WHO EXPERIENCE SOCIAL PROBLEMS, OR WHO FIND THEMSELVES ON THE CASELOADS OF SOCIAL AGENCIES?

As alluded to earlier, there are a multitude of studies that have addressed this question. Usually analyses are undertaken as a part of larger studies that have also examined incidence or participation rates.

While it is difficult to generalize about the results, these studies have tended to show that the social problems experienced by Aboriginal people have an early onset, and are commonly experienced and deeply rooted in Aboriginal families and communities. These studies also often show that a multitude of closely related problems are often experienced simultaneously.

An example may best serve to illustrate the types of findings that have been reported. Typical adult Aboriginal offenders are often found to have a history of mental health, physical health, substance abuse, and criminal justice problems. They are frequently the product of broken homes, may have been abused, and likely were young offenders. Their parents, siblings, and extended family may all have experienced similar problems. They are often poor, their families are often poor, and their communities are typically impoverished. They are usually lacking in formal education and training, and do not have any significant employment experience. They have sometimes abused their spouse and children. They are often dependent on social assistance and social housing, and usually have participated in a wide variety of other social programs (Hylton 1981a).

4. WHY DO ABORIGINAL PEOPLE DISPROPORTIONATELY EXPERIENCE SOCIAL PROBLEMS? WHY ARE ABORIGINAL PEOPLE DISPROPORTIONATELY REPRESENTED ON THE CASELOADS OF SOCIAL AGENCIES?

These questions have also frequently been the subject of social research. There are two common approaches to answering these questions.

In the first approach, the questions are raised in quantitative studies that analyze incidence and/or participation rates. The researchers collect information about the background of those experiencing problems (social, economic, demographic, and other information) and attempt to determine the factors that are correlated with incidence or with program participation. When correlations do exist, the researchers will then often make assumptions about the temporal sequence of events so that they can make statements about causation.[3]

These studies typically conclude that social problems are the result of unemployment, poverty, substance abuse, or lack of economic opportunity. Recommendations focus on providing Aboriginal people with opportunities to participate more fully in the social and economic life of Canadian society (for numerous examples, see Havemann et al. 1985).

The second approach to answering these questions is very different from the first. It typically does not involve a quantitative approach. Rather, it involves a historical analysis of the social, economic, and political relations between the Aboriginal Peoples and the dominant society, usually as represented by its governments. This type of analysis is often undertaken by Aboriginal leaders and unabashed supporters of Aboriginal self-determination.

These analyses typically focus on the disenfranchisement of the Aboriginal Peoples, and on the successive attempts by governments to extinguish Aboriginal culture and traditions. Importance is accorded to the paternalism of Canadian governments, and to the dependency and lack of self-sufficiency that this has created in Aboriginal communities (for example, Getty and Lussier 1983; Barron 1984; Pettipas 1988; Cole and Chaikin 1990; Carter 1990).

These analyses typically conclude that the abrogation of Aboriginal culture and traditions has brought about the social and economic disintegration of Aboriginal communities. The social problems now evident in these communities, it is argued, are the direct result of this long historical process. Recommendations usually focus on restoring Aboriginal culture and traditions, abolishing the paternalistic relationship between the Aboriginal Peoples and governments of the dominant society, and restoring Aboriginal self-determination.

5. How Effective Are Existing Social Programs in Ameliorating the Social Problems Experienced by Aboriginal People?

Studies have been carried out to determine the effectiveness of many social programs in ameliorating the social problems experienced by Aboriginal people. While there are some studies that have examined how the introduction of a program has affected an entire community, usually the methodology involves following a sample of clients to see whether or not their participation in a given program has produced a desired outcome.

As will be discussed in greater detail later in this chapter, there are encouraging signs that programs designed and delivered by Aboriginal Peoples are more effective in attaining their objectives than are programs designed and delivered by non-Aboriginal people for Aboriginal people. The literature indicates that the latter type of program usually meets with very limited success. While some exceptions can be found, social programs designed and delivered by non-Aboriginals are generally much less effective in achieving their intended outcome with Aboriginal people than they are in achieving their intended outcome with non-Aboriginal people.

For example, relative to the non-Aboriginal population:

1. Adult correctional programs are not as effective in rehabilitating or deterring Aboriginal offenders, and Aboriginal offenders have higher recidivism rates (Hamilton and Sinclair 1991);
2. The same holds true for young offenders (Hamilton and Sinclair 1991);
3. Family service programs are not as effective in preventing the breakdown of Aboriginal families; foster care and adoption placements more often fail (Johnson 1983; Kimmelman 1985);
4. Employment training programs are not as effective in leading to employment (Department of Indian Affairs 1989);
5. Substance abuse programs are not as effective in leading to sobriety (Brody 1971; Hylton et al. 1990);
6. Income security programs are not as effective in insuring that the basic sustenance needs of Aboriginal families are met (Department of Indian Affairs 1989);
7. Social housing programs are not as effective in improving housing conditions (Department of Indian Affairs 1989);
8. Educational programs are not as effective in providing an adequate level of formal education (Barman et al. 1986); and
9. Health programs are not as effective in improving health status (Department of Indian Affairs 1989).

There are many other examples.

The literature also provides a good deal of information about the reasons for the general inability of non-Aboriginal programs to meet the needs of Aboriginal people (for example, Hamilton and Sinclair 1991). The following factors have frequently been identified:

1. Because programs have not been designed with the needs of the Aboriginal people in mind, they frequently provide services that are not relevant or, alternatively, fail to provide services that are needed;
2. Policies, procedures, and expectations associated with non-Aboriginal programs often fail to take into account the unique language, culture, traditions, and current life situation of Aboriginal clients;
3. Because non-Aboriginal programs typically employ non-Aboriginal staff, there is often a knowledge gap, and a corresponding lack of trust, between the non-Aboriginal service providers and the Aboriginal clients;
4. Because Aboriginal communities have had limited or no involvement in designing and delivering the programs, there is typically limited community ownership or support. In some cases, for example, when the

circuit court or the child protection worker comes to town, the community may feel that it has been invaded by a foreign power; and

5. Because non-Aboriginal programs are seldom "resident" in Aboriginal communities, Aboriginal people usually have limited access to them. In addition, there is typically a high turnover rate among the non-Aboriginal, non-resident staff. Therefore, services are not consistently or sensitively provided and there is usually an absence of meaningful follow-up.

In light of these realities, it is not difficult to understand why non-Aboriginal service providers have so often become frustrated that their programs are not more effective.

6. What Is the Subjective Experience of Aboriginal People Who Are Served by Non-Aboriginal Social Programs?

As alluded to above, numerous studies have documented the unhappy experiences of Aboriginal clients who have been served by non-Aboriginal social programs (for example, Ryan 1978; Krotz 1980; Hobbs-Birnie 1990). Results indicate that Aboriginal people feel poorly and insensitively treated by non-Aboriginal personnel who have limited understanding and sympathy for their predicament. Inappropriate expectations, inadequate communication, fear, and mistrust seem to characterize relations.

It is significant that Aboriginal people seldom choose to receive services from non-Aboriginal social programs. Rather, they do so out of necessity, or because the state has compelled their participation. When Aboriginal people have a choice between being served by an Aboriginal or by a non-Aboriginal agency, the data indicate they almost always elect the Aboriginal agency.

7. What Are the Attitudes of Canadians, Social Agency Personnel, and Others Toward the Aboriginal Peoples?

There has been a good deal of public opinion and public attitude research conducted in Canada to determine how Canadians view the Aboriginal Peoples (for example, Gibbins and Ponting 1978; Department of Indian Affairs 1980; Hylton 1981b; Cooke 1984). Studies have also examined the attitudes of program personnel (corrections officers, social workers, the police, etc.) toward the Aboriginal Peoples.

Generally, these studies have found that the community has very limited appreciation for the current circumstances of the Aboriginal Peoples. In fact, studies have often revealed a variety of negative attitudes and racial stereotypes. There is some evidence, however, that as a result of the protracted constitutional discussions, more and more Canadians are becoming sympathetic to the aspirations of the Aboriginal Peoples.[4]

Results of studies involving agency personnel have been cause for particular concern. These studies show that personnel, particularly those involved in the exercise of social control functions (for example, welfare workers, child welfare workers, police, corrections officers, etc.) often harbor very negative racial stereotypes (for example, Hylton 1980).

This section has focused on what is known about the social problems experienced by Aboriginal people and on the difficulties they experience in attempting to receive services from programs that are not designed with them in mind. Generally, there is an extensive research literature, and much is known about these problems.

THE CREATION OF PARALLEL SOCIAL PROGRAMS RUN BY ABORIGINAL PEOPLES FOR THEMSELVES

The failure of non-Aboriginal social programs to effectively meet the needs and aspirations of Aboriginal people has led to a good deal of interest in establishing parallel programs that are run by the Aboriginal Peoples for themselves. As this book attests, there are now numerous examples of parallel Aboriginal social programs in Canada. They include programs in child and family services; justice services (including policing, corrections, and court services); alcohol and drug abuse programs; recreation and community development programs; health care services (including hospitals); educational programming (including secondary and post-secondary educational institutions); child care and day care services; and many others.

While much more needs to be known about the effectiveness and potential of parallel Aboriginal social programs, some evaluative studies have been completed. The results are encouraging. While there are always dangers in generalizing, some common findings are beginning to emerge from these studies (for example, Morse 1980; Social Policy Research Associates 1983; Coopers and Lybrand 1986; Hurd and Hurd 1986; Hudson and Taylor-Henley 1987).

It appears the Aboriginal programs are more successful than the corresponding non-Aboriginal programs in:

1. Incorporating principles, beliefs, and traditions that are a part of Aboriginal culture;

2. Attracting and retaining Aboriginal staff;
3. Involving the Aboriginal community in the design and delivery of programs;
4. Fostering greater acceptance by the individual client and the Aboriginal community;
5. Creating economic benefits for Aboriginal communities;
6. Extending services that were previously unavailable through the non-Aboriginal program;
7. Drawing attention to social issues in Aboriginal communities and generating interest, involvement, and support for social programs in Aboriginal communities;
8. Providing levels of service that approach or equal levels of service available to non-Aboriginal communities;
9. Reducing the need for the intervention of the state in the lives of Aboriginal people and communities; and
10. Providing services at a cost that is no more, and sometimes less, than the cost of corresponding non-Aboriginal programs.

It is important to note that a substantial body of historical research now exists on traditional Aboriginal approaches to dealing with many social issues and social problems (for example, Morse 1983; Hylton et al. 1985; Coyle 1986; Clark 1990; McDonnell 1991, 1992). There has been a strong interest among the Aboriginal Peoples in adapting this knowledge about what has worked in the past to present-day circumstances. As a result, many parallel social programs that have been developed by the Aboriginal Peoples have incorporated unique approaches to the problems that Aboriginal people face today. There are many examples.

Aboriginal justice programs, unlike the justice programs of the dominant society, have tended to accord much less importance to a formalized process of adjudication. In addition, unlike Canadian justice services, they have not been preoccupied with the punishment of offenders. Rather, these Aboriginal programs have emphasized the traditional practice of restoring peace and harmony in the community. There is no schedule of penalties for different offenses and, in many instances, no formal adjudication process. What is important in the Aboriginal approach is that the offender, the victim, and the community feel that a transgression has been dealt with appropriately, and that any divisiveness in the community is healed.

Historically, Aboriginal children were not viewed as possessions of their parents. Child care was a community responsibility, and the extended family, and the community as a whole, had important roles to play in teaching and safeguarding children. Whereas the dominant non-Aboriginal society has tended to view children as the primary responsibility of their parents and has removed children from their parents in cases deemed to involve neglect or abuse, Aboriginal child welfare programs often avoid apprehensions by enlisting the support of the extended family and the community.

Health care practices of the dominant society have emphasized the treatment of physical disorders by health care experts. In Aboriginal approaches, health is a holistic concept that goes beyond physical health to involve spiritual and psychological dimensions. Whereas modern medicine has only recently recognized that many disorders have an underlying cause that is not physical, this has been an important principle underlying Aboriginal approaches to health and well-being for centuries.[5]

Despite the many positive accomplishments of parallel Aboriginal social programs, the literature also suggests there are a number of common problems (for example, Bryant et al. 1978; Singer and Moyer 1981; Coopers and Lybrand 1986; Hurd and Hurd 1986; Hudson and Taylor-Henley 1987):

1. Financial resources provided to these programs are typically inadequate when compared with the resources made available to corresponding non-Aboriginal programs;
2. The future of these programs is often in doubt. Budgets are subject to review as the programs are usually viewed by funders as "experimental" in nature;
3. An absence of resources forces many agencies to focus all their energies on crisis management. Prevention and community development activities are not properly recognized or funded;
4. Programs frequently have to operate without a proper infrastructure of personnel and program policies and procedures. Funders seldom recognize the importance of developing this infrastructure;
5. Relationships between Aboriginal programs and the dominant non-Aboriginal programs are often characterized by uncertainty about respective roles and responsibilities; and
6. Typically, Aboriginal programs are confined to a particular geographic area. It is often uncertain how members of the Aboriginal community who are outside the geographic boundaries of the program ought to be served by Aboriginal and non-Aboriginal agencies. This is a particular problem, for example, with off-reserve Indians.

Clearly, the findings to date point to the positive potential of social programs operated by Aboriginal Peoples for themselves. Yet, if this approach is to move beyond isolated "experimental" programs, so that it can be accepted as the usual and proper approach to service delivery, a much stronger commitment is required.

CONCLUSION

There is no need to further document the social problems faced by the Aboriginal Peoples in Canada. Nor is there a need to further document the failure of non-Aboriginal programs to effectively respond to the needs and aspirations of the Aboriginal Peoples. While the review and updating of existing findings may be required from time to time, there now exists an adequate information base upon which to formulate public policy.

Solutions, not problems, should drive public policy development in Canada. There is ample evidence to suggest that these solutions lie in the direction of programs run by Aboriginal Peoples for themselves, that is, self-government.

NOTES

1   This paper is based in part on a literature review prepared for the Royal Commission on Aboriginal Peoples. See Hylton (1992).
2   For example, a bibliography, without annotations, prepared by Horn and Griffiths (1989) runs some 275 pages, and the subject matter is limited to criminal justice issues affecting Aboriginal Peoples.
3   In fact, these types of analyses are typically cross-sectional analyses that examine relationships among variables. Often, the data are collected at one time and describe conditions as they existed at another time. Therefore, the data usually do not permit definitive statements to be made about what came first to cause something else that came later.
4   For example, see the March 16, 1992, issue of *Maclean's* magazine, and the Berry and Wells chapter in this volume.
5   The Canadian Mental Health Association, for example, estimates that as many as 50 percent of visits to family doctors may be for mental health problems.

REFERENCES

Barman, Jean, et al. 1986. *Indian education in Canada*. Vancouver: University of British Columbia Press.

Barron, Laurie. 1984. A summary of Canadian Indian policy in the Canadian West. *Native Studies Review* 1:28–39.

Brody, Hugh. 1971. *Indians on skid row*. Ottawa: Information Canada.

Bryant, V. M., et al. 1978. *Evaluation of the Indian special constable program (option 3b)*. Ottawa: Department of Indian Affairs and Northern Development.

Cardinal, Harold. 1969. *The unjust society: The tragedy of Canada's Indians.* Edmonton: Hurtig.

Carter, Sarah. 1990. *Lost harvests: Prairie Indian reserve farmers and government policy.* Montreal and Kingston: McGill-Queen's University Press.

Clark, Scott. 1990. *Aboriginal customary law: Literature review.* Winnipeg: Aboriginal Justice Inquiry.

Cole, Douglas, and Ira Chaikin. 1990. *An iron hand upon the people: The law against the potlatch on the northwest coast.* Vancouver: Douglas and McIntyre.

Cooke, Katie. 1984. *Images of Indians held by non-Indians: A review of the current Canadian research.* Ottawa: Department of Indian Affairs and Northern Development.

Coopers and Lybrand Consulting Group. 1986. *An assessment of services delivered under the Canada-Manitoba northern Indian child welfare agreement.* Winnipeg: Coopers and Lybrand.

Coyle, Michael. 1986. Traditional Indian justice in Ontario: A role for the present. *Osgoode Hall Law Journal* 24:605–33.

Department of Indian Affairs. 1989. *Highlights of Aboriginal conditions, 1981–2001.* Ottawa: Department of Indian Affairs.

———. 1980. *An overview of some recent research on attitudes in Canada towards Indian people.* Ottawa: Department of Indian Affairs and Northern Development.

Dosman, Edgar J. 1972. *Indians: The urban dilemma.* Toronto: McClelland and Stewart.

Frideres, J. S. 1974. *Canada's Indians: Contemporary conflicts.* Scarborough, ON: Prentice-Hall.

Getty, A. L., and A. A. Lussier. 1983. *As long as the sun shines and the river flows: A reader in Canadian native studies.* Vancouver: Nakota Institute and University of British Columbia Press.

Gibbins, Roger, and J. Rick Ponting. 1978. *Canadian opinions and attitudes towards Indians and Indian issues: Findings of a national study.* Ottawa: Department of Indian Affairs and Northern Development.

Hamilton, A. C., and M. Sinclair. 1991. *Report of the Aboriginal justice inquiry of Manitoba.* Winnipeg: Government of Manitoba.

Havemann, Paul, et al. 1985. *Law and order for Canada's indigenous people: A review of recent research literature relating to the operation of the criminal justice system and Canada's indigenous people.* Regina: Prairie Justice Research Consortium.

Hawthorn, H. B. 1966. *A survey of contemporary Indians of Canada: Economic, political, educational needs and policies.* Ottawa: Department of Indian Affairs and Northern Development.

Hobbs-Birnie, Lisa. 1990. *A rock and a hard place: Inside Canada's parole board.* Toronto: Macmillan.

Horn, Charles, and Curt T. Griffiths. 1989. *Native North Americans: Crime, conflict, and criminal justice.* 4th ed. Burnaby, BC: The Northern Justice Society.

Hudson, Peter, and Sharon Taylor-Henley. 1987. *Agreement and disagreement: An evaluation of the Canada-Manitoba northern Indian child welfare agreement.* Winnipeg: University of Manitoba.

Hull, Jeremy. 1987. *An overview of registered Indian conditions in Manitoba.* Ottawa: Department of Indian and Northern Affairs.Hurd, Carroll P., and Jeanne M. Hurd. 1986. *Evaluation: Implementation of the Canada-Manitoba-Brotherhood of Indian Nations child welfare agreement.* Edmonton: McKay-Hurd Associates.

Hylton, John H. 1992. *Social problems, social programs, and the human services: Towards the development of a research program for the Royal Commission on Aboriginal Peoples.* Ottawa: Royal Commission.

———— et al. 1990. *Alcoholism treatment for impaired drivers.* Queenston, ON: Edwin Mellen.

———— et al. 1985. Customary law. In Hylton et al., *Reflecting Indian concerns and values in the justice system.* Ottawa: Department of Justice.

————. 1981a. *Reintegrating the offender: Assessing the impact of community corrections.* Washington, D.C.: University Press of America.

————. 1981b. Some attitudes towards Natives in a prairie city. *Canadian Journal of Criminology* 23:357–63.

————. 1980. Public attitudes towards crime and the police in a prairie city. *Canadian Police College Journal* 14:243–76.

Johnson, Patrick. 1983. *Native children and the child welfare system.* Toronto: Lorimer.

Kimmelman, Edwin C. 1985. *No quiet place: Review committee on Indian and Metis adoptions and placements.* Winnipeg: Manitoba Department of Community Services.

Krotz, Larry. 1980. *Urban Indians: The strangers in Canada's cities.* Edmonton: Hurtig.

McDonnell, Roger. 1992. *Justice for the Cree: Customary beliefs and practices.* Quebec: Grand Council of the Cree.

————. 1991. *Justice for the Cree: Customary law.* Quebec: Grand Council of the Cree.

Morse, Bradford W. 1983. Indigenous law and state legal systems: Conflict and compatibility. Pp. 381–402 in *Proceedings of the symposium on folk law and legal pluralism,* ed. Harald W. Finkler. Ottawa: Department of Indian Affairs and Northern Development.

————. 1980. *Indian tribal courts in the United States: A model for Canada?* Saskatoon, SK: Native Law Centre.

Nagler, Mark. 1973. *Indians in the city*. Ottawa: Canadian Research Centre for Anthropology.

Pettipas, K. A. 1988. Serving the ties that bind: The Canadian Indian Act and the repression of indigenous religious systems in the prairie region, 1896–1951. Ph.D. diss., University of Manitoba.

Ponting, J. Rick, and Roger Gibbins. 1980. *Out of irrelevance: A socio-political introduction to Indian affairs in Canada*. Toronto: Butterworths.

Ryan, Joan. 1978. *Wall of words: The betrayal of the urban Indian*. Toronto: Peter Martin.

Singer, Charles, and Sharon Moyer. 1981. *The Dakota-Ojibway tribal council police program: An evaluation*. Ottawa: Solicitor General of Canada.

Social Policy Research Associates. 1983. *National evaluation overview of Indian policing*. Ottawa: Department of Indian and Northern Affairs.

CHAPTER 3

ABORIGINAL SELF-GOVERNMENT: IMPLICATIONS OF THE AUSTRALIAN EXPERIENCE

JOHN W. EKSTEDT,[1] SIMON FRASER UNIVERSITY

This chapter defines and discusses some important policy issues relevant to the quest for Aboriginal self-determination in Canada. These issues are examined through a comparison with experiences in Australia. Although some reference is made to the United States and New Zealand, Australia is singled out for discussion, in part because it shares much with Canada in terms of European history, politics, and law.

Policy is used here to refer to the judgments that political organizations and governing bodies make about alternative courses of action. It serves as a guide for settling disputes by declaring and reinforcing desired social values. This focus, therefore, highlights the underlying values and beliefs that are at stake in disputes over control of important elements in public life (for example, land rights, health, education, etc.).

Self-determination is used here to refer to the right of a people "to exercise control over those political, cultural, economic, and social issues of concern to them" (Fleras and Elliot 1992, p. 23). It is the policy goal of political organizations representing Indigenous Peoples. *Self-government*, on the other hand, is the authority to create and maintain the organizational structures necessary to manage day-to-day community affairs. Self-government is the means employed within particular communities or regions to put self-determination into practice. Therefore, self-determination can be realized through any number of structures for self-government.

In Canada, the Aboriginal Peoples have been building up momentum toward assuming greater control over their own affairs. This has generated considerable reaction and response within the larger society, as witnessed recently in the referendum on the Canadian Constitution.[2] While the result of the referendum caused disappointment and anger within much of the Aboriginal community, the debate served to clarify the conflicting demands that will have to be addressed in order for Aboriginal self-determination to be realized. This is an area where lessons from the Australian experience are particularly useful.

Many authors have drawn attention to the importance of the Australian

49

experience for Aboriginal policy in Canada. A decade ago, for example, Morse (1984) suggested that Canada could learn from Australian approaches in a number of areas, including the definition of Aboriginality; the method for addressing land rights; various experiences with Aboriginal control over economic initiatives; and developments in a variety of other specific program areas, such as research, legal services, health, housing, and post-secondary education.

LAND RIGHTS

In both Canada and Australia, the Indigenous Peoples do not generally possess a formalized traditional court system. Therefore, it is necessary for them to litigate their asserted land rights before the general courts of the country. The attitude of the courts about whether Indigenous Peoples enjoy traditional or common law rights to their land has, therefore, been critical to the evolution of relationships between Aboriginal Peoples and the larger society.

The existence of traditional land title has been recognized as a principle of law by the courts in Canada for some time, but not until very recently in Australia.[3] This difference has set the tone for a number of other important issues (Hanks and Keon-Cohen 1984), and has led to distinctive procedures and practices in several areas. This is partly due to the different strategies employed by occupying peoples as they confronted Indigenous populations in the territories now known as Canada and Australia. In Canada, negotiated agreements or understandings concerning the occupation of land and other matters often resulted in the establishment of treaties from which further negotiations could proceed. In Australia, there are no historical treaties on which negotiations related to land claims and other matters can be based. Consequently, and only since the 1960s, settlements have been reached through legislated schemes. These have usually had to do with rights of occupation to "leasehold" lands and with arrangements between governments, private enterprise, and Aboriginal Peoples to exploit the resources available on those lands or on other places regarded as "sacred" by Aboriginal tribal groups.

In Canada, it is more likely that governments will consider negotiation as a viable method of responding to the demands of the Indigenous Peoples for self-determination and self-government. Because of this, there has been a historical difference in the matters considered when negotiating Aboriginal land claims in Canada and in Australia. The fundamental difference in assumptions between the two countries related to land title also affects the involvement of the Indigenous Peoples in the constitutional processes in the two countries. In Canada, Indigenous Peoples are involved in constitutional discussions in a manner not experienced by Aboriginal Peoples in Australia.

While it might appear from the above discussion that the Canadian situation is more advanced than the Australian one, this is not necessarily the case. As Morse (1984, p. 108) has pointed out, Australians have avoided the Canadian tendency to concentrate on resolving disputes as a matter of law and "lawful obligation" (although that may be changing). Rather, Australians are more likely to address "fundamental concerns of fairness, justice and morality in the broadest sense at a political and ethical level."

1. A Note on the United States and New Zealand[4]

Before proceeding to a discussion of specific lessons in this cross-jurisdictional analysis, it is useful to acknowledge two other countries whose experiences with the conflict between Aboriginal and non-Aboriginal populations continue to be instructive. These are the United States and New Zealand. While these countries share some similarities with Canada and Australia, there are also important differences.

In the United States and New Zealand, as in Australia and Canada, historical policies emerging from first contact sought to impose the will of land "discoverers" on those who were land "holders." These policies ranged from genocide on one extreme, to assimilation, to various forms of partnership agreements. In all of these countries, however, new paradigms are emerging, which are based on a genuine desire to improve the conditions under which people live together.

One of the distinctions between Canada and the United States and New Zealand is that both the latter countries have long-standing national agreements governing some aspects of Aboriginal affairs. In the United States, the Constitution has been the basis for establishing the government of the occupying peoples, and it has provided the framework for resolving domestic and foreign matters in dispute since the "founding" of the country by non-Indigenous peoples over three centuries ago. Therefore, it has provided the context for treaty arrangements and other settlements. Because of this, agreements about land and other matters in the United States seem to depend on the existence of the political will required to assure the inclusion of Indigenous Peoples in constitutional understandings that are already in place.

In New Zealand, the historical agreement is the Treaty of Waitangi. This document of understanding is specifically intended to address Maori sovereignty. However, as in the United States, the implementation of this understanding has been dependent on the exercise of political will. It has been argued that since the Treaty was established, there have been few occasions when the political will has been sufficient to maintain the intent of the Treaty, namely, to provide consistency and fairness in the relationship between the Aboriginal and non-Aboriginal populations. In contrast, while there have been expressions of political will in Canada,[5] these expressions have occurred in the absence of an accepted national model of understanding.

In both the United States and Australia, negotiations between the Aboriginal and non-Aboriginal peoples are complicated by the type of federalism at work. The preeminence of state responsibility in a number of areas, with the federal government taking leading initiatives specific to Aboriginal populations, sometimes causes federal decisions to result in conflict between the states and Aboriginal populations. While such conflicts and tensions do exist in Canada, the more centralized federalism of Canada means that political will is more easily acted upon once it exists.

2. ABORIGINAL TITLE IN AUSTRALIA: A NEW ERA—*MABO V QUEENSLAND*

In the northeast portion of the Torres Strait lies a group of islands known as the Murray Islands. These islands are occupied by a group of people known as the Meriam. In May 1982, the Meriam initiated legal proceedings against the State of Queensland. They claimed that they had continuously occupied the islands "since time immemorial," and had established communities with a clear social and political organization. While they did not dispute that the islands came under the sovereignty of the Crown, they asserted that this sovereignty was subject to the rights of those who had historically occupied the land.

Mabo v Queensland has proved to be extremely important in the struggle for recognition by the Indigenous Peoples of Australia. While Aboriginal title at common law had been the doctrine accepted in the United States, Canada, and New Zealand, it had not been accepted in Australia. In fact, in 1971, Australian courts in *Milirrpum v Nabalco* reviewed the jurisprudence on the common law doctrine and concluded "that the doctrine does not form, and never has formed, part of the law of any part of Australia."[6]

In 1992, the High Court of Australia concluded that: the Murray Islands had been settled for some generations by people of Melanesian origin, probably from Papua New Guinea; prior to European contact these islanders had an evolving social organization; the land was managed by individuals or family groups, and there was no apparent concept of public or general community ownership; the relationship of the islanders to land and sea was "strong" and "enduring"; prior to contact there was no chieftainship system (social cohesion was maintained by peer pressure, spiritualism, and force); and the system of governance introduced by Europeans did not acknowledge the social organization of the islanders prior to contact but, nevertheless, had become a dominant influence on the lives of the people (Bartlett 1992). This decision had the effect of bringing the common law of Australia into line with the rest of the common law world. Aboriginal title or "native title," was recognized at common law.

This case has many important characteristics, some of which have application to the dialogue surrounding Aboriginal title in Canada. The decision declares that general public lands legislation does not of itself extinguish Aboriginal title. Just because the land has been designated, under European law, for public or private use, it does not follow that the question of Aboriginal title has been resolved. As Bartlett (1992) points out, this may have some considerable significance in Canada concerning the question of whether Aboriginal title was ever extinguished in British Columbia. It is, perhaps, even more important that the decision puts Canada, the United States, New Zealand, and Australia on the same footing in terms of the law as it affects Aboriginal title. Therefore, there are significant opportunities for discussion and collaboration among these countries.

The recognition of Aboriginal title in Australia also poses a danger, however. The decision places the Aboriginal Peoples in Australia in the position of negotiating land rights on the basis of law, rather than on the basis of the more fundamental questions of fairness, justice, and morality referred to earlier. In Canada, for example, it cannot be said that the recognition of Aboriginal title at common law has substantially addressed the grievances and concerns of the Indigenous Peoples.

EDUCATION

While there are parallels between the Canadian and Australian experiences in the area of land rights, there are also parallels in other areas that are important in achieving Aboriginal self-determination and self-governing status. One of these is education—the process by which culture, language, and values are communicated within generations and between them.

The key to the educational process is the organization of formal instruction for the young. In Australia, as in Canada, the history of education is bound up with attempts by Europeans to usurp control over the Aboriginal educational experience. In Australia, a number of cases analogous to Canada's "mission schools" have been documented. One such case is the Oombulgurri School, located on the Forrest River in the northwest of Australia (Green 1987). The Oombulgurri experiment is a useful case study of an attempt by an Australian community to reestablish its self-identity, and to achieve self-determination, after its "mission experience."

1. THE OOMBULGURRI SCHOOL

In 1887, a pastoral farming company took up a lease in the region later occupied by the school but was forced out after a year by the local Aboriginal people, who objected to its presence. In 1898, an attempt to establish a mission on the same site met a similar fate when the missionaries were attacked. In 1912, the Anglican Mission of St. Michael of All Angels successfully established a mission program in the area that ran continuously until March 1968. The mission left the community because of an accumulation of debt. However, for fifty-six years, or nearly two generations, this Aboriginal community had been placed under the supervision and control of the mission, and had become dependent on it.

When the mission left the area, local residents were moved to an adjoining area and left to fend for themselves. The church's freehold rights were sold to the government to pay outstanding debts; the cattle were offered for sale to neighboring stations; the mission was sold and the records, personal documents, and mission journals, dating back to 1913, were abandoned. Thus, the history of a generation of people was effectively lost.

In 1970, two elders, accompanied by social workers from a nearby community, returned to the abandoned settlement. Many of the buildings were still habitable, although most of the equipment had been lost or vandalized. One of the elders, in a written statement entitled "Why We Should Return to Forrest River" (Taylor 1970), said: "Where the houses are standing, that was the aboriginal main camping and tribal meeting ground. Now today stands a big group of buildings because the white man took the land away from them because we had no hope for our own land."

This visit started an attempt at recovery of the land at Forrest River, and the development of a school that would return the responsibility of formal education for Aboriginal people to the Aboriginal community itself.

In 1972, the mission was renamed Oombulgurri, which is the traditional name for the flood plain that, in the days before white settlement, had been an important meeting place. That year, thirty men, women, and children returned to Oombulgurri. They began clearing land and planting crops. The following year, the Oombulgurri community invited the Ecumenical Institute, a semi-religious organization, to assist them in developing a sound economic base. Between August 1973 and September 1978, the institute maintained a staff of Australian and American advisors at Oombulgurri.

By October 1973, approximately fifty people were living at Oombulgurri, and, in that month, a teacher was employed to open a school in the education department building that had been unoccupied for nearly seven years. In 1974, Oombulgurri became the first independent Aboriginal school in Australia, and the first to bypass the state system and receive direct funding from the federal government.

While the return to the land carried great significance for these people, and they labored to establish a working economy for the community in planted crops and cattle, the most important achievement was the initiative to provide a new model (as opposed to the mission model) for the education of the children. The community had difficulty determining what was wanted from the educational experience, but, finally, agreed that the school should be a place where children would learn to read, write, and find out about their culture. The desire to revive the culture expressed the deep sense of loss that had occurred during the mission years.

The choice to be a numerate, literate people with their own culture became known as the "two schools" concept, and this same approach was later developed at other independent Aboriginal schools. The "two schools" concept recognized that Western education is important for survival in the larger Australian culture. It also recognized that there is an important body of traditional knowledge and community history that the children must acquire. The Western education component was made the responsibility of European teachers who were brought into the community, while the traditional knowledge was imparted by the elders.

In August 1985, a "consult" was held at Oombulgurri. Farmers, engineers, other professionals, teachers, and community members met to consider the education program at Oombulgurri. Their purpose was to determine the future direction of the school. At this "consult" it was determined that the program needed revision. It was apparent that, in practice, the "two schools" concept was not working to the satisfaction of most of the participants.

The Ecumenical Institute (by this time renamed the Institute of Cultural Affairs—I.C.A.) was given responsibility for redrafting an educational program for the community. It was decided to discard the regular curriculum that emphasized reading, writing, and arithmetic. Instead, an innovative program, referred to as "imaginal education," was introduced. This program was drawn from the American experience with a program called the Fifth City Project, which had been introduced in the black ghettos of Chicago, Illinois.

This new program was organized around five principles:

1. DELIMITED AREAS: creating an identity for the local area that reflects local "ownership" and values;
2. DEPTH, HUMAN PROBLEMS: creating new and positive self-concepts for the children of the area;
3. AN HOLISTIC APPROACH: tackling community development on all fronts;
4. EVERY AGE GROUP: involving everyone in the community in some form of activity; and
5. POWER OF SYMBOLS: finding ways of visually representing the hopes and aspirations of the community.

These principles were intended to reinforce a new identity among the people of Oombulgurri, especially its children, and many apparently useful initiatives emerged out of the new approach.

While many lessons were learned from this experiment, the program quickly became identified as a failure in achieving the ends anticipated by the elders, and by the community as a whole. The I.C.A., though well intentioned, represented a paternalistic structure not dissimilar to the old mission concept. Although the initiatives of the I.C.A. did foster new feelings of self-identity among the people, these feelings did not come from the people themselves. Thus there was a continuing struggle to overcome influences of the past, when mission superintendents made all the decisions.

Although there had been a significant attempt to organize an economic base, and to create symbols that the people could relate to, these projects emphasized Western urban values rather than community values. Therefore, the symbols that emerged in the search for a unique community identity actually imposed alien values, which were a curious combination of urban Australian values mixed with those of the American Fifth City Project.

The Oombulgurri school closed in August 1978 and was reopened in February 1979 with Australian teachers assisted by community education aides. It continued as an independent school until 1982, when the Western Australian Education Department appointed four teachers. In 1986, the school had a population of forty-two children, taught by four teachers and two community education workers (Green 1987).

The Oombulgurri experience illustrates how difficult it is for members of a community that has been dislocated from its roots and subjugated to paternalistic control for so long to reestablish their community identity and community life. Many comparable Canadian situations reinforce the principle that significant effort is required to move away from the ingrained state of dependency and uncertainty toward self-initiative and self-control.

One of the persons who reported on this experiment (Green 1987, p. 60), quoted from Julius Nyerere, the then-president of Tanzania, about the problems of foreign intervention:

> Development brings freedom, provided it is the development of people. But people cannot be developed; they can only develop themselves. For while it is possible for an outsider to build a man's house, an outsider cannot give the man pride and self-confidence in himself as a human being.

2. ABORIGINAL INVOLVEMENT IN EDUCATION IN AUSTRALIA

Aboriginal Australians have identified education as a key factor in achieving a clear sense of identity and social purpose. Nereda Blair (1987, p. 1), an Aboriginal Australian educator, expressed the point this way:

> We want education, we want success and we want to live, not just to survive. On our own terms. As aboriginal Australians we have had and still maintain our own concepts of learning and teaching, of knowing and understanding, no matter how buried they have become within the imposed system of education. We have something to offer our colonial invaders, we have something to teach them about education, if only they would listen, and if only we could decolonize our thinking to fully appreciate and recreate our own models.

Lessons from the past, particularly flowing from the "two schools" policy, have resulted in a number of initiatives to take back the educational experience. A national Aboriginal Education Committee has been established to work on the development of a national pedagogy. The Australian Institute of Aboriginal Studies has developed a research program for curriculum development from an Aboriginal perspective. At least one teacher's college has developed a degree in Aboriginal education. There has been discussion about the development of an Aboriginal college that would take account of Aboriginal pedagogy and epistemology, and reflect these principles in the higher education of Aboriginal persons.

While there is interest in establishing a national Australian effort related to Aboriginal education, the very essence of Aboriginal pedagogy is that it both reflects, and emerges from, the local culture. The Pintupi teachers at Walungurru School in Kintore, Northern Territory, for example, express the concept this way: "The school must be strengthened by and assist to strengthen Pintupi culture. The school can do so through an emphasis on the education of a child as a whole person" (Blair 1987, p. 13).

In discussing the work at this particular school, Keefe (1987, p. 5) noted that: "The belief of these aboriginal teachers in the need for schooling to grow from and be part of the social and cultural reality of the community is clear, unambiguous and powerful."

3. THE LAND AND LEARNING

There is an important relationship between the land and learning in Aboriginal thought, both in Australia and Canada. In a publication of the Institute of Applied Aboriginal Studies in Western Australia (1986, p. 12), the strong identification by Aboriginal people with the land was explained in this way:

> Before the dreaming, according to aboriginal tradition, the land existed but was without shape or life. The "spirit beings" or "dream time figures" travelled over the land creating the natural environment as it now exists—the physical features and all living things including the people. The spirit beings also, according to tradition, gave the people their own tracts of land along with their languages and social institutions. Particular features of the landscape are believed to retain part of the spiritual essence of the dreamtime heroes who created them. . . . Even when aborigines have been dispossessed of their land, they retain their sense of "place." . . . This affinity means that, without their land, they cannot be "whole" people. They need their land if they are to have their full dignity, pride and social standing restored to them.

According to Keefe (1987, p. 5), the Yanangu teachers in the Pintupi culture speak of the relationship between education and "place":

> The experience of attending schools where the domain of the person is neglected or ignored is a different and traumatic experience. Students who try to be educated in a context that does not support Yanangu ideas usually fail. People who try to downplay or ignore their own Yanangu aspects, have great difficulty in replacing it with a Walypala, or non-aboriginal, persona.

This separation of personhood and learning results in a variety of maladies, many of which affect the physical health of the people. The teachers in Pintupi have acknowledged the relationship between this separation and the tendency toward petrol sniffing and drunkenness in the community.

HEALTH

In the areas of health and social service programs, the Australian experience is more advanced than the Canadian one. Much can be learned from the various initiatives of the Australian Aboriginal Peoples, particularly about the problems of relating to the dominant culture.

In Australia, it has been recognized that, in the area of health, as in so many other areas of social concern, attention to the needs of Aboriginal people can only be truly successful when Aboriginal communities take control of their own programs. The Australian experience thus reinforces what has been learned in many developing countries, such as Tanzania and Papua New Guinea, as well as with the Barefoot Doctors of China. Training must be provided to primary health workers from the community, who are chosen by the people themselves.

In Australia, a strong link between the land and personal well-being is also recognized. This link has important implications for physical health and social behavior. In "Generations of Resistance," for example, Lippmann (1981, p. 115) observes:

> The granting of land rights, according Aboriginals a sure base on which
> to enhance their communities, is a first step in the long march toward
> better health; a feeling of power and control over one's own destiny
> brings with it the ability to identify and work towards solutions.

Cultural values and beliefs are also recognized as playing an important role in health and health care. In practical terms, health problems not only involve attention to the "whole person" in the context of their beliefs and values, but treatment responses aimed at alleviating the symptoms of ill-health must also take these values and beliefs into consideration.

In the mid-1980s, there were no Aboriginal people in Australia trained as physicians in the Western tradition. However, a modular system of education for primary health workers had been introduced in the Northern Territory in the mid-1970s. Those who completed this training were able to cope with the most common health problems of their own communities. Serious cases were referred to the formal health system. By 1979, the national Aboriginal and Islander Health Organization had been established, comprising seventeen Aboriginal-controlled health services throughout Australia (Lippmann 1981). Numerous proposals aimed at improving health services for Aboriginal people have been submitted through this organization. A major goal of the organization is to promote Aboriginal control of all health services in Aboriginal communities.

LAW

Aboriginal customary law is an integral part of traditional Aboriginal societies wherever such societies continue to exist. It incorporates a wider system of social control than Western legal systems, because it includes elements of "private law" (for example, interpersonal relations and dispute-resolution); "public law" (for example, community government); and religious beliefs and practices. It has important implications for gender relationships; hunting, fishing, and gathering practices; rights and duties in respect of land, sacred sites, and objects; spiritual beliefs and practices; and many other areas of community life.

Many aspects of Aboriginal customary law are inaccessible to others, for a variety of reasons. These include the fact that the law varies from community to community, that it is usually not recorded in writing, that some of it is secret or confidential, that it can usually only be learned orally in the relevant Aboriginal language, and that it is based on ideas and concepts radically different from Western ideas and concepts.

In Australia, considerable attention has been paid to the problem of the relationship between Aboriginal customary law and European law. In part, the developments have centered on finding ways in which Aboriginal customary law may be employed in Aboriginal communities, without conflicting with the European law practices that may be dominant in those communities. While achieving this type of accommodation has been difficult, there is evidence that progress is being made. In the area of criminal law, for example, including law-enforcement practices in Aboriginal and non-Aboriginal communities, a number of specific programs have been proposed in Australia that allow Aboriginal and Western systems to coexist. Some of these models could have real applicability to the Canadian experience.

In both Canada and Australia, one mechanism for breaching the gap between European law and customary Aboriginal law is alternative dispute-resolution or settlement. Very often these alternative practices seek to merge European practice and procedure with some elements of customary ritual. As such, they can be successful in satisfying parties on all sides.

In Australia, dispute-resolution mechanisms tend to take the form of the "two schools" concept described earlier. For example, it has been the case for some time that disputes between Aboriginal members of the remote Edward River community, located on the west side of Cape York Peninsula, are not necessarily handled by the Queensland court system. In this community, disputes may be handled either by the local Aboriginal court or according to the customary law in that area. The roles and responsibilities of these two Aboriginal systems overlap, and jurisdiction is decided on a case-by-case basis. On the whole, customary law systems handle transgressions of local members against customary law. The Aboriginal community court, on the other hand, handles transgressions against members and applies punishment to members who have broken the "white man's law" (Law Reform Commission 1986).

In Australia, according to the Law Reform Commission (1986, vol. 2, p. 19), breaches of customary law might include one or more of the following:

1. Failure of kinship duties, particularly in the provision of food and gifts to appropriate kinsmen;
2. Mistreatment and infidelity toward kinsmen;
3. Breaches of marriage arrangements;
4. Insult, injury, or the threat of injury;
5. Trespass upon someone else's country or resources;
6. Failure to consult or acknowledge the rightful decision-making authority; and
7. Breach of ceremonial or ritual codes.

As in many Indigenous societies, a breach of customary law in Australia is believed to bring about automatic retribution from supernatural agencies. Community retaliation and punishment may also follow, particularly if a victim of an offense seeks public redress. It has been through this process of public exposure and search for redress, that Aboriginal skills in dispute-resolution have been developed. The Aboriginal community court system extends this skill of dispute-resolution into a defined and limited arena for settlement under Western law.

To some extent, customary sanctions— such as public "growling," public shaming, elder supervision, or even banishment from the community—can be merged with, or added to, community court sanctions of fines, community service orders, or imprisonment. By this process, Aboriginal communities administering community justice programs have created a link between Aboriginal customary law and the general legal system in Australia (Law Reform Commission 1986).

This is not to say that the accommodation of the two systems has always worked smoothly. There was, for example, an incident at Fitzroy Crossing in Western Australia where the community's application of customary law practice and the white court's judicial review produced different results. Steve Hawk, an Aboriginal spokesman commented:

> Look like that two law, white man law and aboriginal law. White man law not believing in aboriginal law, same way aboriginal law not believing on white man's side. Might be that aboriginal law is on the people's side. . . . Now this is the way that we're thinking—to pull the white man from the ears to listen to what the aboriginal law will say . . . . We are looking that something be changed. . . . They talk in the parliament for making laws, and they've been pushing into aboriginal people. Now we are looking for that law we can put up that can help people. (Lippmann 1981, p. 171)

CONCLUSION

Some Australian and Canadian experiences in the areas of land rights, education, health, and law have been examined in this chapter. Although it could be argued that neither country has resolved the relationship between Indigenous Peoples and the conquering peoples in anything like a satisfactory way, there are shared experiences between the two, as well as unique frustrations and successes, that are instructive. Both countries have much to learn from each other.

In Australia, the relative isolation, especially from the North American experience, appears to have allowed a greater sense of attachment, by both Indigenous and non-Indigenous peoples, to traditional Aboriginal concepts and lifestyles. For example, it is no accident that some of the best contemporary work on Aboriginal customary law, and certainly the most complete, comes from Australia. Moreover, the attention to basic questions of human need, in areas such as education and health, seem to be more advanced in Australia, particularly for Aboriginal Peoples living traditional lifestyles in isolated areas.

In Canada, the constitutional and political organization of relationships between Indigenous and non-Indigenous peoples appears better articulated. Alternative means of dispensing justice in ways that more adequately reflect the desire and beliefs of Indigenous Peoples are also further advanced.

In both countries, difficulties have been experienced in using European approaches to achieve greater self-determination for the Indigenous Peoples. The "two schools" concept, as it applies to law, education, and health, has presented numerous difficulties, largely because the "two schools" are in the hands of the dominant society. While there is probably little argument that Indigenous Peoples must function within the larger society, it appears clear that efforts that are successful in promoting self-determination will be ones that are organized from the perspective of Aboriginal interests.

What can be concluded from this analysis? It is evident that to achieve self-determination, Aboriginal Peoples must gain control of the "two schools" concept and determine, among other things, how they can best recover and maintain their values while, at the same time, relating to the larger society. In relation to self-government, it is evident that there must be local management of essential services in order to ensure that structures of conflict-resolution, learning, and healing reflect the traditional beliefs that are the essence of Aboriginal life. The sense of "place," as part of these beliefs, requires that this management process emerge from a clearly defined and understood relationship with the land.

NOTES

1   While a visiting fellow at the University of Western Australia Law School, the author of this chapter spent a year in Western Australia, visiting and studying with the Indigenous Peoples in that part of Australia. This was followed by a cross-cultural exchange program between Canada and Australia in 1988.

2   On October 26, 1992, a referendum question was put before the Canadian people. The question was "Do you agree that the Constitution of Canada should be renewed on the basis of the agreement reached on August 28, 1992 [Charlottetown Accord]?" The majority vote was "No." There was strong Aboriginal participation in these talks and the Charlottetown agreement included a major section on Aboriginal rights.

3   See the discussion below on *Mabo v Queensland*.

4   For a complete discussion of conditions in Canada, the United States, and New Zealand, see Fleras and Elliot (1992).

5   For example, all federal and provincial government leaders supported the Aboriginal rights package contained in the Charlottetown Accord.

6   *Milirrpum v Nabalco* (1971), 17 F.L.R. 141 (N.T.S.C.).

REFERENCES

Bartlett, Richard H. 1992. The landmark case on Aboriginal title in Australia: *Mabo v. State of Queensland.* Case Comment, 3 C.N.L.R., pp. 4–19.

Blair, Nerida. 1987. Education and its role in the destruction of indigenous cultures. Paper presented to the World Conference on Indigenous People's Education, June 8–13, 1987, Vancouver, Canada.

Fleras, Augie, and Jean Leonard Elliot. 1992. *The nations within: Aboriginal state relations in Canada, the United States, and New Zealand.* Toronto: Oxford University Press.

Green, Neville. 1987. Education at Oombulgurri: An American model. *Wikaru* 14:50–62.

Hanks, Peter, and Bryan Keon-Cohen. 1984. *Aborigines and the law.* Sydney: George Allen and Unwin.

Institute of Applied Aboriginal Studies. 1986. *Aboriginal land rights: A moral issue of national importance.* Australia: Western Australia College of Advanced Education.

Keefe, K. 1987. *Curriculum development in Aboriginal studies for schools: Initial report.* Australia: Australian Institute of Aboriginal Studies.

Law Reform Commission. 1986. *The recognition of Aboriginal customary law.* Canberra: Australian Government Publishing Service.

Lippmann, Lorna. 1981. *Generations of resistance: The Aboriginal struggle for justice.* Melbourne: Longman Cheshire.

Milirrpum v Nabalco. 1971. 17 F.L.R. 141 (N.T.S.C.).

Morse, Bradford W. 1984. *Aboriginal self-government in Australia and Canada.* Kingston: McGill-Queen's University Press.

Taylor, Les. 1970. Why we should return to Forrest River. In Neville Green, Education at Oombulgurri: An American model. *Wikaru* 14:50–62.

PART II

TRENDS IN THE
IMPLEMENTATION OF SELF-GOVERNMENT

CHAPTER 4

COMMUNITY HEALING AND ABORIGINAL SELF-GOVERNMENT: IS THE CIRCLE CLOSING?

JOHN D. O'NEIL AND BRIAN D. POSTL[1]
UNIVERSITY OF MANITOBA

Aboriginal self-government has important implications for the way health and medical services are administered in Canada, and also for the health of the Aboriginal Peoples. The emergence of self-governing Aboriginal nations and communities will result in radically different institutional arrangements for the provision of services. Self-government, however, is also a foundation for social development, and social development will contribute to improved health by supporting the healing process that is already under way in many Aboriginal communities. Therefore, self-government will affect not only the administration of services, but also the general well-being of Aboriginal populations.

This chapter examines the implications of self-government for health and health care in the context of the history of Aboriginal health in Canada. Following a brief review of current health conditions, the chapter provides a detailed examination of the historical relationship between Aboriginal communities and the health care system. It then describes several approaches to developing self-governing health care systems in Canada. Finally, the chapter addresses the long-term expectation that self-government will be about more than politics, power, and the administration of services. Fundamentally, it will also be about community well-being.

HEALTH CONDITIONS AMONG THE ABORIGINAL PEOPLES

There is no lack of data describing the disproportionate burden of illness suffered by the Aboriginal Peoples. Although the large catalogue of literature will not be fully described here, it is useful to review the salient health epidemiology of Aboriginal people.

Mortality rates across all age groups are well in excess of Canadian rates. Infant mortality, largely a measure of socio-economic development, is roughly twice the national average. Causes of death also vary. One-third of Aboriginal deaths are associated with injury and violence; and adolescent suicides, which may be taken as a measure of the hopelessness felt by Aboriginal youth, are four to six times the national average (Health and Welfare Canada 1991). Mortality statistics, however, reflect only the tip of the epidemiological iceberg.

The burden of illness on Aboriginal people now comprises both infectious diseases, largely controlled in the non-Aboriginal community, and burgeoning chronic conditions that are relatively new in the Aboriginal collective "health" experience. Aboriginal children, for example, suffer excessive rates of meningitis, otitis media, and iron deficiency anemia (Dufour and Therien 1990; Carson and Postl 1991; Moffatt 1991). Moreover, the prevalence of diabetes mellitus has increased dramatically in Aboriginal adults. And cancer of the lung and cervix is also relatively high (Young 1983).

The high incidence of illness has lead to a high rate of utilization of services, including a high rate of hospitalization, in virtually all age groups (Health Advisory Network 1992). Hospitalizations tend to occur at sites remote from the home communities of Aboriginal people, further accentuating the stress of illness suffered by both individuals and families. Moreover, most of the services provided to the Aboriginal Peoples are provided by non-Aboriginal professionals, health workers, and institutions. Although efforts have been made in some jurisdictions to enhance services, Aboriginal patients remain largely alienated from the "caring system" they must access (Kaufert and Koolage 1984).

The provision of services by a largely alien caring system has also served to diminish the role of traditional values related to the maintenance of health within an Aboriginal "caring system." Colonial medical practice in Aboriginal communities has contributed to the "intimate enemy"—the "new values" that are transmitted by external institutions convince the subordinate population that their own values and beliefs are no longer valid (Nandy 1983; O'Neil 1986). This effect has been particularly insidious.

THE HISTORY OF THE HEALTH SERVICE DEVELOPMENT

Prior to the mid-nineteenth century, distinct, self-governing Aboriginal societies lived in a harmonious relationship with different ecological regions across the country (Young 1988a). Within these environments, Aboriginal societies developed healing systems that emphasized the balanced integration of human beings with the physical, social, and spiritual environment (Speck 1987). By living balanced lives according to the principles of their respective traditions, Aboriginal people largely avoided sickness (Garro 1988).

In each society, some individuals had special abilities. Through ceremonial activity, they were responsible for assisting individuals and communities to maintain ecological, social, and spiritual balance (Jilek and Todd 1974; Hoffman 1981). Additionally, some individuals had specialized knowledge of the medicinal properties of plant and animal parts that were effective in the cure of common ailments (Obomsawin 1980; Young, Ingram, and Swartz 1989). However, all members of the community shared the responsibility to live balanced lives, and all had some knowledge of traditional medicines.

Illness in Aboriginal belief systems was the result of a failure to respect the basic moral code of the community. Therefore, healing was fundamental to the social structure and self-governing systems of each society. Contact with settlers from Europe, however, undermined the ecological, social, and spiritual balance, and, in the process, threatened the survival of Aboriginal societies.

It is beyond the scope of this chapter to address in any detail the social changes resulting from Aboriginal–Euro-Canadian contact, except to say that high mortality and morbidity rates resulted from the introduction of infectious diseases to which the Aboriginal Peoples lacked immunity. Although this has often been overlooked in historical discussions of contact, the impact of infectious diseases such as smallpox, influenza, diphtheria, poliomyelitis, and tuberculosis was significant. In terms of mortality, averages of 40 percent to a high of 90 percent in some parts of Aboriginal North America were reported (Thorton 1985; Norris 1990). In addition, these diseases resulted in the major dislocation of individuals, communities, and entire social systems. Since most of the mortality was among productive adults, particularly elders, it is an indicator of the strength of Aboriginal traditions that they have endured and flourished.

Aboriginal leaders sought to negotiate agreements with representatives of the Euro-Canadian state that would ensure the survival of their societies. As compensation for the use of their land and resources, some Aboriginal leaders agreed to relocate their peoples into villages and reserves, provided the Crown guaranteed the welfare of future generations (Gibbins and Ponting 1986). Given the vastly different traditions and languages in which these agreements were negotiated, it is not surprising that Euro-Canadian representatives interpreted their obligations in many different ways (Stanley 1983).

Of particular relevance to today's discussion is the conflict surrounding the interpretation of federal responsibility for health. The so-called medicine chest clause in Treaty 6, which was signed with the Plains Cree, is the only specific reference to health in any treaty. This clause requires the federal government to provide a "medicine chest" in the house of each Indian agent, while another similar clause charges the federal government with the responsibility to protect Aboriginal people from pestilence and famine. The Aboriginal perspective on these clauses is clearly articulated in the records of Alexander Morris (1880, p. 177), the treaty commissioner at the time:

> The Indians were apprehensive of their future. They saw the food supply, the buffalo, passing away, and they were anxious and distressed. . . . They desired to be fed. Smallpox had destroyed them by hundreds a few years before, and they dreaded pestilence and famine.

Fumoleau (1973, p. 113) has pointed out that the treaty commissioners who negotiated Treaty 8 promised medicines and medical care. He cites a 1919 report by the then-assistant deputy and secretary of Indian Affairs, who wrote that Indians were to be "assured . . . that the government would always be ready to avail itself of any opportunity of affording medical service." Fumoleau also argues that the perceived need among the Aboriginal Peoples for a treaty in the far North was because of the poor health conditions of the Dene in that region.

Further legislative authority for the federal government's obligation for Aboriginal health may be found in subsections 73(1)(f), (g), and (h) of the Indian Act. Here, containment of on-reserve epidemics, provision of medical services, compulsory hospitalization for infectious diseases, and provision of sanitary conditions on reserves are described as federal responsibilities (Young 1984). While First Nations representatives view these provisions as the basis for a full federal obligation for the health of First Nations people, the federal government has adopted the position that the provision of medical care is a matter of policy, not of right (Mayhurst Consulting Group 1993). This position has been supported by the courts.

Later revisions to the Indian Act prohibiting healing ceremonies, such as the potlatch and sun dance, further extended the external society's regulatory control of everyday life in Aboriginal communities, and contributed to the suppression of traditional healing practices (Titely 1989). The penultimate act of this assimilation effort was to force Aboriginal children into residential schools. Over a fifteen-year period, tuberculosis killed 24 percent of all the children who attended (Bryce 1922). In the words of Duncan Campbell Scott (quoted in Miller 1989), deputy minister for Indian

Affairs at the time: "It is quite within the mark to say that fifty percent of the children who passed through these schools did not live to benefit from the education which they had received therein." Of those who survived, harsh discipline, and incidents of sexual and physical abuse, coerced children away from their language and tradition and inflicted psychological scars that remain to this day (Caribou Tribal Council 1991).

Resistance to these destructive forces was, for the most part, underground. The most visible symbol of opposition, the 1885 Métis resistance in Manitoba and Saskatchewan, in part provoked by the perceived failure of the Crown to provide food during a period of famine, was crushed through armed force (Brogden 1991). Imprisonment, fines, and relocation were used in other regions of the country to enforce assimilationist policies (Titely 1989). Otherwise, the "welfare" of Aboriginal societies was systematically neglected (Bryce 1922; Graham-Cumming 1967; Vanast 1991a). Famine and disease were allowed to virtually decimate Aboriginal communities. Communities were unaided, except that survivors were relocated to state institutions. The "housing" provided was of the poorest quality, and health care and education were, until quite recently, left to the church (Vanast 1991a).

Western health care providers generally assumed that Aboriginal medicine had disappeared. When Western medical practitioners were aware of traditional healing, it was characterized as "superstition" or "witchcraft." In most cases, however, it was assumed to no longer exist (Jilek 1982; Gregory 1988).

In many communities, the church had successfully convinced much of the population that traditional spirituality and healing were evil. Therefore, those few elders who retained traditional knowledge, and who sought to practice healing ceremonies in public, were sometimes viewed with skepticism and suspicion by the younger generations.

After decades of ignoring the health of the Aboriginal Peoples, in the 1950s the Canadian state began to develop a system of primary care clinics, a public health program, and regional hospitals. Initiated primarily in response to the threat that epidemics of tuberculosis posed to the external society, this system adopted an authoritarian approach, where Aboriginal people were forced to become dependent on Western medical institutions (O'Neil 1986, Vanast 1991b). In practice, this meant Aboriginal people had little choice but to undergo treatment in medical facilities away from their communities. Furthermore, they had to accept public health campaigns that were often insensitive to local social and cultural systems. In the worst cases, they had to unwillingly accept invasive medical procedures, such as sterilization (O'Neil and Kaufert forthcoming).

Until quite recently, virtually all providers of services in Aboriginal communities were non-Aboriginal, and they behaved according to Euro-Canadian cultural standards. Little interest was shown in the cultural practices or values of Aboriginal "clients." Encounters were often clouded by suspicion, misunderstanding, resentment, and racism (Speck 1987; O'Neil 1989; Kaufert and O'Neil 1990).

It was not until the 1960s that the Canadian state's disinterest in fulfilling its obligation to Aboriginal societies was met with systematic Aboriginal resistance. Aboriginal organizations formed to represent the interests of their people in the courts and legislatures of Canada (Ponting and Gibbins 1980).[2] Fundamental to these initiatives were:

1. The interpretation of treaties as understood by the Aboriginal Peoples;
2. The assertion of Aboriginal identity and rights by those excluded from the treaties;
3. The establishment of Aboriginal claim to traditional territories; and
4. The assertion of the right to self-government (Little Bear et al. 1984).

Moreover, these initiatives sought to recast the institutions responsible for structuring the relationship between Aboriginal communities and Canadian society (that is to say, schools, legal and social services, and medical care) in a way that would recognize Aboriginal cultural principles, including community autonomy (Cassidy and Bish 1989; Hawkes 1989).

Throughout this period, growing evidence was accumulating that Aboriginal health status was poor and that it required extraordinary efforts to resolve (Postl 1986). Chronic diseases such as diabetes and heart disease supplanted earlier infectious disease epidemics, such as tuberculosis, as major causes of morbidity and mortality; however, minimal overall reduction in mortality rates was evident (Young 1988b). More recently, injuries and violence, particularly young adult suicides, have become the principal cause of death in many Aboriginal communities (Garro 1988; Health and Welfare Canada 1991).

Statistics, however, do not provide a complete picture of Aboriginal health status. First, most statistics, including those collected and reported by the federal government, typically do not describe the health conditions of Métis and off-reserve and urban Indians (Waldram 1989; Royal Commission on Aboriginal Peoples 1993). Second, they do not provide a clear picture of mental health conditions and social problems in Aboriginal communities, even though family violence, child abuse, and fetal alcohol syndrome are priority areas of concern, particularly among Aboriginal women's organizations (Voices of Aboriginal Women 1989; Femmes

Autochthones du Québec 1991). Third, these data have typically been collected and interpreted by government and university agencies external to Aboriginal communities, without Aboriginal input. Finally, the picture of health conditions that emerges from these statistics often focuses attention on medical services, even though there is substantial evidence to indicate that solutions to Aboriginal health problems do not lie in improved medical services. Rather, the solutions lie in improvements in the conditions of Aboriginal life, including, for example, better local economies, access to nutritional foods, improved housing, better sanitation systems, and community-based healing programs that involve traditional medicine (Young 1988a; Assembly of Manitoba Chiefs 1991).

In the 1970s, a number of consultations and position papers were completed, culminating in a 1979 federal government document on Indian health policy. This policy established both traditional medicine and community control as important components of an Aboriginal health system (Department of Health and Welfare 1979). Also in the seventies, the James Bay and Northern Quebec Hydroelectric Agreement established self-governing structures for health care among the Cree and Inuit of northern Quebec (Peters 1989). Elsewhere, the first Aboriginal health authorities, such as the Alberta Indian Health Commission and the Kateri Memorial Hospital in Quebec, were established (Nuttall 1982; Macaulay 1988).

In the eighties, these initiatives gained momentum:

1. Widespread dissatisfaction with a paternalistic system fueled demands for community control over health services (O'Neil 1981);
2. The federal government initiated a program to devolve responsibility for health and social services to First Nations and the Inuit (Dion-Stout 1991; Gregory et al. 1992);
3. Increased interest in traditional healing at the community level, part of a resurgence of interest in Aboriginal identity, resulted in wider visibility and public acceptance (Young, Ingram, and Swartz 1989; Young and Smith 1992);
4. Professional interest in the cultural values underlying health, and in broader health promotion frameworks, contributed to less paternalistic approaches to providing services (Hagey 1984); and
5. Community healing, as an integrated and holistic effort to approach community well-being from a traditional cultural perspective, began to flourish.

In the nineties, many of the grass-roots initiatives undertaken in the eighties have stalled, and participants have become frustrated by a policy environment resistant to real structural change (Speck 1989; O'Neil 1990). The inequities in health and health services for non-status Aboriginal people have also become more generally apparent. This has been evident in Métis communities and among non-status Aboriginal people living in urban areas. They have increased pressure on federal and provincial governments to acknowledge their historic obligations to all Aboriginal people (Martin 1991; McClure et al. 1992). Meanwhile, representatives of some First Nations have expressed concerns about so-called tripartite agreements involving federal, provincial, and Aboriginal governments. They fear that these agreements could undermine efforts to have the federal government broaden its interpretation of treaty obligations. In turn, they are concerned that this could jeopardize the prospect of having these obligations entrenched in constitutional reform (Hawkes 1989).

In broad terms, Aboriginal health development has come full circle. Community healing was once the essence of the Aboriginal approach to health, and it has once again become the critical element of a holistic concern for community well-being. Nonetheless, impediments to achieving success with community-based initiatives continue to flow from the inconsistent and inequitable policies and practices of state institutions.

SELF-GOVERNMENT AND COLONIAL (WESTERN) MEDICINE

The first Aboriginal initiative to take control of the colonial medical system occurred in 1978, when the federal government attempted to reduce the provision of uninsured services to status Indians.[3] This action provoked a forceful reaction from Indian organizations, such as the National Indian Brotherhood, who argued that treaty rights were being abrogated.

Following a national election, the federal government brought forward a new policy, commonly referred to as the Three Pillars policy. It was intended to restore Aboriginal health through community development and to reaffirm the traditional relationship between the Aboriginal Peoples, the federal government, and the Canadian health care system (including provincial and private medical services). This document has been further interpreted as providing a stimulus both for the recognition of the important role for traditional medicine and for greater Aboriginal involvement in the delivery of services.

Also in 1979, the *Report of the Advisory Commission on Indian and Inuit Health Consultation,* authored by Justice Thomas Berger, provided the first systematic inquiry into Aboriginal dissatisfaction with the health care system. Berger recommended that Inuit and Indian health be addressed separately, given the vastly different traditions and problems faced by each group. He further recommended that funding be provided to a commission on Indian health, a sub-committee of the National Indian Brotherhood, to develop a national Indian health council. This council was intended to assist First Nations communities in developing locally controlled health care systems. With respect to the Inuit, Berger felt their health care needs should be dealt with largely in the context of land claims and ongoing political development (Advisory Commission on Indian and Inuit Health Consultation 1979).

Prior to these national initiatives, the James Bay and Northern Quebec Agreement was signed by representatives of the James Bay Cree, the Inuit of Nunavik, and the federal and Quebec governments. In the process, the first Aboriginal health and social service boards in Canada were created. While debate continues as to whether this agreement serves as a model for Aboriginal self-determination, there have been significant changes in the approach to health and social services as a result of this agreement.[4] In Povungnituk, for example, the Inuit-controlled hospital board has established an Indigenous midwifery program where Inuit midwives provide a full range of care. The program is unique, not only among Aboriginal communities, but for the whole of Canada, and it provides a model for Inuit in other jurisdictions, many of whom regard the expropriation of childbirth from their communities by external authorities as possibly the most significant contemporary threat to community development (O'Neil and Kaufert forthcoming).

One of the first federal health programs to be devolved to Aboriginal administrative authority was the National Native Alcohol and Drug Abuse Program (NNADAP). Established in 1975, it has been responsible for the creation of hundreds of community-based alcohol prevention and treatment projects across the country. Since the early eighties, this program has contributed to the emergence of some of the most significant Aboriginal health initiatives in the country, including the Four Worlds Development Project, the Nechi Institute, the Alkali Lake prohibition strategy, and the more recent Healing the Spirit Worldwide conference in Edmonton. However, recent evidence suggests that despite the remarkable efforts and success of Aboriginal organizations involved in community mental health and alcohol treatment, frustration remains with the extent to which this program is responsive to community needs.[5]

Community Health Representative (CHR) programs, developed as community-based components of the health care system, were also devolved early to community control. The role of the CHR, however, remains a difficult and often poorly defined one.

The federal government initiated the Community Health Demonstration Program (CHDP) in 1981, in an attempt to assess the costs, timing, and implications of future transfers of control (Department of National Health and Welfare 1981). The program, although portrayed as an exercise in self-determination, was roundly criticized by Aboriginal organizations because it was implemented without prior consultation and because "demonstration" implied that long-term transfer was not possible (Indian Management Systems 1985). Just thirty-one projects were funded, and only seven directly addressed the transfer of community health services.

One CHDP project, the Sandy Bay reserve in western Manitoba, has been evaluated by Garro et al. (1986). They found that the CHDP contravened the principles set out in the Berger Inquiry by negotiating directly with the band. This inhibited the important role of regional and national Aboriginal organizations in the monitoring of government policy. These authors also argue that real local control was lacking in the CHDP, because global budgeting was not available and training resources were withheld. Therefore, the program was prevented from developing a truly community-based health plan.

Other examples of community control initiatives, which provide a further understanding of the relationship between self-government and health services, have emerged in the last decade. Some of these are particularly significant because they include non-treaty, urban, and Métis communities:[6]

1. The Alberta Indian Health Commission (AIHCC) was established in 1981 to promote First Nations health concerns in the province. In addition to consultation and liaison with various Aboriginal and provincial organizations, the AIHCC provides administrative support to a provincial CHR organization and has established urban community health representatives in Edmonton and Calgary;[7]

2. The Labrador Inuit Health Commission (LIHC) was created in 1979. Owing to a dispute relating to their rights, the Labrador Inuit Association refused to witness the signing of the 1986 Canada-Newfoundland-Native People's of Labrador Health Agreement and, instead, established the LIHC. It concentrates on CHR-delivered health education and promotion (Allen 1990);

3. The Kateri Memorial Hospital Centre was established in 1955, when a local elder, a Mohawk woman, secured funding from the Mohawk Council of Kahnawake and the Quebec government to continue operating the local hospital. Through almost four decades of tumultuous relations with federal, provincial, and university (McGill) agencies, the hospital has continued to provide curative and preventive services to

Aboriginal residents of the Kahnawake reserve and nearby Montreal (Macaulay 1988); and

4.   Anishnawbe Health Toronto (AHT) was funded in 1988 by the provincial government. It is a multiservice, urban community health center grounded in the principles of the medicine wheel. It is mandated to continue a thirteen-year history of providing services to the off-reserve First Nations, non-status, and Métis Aboriginal population of Toronto (Johnston 1990; Shah 1988).

The majority of community health development in Aboriginal communities in Canada has occurred under the auspices of the 1986 Transfer Initiative of the Medical Services Branch of Health and Welfare Canada. Significant funding has been made available for this program. As of September 1991, there were seventy-nine pre-transfer projects, representing 244 bands, and fourteen signed transfer agreements, representing 55 bands (Gibbons and Associates 1992). Transfer agreements apply only to administrative control of federally sponsored programs, however, not to absolute control of planning, implementation, and evaluation.

The transfer program has been the subject of considerable criticism. Speck (1989), for example, has argued that the transfer initiative may be driven by federal efforts to offload programs and contain costs, not by an interest in responding to Aboriginal community needs. Her concerns are also reflected in some Aboriginal evaluations (Assembly of First Nations 1989; Dion-Stout 1991; Union of Ontario Indians and Assembly of First Nations 1991). This cautious acceptance of the program has been articulated by the Swampy Cree Tribal Council (Connell, Flett, and Stewart 1990):

> Overall, this policy direction has been criticized as an attempt to abrogate treaty rights and have Indian people administer their own misery. Nevertheless, we entered the transfer process with our eyes wide open. We saw transfer as a way to achieve some of our objectives and we felt we could look after ourselves in dealing with government.

Gregory et al. (1992) have provided a critical evaluation of one First Nation's experience with the program. They conclude that the policy does little to address the wider socio-economic and environmental sources of ill health. They argue that the transfer policy reinforces the dominance of a medical model of health that, by definition, maintains relations of power over Aboriginal Peoples. These authors also report that the Gull Lake First Nation in Ontario has suspended transfer proceedings. They are developing a more comprehensive community health development plan.

Others, however, describe a more positive picture for locally controlled health services. Gibbons (1992) has concluded that most First Nations are generally satisfied with the transfer process. Nonetheless, a number of problems remain:

1. Unclear relationship with self-government;
2. Lack of recognition of treaty rights to health;
3. Lack of legislative authority to enforce public health laws; and
4. Need for program enrichment to meet new needs.

In Montreal Lake, Saskatchewan, a recent study (Moore, Forbes, and Henderson 1990) concludes that the provision of primary care under band control has resulted in the following positive changes:

1. People feel the reserve is safer;
2. People feel better cared for;
3. Confidentiality and trust of health care staff has been enhanced;
4. Elders feel better cared for;
5. Healthy changes in lifestyle were reported;
6. Children were hospitalized less often;
7. Less violence was reported in the community;
8. There was less alcohol and more "dry" activities;
9. Coordination with hospitals was better;
10. More comprehensive services were provided;
11. There were better emergency and acute care services;
12. Earlier intervention in the disease cycle was reported, with projected lower hospitalization rates; and
13. Health center staff were perceived as role models for community health development.

Devolution of health services in the Northwest Territories was initiated in the early 1980s. Devolution was in response to pressure from Inuit Tapirisat of Canada, although the Dene Nation expressed serious reservations about the potential impact on land claims. By 1988, the transfer of authority for health to the territorial government and regional health boards was completed.

Evaluations of the NWT process have been largely critical. O'Neil (1990, 1991), for example, has argued that little real empowerment of regional health boards has occurred, resulting in increasing tension and alienation between Yellowknife and Inuit in the regions. A recent audit of the health devolution process by the auditor general of Canada (1992) echoes these concerns. Moreover, the Inuit have expressed the desire to have control over health services embedded in self-government agreements, particularly in the creation of Nunavut. The territorial bureaucracy has resisted this process. Recent developments suggest many of the problems cited above are the result of the federal government's failure to provide sufficient funding to support the development of a health care system grounded in Inuit, Dene, and Métis social values.

SELF-GOVERNMENT AND TRADITIONAL MEDICINE

Canada is one of the few countries in the world where medical pluralism is not taken for granted. The medical profession in Canada has assumed greater control over healing activities than anywhere else either in the industrialized world or in the developing world. Perhaps the best example of this is midwifery.

In Canada, midwifery is defined as a medical act, whereas it is a separate, legal, and widely used professional service in most of the rest of the world (including the United States, Europe, and Australia). Other healing systems, such as homeopathy, chiropractic medicine, acupuncture, and naturopathy, are also well-established professions in other countries and, in some instances, are state supported through health insurance (for example, in Britain). Ayurvedic and Chinese medicine are examples of ancient and widely used healing systems for much of the world's population (in India and China respectively).

It is beyond the scope of this paper to address the social history of Aboriginal medicine in Canada. However, it must be pointed out that traditional medicine has been, and continues to be, misunderstood and underestimated by mainstream health care providers. Indeed, for a period of time, one might describe the interaction as systematically condescending and discriminatory toward the traditional healing methods employed by Aboriginal healers.

Although traditional Aboriginal medicine has always fascinated external observers, and much has been written that purports to describe and analyze beliefs and practices, very little of this literature is useful in understanding the history of traditional medicine or contemporary Aboriginal perspectives. Much of what has been written is from what anthropologists refer to as an "etic" perspective—the phenomenon is understood according to the explanatory frameworks of the external observer. For example, traditional medicine is described as a mechanism of social control, in an effort to provide a "rational" explanation for a phenomenon which, to the Western scientific mind, is irrational and unintelligible. Rarely have "emic" explanations been attempted—explanations that attempt to understand Aboriginal medicine in its own terms, according to the world view of its practitioners.

Unlike some of the other pluralistic traditions described above, Aboriginal medicine does not have a large literature documenting its knowledge base. This is because Aboriginal medicine is an oral tradition, and oral traditions require a social environment that is supportive and protective of knowledge transmission from generation to generation. The catastrophic population losses described earlier, combined with federal legislation and religious oppression, have served to severely threaten the knowledge base of Aboriginal medicine.[8]

Traditional Aboriginal medicine in Canada, historically at least, should be understood as a diverse and heterogeneous phenomenon, albeit with some consistent principles and values, including the importance of spiritual well-being and balance in everyday life. Nonetheless, considerable variation exists from the medicine societies of the Kwakw*aka*'wakw and Anishina'beg, to the family-based *angatquq* of the Inuit. Additionally, within each society, other healers, such as midwives and herbalists, are recognized.

In those Aboriginal societies where traditional healing was organized into a more institutional framework, resistance to the destructive forces described above was possible. In communities where healers functioned independently, however, such as among the Inuit, resistance was weaker.

It would be a mistake to characterize all Aboriginal communities and individuals as participants in traditional medicine. Many communities, and many individuals, have adopted Christianity as a spiritual basis for well-being. They remain skeptical of "Indian medicine." Many Inuit and Métis communities regard Christian spirituality as a legitimate and important component of their culture, and they look to these values as a basis for community healing.

Traditional medicine must also be understood in more holistic terms than Western medicine. Attempts to compare the two systems from a Western institutional perspective fail to grasp the pervasive way that Aboriginal medicine underpins Aboriginal culture. Aboriginal medicine is independent of the state-imposed regulatory structures that affect so many other aspects of contemporary Aboriginal life. It "works" largely because participants accept the authority of medicine people to effect changes in their everyday lives. This authority derives from an altogether different source than the authority delegated from the Canadian state. Aboriginal medicine, in this sense, is a way of life, complete with guidelines for behavior, systems of authority, and, in some instances, punitive mechanisms.[9]

Although traditional medicine should be considered in the context of self-government, it is not a system that can be regulated by community, band, or tribal governments in the way that the Canadian state can regulate the institutions of colonial medicine. In fact, in some communities, it is more likely that various levels of Aboriginal government will be regulated by the authority structure of traditional medicine.

An example of the role that traditional medicine potentially can play in community health programs under self-government can be found in the experience of the Peguis First Nation in Manitoba (Cohen 1993). During the 1980s, increasing numbers of band members approached health center staff (the health center had previously been transferred to band control) for assistance in accessing traditional healers. In 1985, health center staff negotiated with the Medical Services Branch of Health and Welfare Canada for the provision of travel costs to facilitate referral to traditional healers. Demand for these services has grown to the point that a traditional healer now travels to Peguis at least once every three months to hold "clinics" at the Matootoo Lake traditional healing center.

The Matootoo healing center was established by Mide Megwun Bird, one of seven traditional chiefs appointed by the female elders of the Three Fires (Midewiwin) Society. "Clinics" held at the center usually see an average of thirty to forty clients. Between July 1991 and March 1993, for example, the center reported there were 325 referrals for traditional healing, and these numbers do not include those who approached healers directly.

The success of the traditional clinic has raised questions about the limitations of the support provided by the Medical Services Branch of Health and Welfare Canada, and about the limitations of referral systems with hospitals and regulatory systems to ensure quality of care. For the Peguis people who are involved in the healing center, raising the awareness of Western health professionals and maintaining Aboriginal community-based control over the regulation of traditional practices are essential for future development.

The purpose of this brief review is to underscore the historical basis for contemporary differences in Aboriginal responses to the renewal of traditional medicine.[10] The resurgence of ceremonial activity for healing purposes has caused a profound change in the lives of many Aboriginal people and now constitutes a widely used alternative to Western medicine in many communities, particularly in western Canada. Moreover, there is increasing interest in its potential by Western health care providers, as evidenced in the increasing demand on traditional healers to introduce and orient health care workers to the concepts of traditional Aboriginal medicine.[11]

SELF-GOVERNMENT AND HEALTH

What is the connection, then, between self-government and health?[12] It is not easy to establish a causal link. This stems from the remarkable web of causation of ill health that extends into all aspects of the social, cultural, and political life of the Aboriginal Peoples. Nonetheless, by examining the key components of the web, it is possible to speculate about the probable consequences that self-government will have on Aboriginal health status.

Poverty has been known to be an important determinant of health for fifty years. Mortality, for example, is significantly correlated with social class (Black et al. 1982; Whitehead 1992). Likewise, longevity can be linked to income (Berkman and Breslow 1983). Aboriginal people suffer a high degree of unemployment, a high dependency on social assistance, and low incomes relative to other Canadians. In short, they live in poverty (Hagey, Larocque, and McBride 1989). This helps to explain the dispropor-tionate mortality rates described earlier. If self-government improves the economic status of Aboriginal people, it is reasonable to expect that health status will improve.

The likely sources of improved economic status associated with self-government are at least twofold. First, when self-government is linked to land and land claims, the satisfactory conclusion of these claims will provide resources (cash, land, or both) to Aboriginal people. Second, with self-government, job creation, or job displacement, will favor Aboriginal people. This would provide wage employment for an expanded proportion of the Aboriginal population.

Self-government is grounded in the traditional values of the Aboriginal Peoples, and it promotes social, political, and cultural development. Traditional health networks will be fostered under self-government, and the policy-setting agenda for health will no longer be set externally. This rebalancing of the system in favor of Aboriginal values will lead to empowerment and to improvements in self-esteem for those working within the system, as well as for those served by it. Improvements in health will result from the self-esteem and empowerment that self-government brings about (International Conference on Health Promotion 1986).

The link between health, self-esteem, and control over conditions in one's community is well established.[13] If crowding can be reduced, and water and sewage systems improved, for example, there will be a reduction in the incidence of infectious diseases. If employment, self-esteem, and personal empowerment are improved, there will be fewer injuries, suicides, and homicides.

Finally, with the control implicit in self-government, Aboriginal people will assume roles now filled by non-Aboriginals. The positive impact of this role modeling on young Aboriginal people could reasonably be expected to result in diminished alcoholism, drug dependency, and violence within the community.

Self-government, then, will constitute an enormous step in breaking the cycle of poverty, disadvantage, and hopelessness that now causes an extensive burden of illness in Aboriginal communities. While self-govern-ment will improve the effectiveness of health care services, its more important result will be to prevent the causes of ill health in the first place. From the standpoint of Aboriginal rights, as well as from humanistic and economic points of view, this is a goal well worth striving for.

NOTES

1   Sections of this paper are derived from research for the Royal Commission on Aboriginal Peoples. The authors are grateful for their support. Case study materials on Peguis First Nation and Povungnituk were provided by Benita Cohen and Christopher Fletcher respectively. The authors would also like to thank the faculty and staff of the Northern Health Research Unit at the University of Manitoba for their contributions. Joan Mollins contributed significantly to the bibliographic work.
2   Aboriginal political development was kindled, in part, as a critical response to the federal White Paper of 1969. This document was perceived as an effort to dismantle the Indian Act. While the act was considered by many as colonial and genocidal, it was perceived by others as "protective," in that it set out the federal responsibility for Aboriginal Peoples.
3   Uninsured services are those, such as drugs and eyeglasses, that are not provided to all Canadians through the medicare system.
4   For contrasting perspectives on this debate, see Salisbury (1986) and Weaver (1990).
5   Concerns about NNADAP have been expressed by the Four Worlds Develop-ment Project (1990).
6   For reasons of space, we provide only a brief listing here. The interested reader is referred to the bibliography by Young and Smith (1992) for more details.
7   For a description of the history and activities of the Alberta Indian Health Care Commission, see Nuttall (1982).
8   Titely (1989) describes amendments to the Indian Act that proscribed

traditional healing ceremonies. They were sponsored by missionaries and Indian agents concerned that these ceremonies were a threat to the conversion of Aboriginal populations to "hard-working" Christian farmers.

9 A somewhat inflammatory article in the Victoria *Times Colonist* (July 18, 1992, "Couple Caught in Cultural Crunch"), describes the practice of initiating new members into a longhouse community, sometimes against their will. This was used as a form of remedial action, when families determined a member was acting inappropriately. In this instance, the individual brought charges against the band and spirit dancers for unlawful confinement.

10 Interestingly, this process was prophesied by Albert Lightning in 1976 at a University of Manitoba Native health conference.

11 For example, in June 1993, the Manitoba Medical Association, together with the Brokenhead First Nation, organized a workshop on traditional medicine that drew over 120 participants, including 45 physicians.

12 Of course, the compelling need for self-government does not rest solely on its likely impact on health status. Rather, it is a recognition of existing and historical relationships. It is also a just and right consequence of a century of colonial rule, oppression, and many, many acts of omission and commission perpetrated against Aboriginal Peoples.

13 In 1986, for example, the Honourable Jake Epp, the federal minister of health, released a document entitled "A Framework for Health Promotion." Within it, he cited the challenges of reducing inequities, increasing prevention, and enhancing coping by self-help, mutual care, and healthy environments. Strengthening community participation is a cornerstone of this framework.

REFERENCES

Advisory Commission on Indian and Inuit Health Consultation (Berger Commission). 1979. *Report of the advisory commission on Indian and Inuit health consultation*. Ottawa: Government of Canada.

Allen, I. 1990. Community health representatives working in Labrador Inuit communities. In *Circumpolar health 90,* ed. B. Postl et al. Winnipeg: University of Manitoba Press.

Assembly of First Nations. 1989. *Draft discussion paper: Health program transfer proposal of Medical Services Branch*. Ottawa: Assembly of First Nations.

Assembly of Manitoba Chiefs. 1991. *Family violence and community healing: A plan of action.* Winnipeg: Assembly of Manitoba Chiefs.

Auditor General of Canada. 1992. *Comprehensive audit of the Department of Health: A report to the Legislative Assembly of the Northwest Territories.* Ottawa: Auditor General of Canada.

Berkman, L. F., and L. Breslow. 1983. *Health and ways of living: The Alameda county study.* New York: Oxford University Press.

Black, D., J. N. Morris, C. Smith, and P. Townsend. 1982. *Inequalities in health: The Black report.* Middlesex, UK: Penguin.

Brogden, Mike. 1991. The rise and fall of the western Metis in the criminal justice process. Pp. 39–68 in *The struggle for recognition: Canadian justice and the Metis nation,* ed. S. W. Corrigan and L. J. Barkwell. Winnipeg: Manitoba Metis Federation.

Bryce, P. H. 1922. *The story of a national crime: An appeal for justice to the Indians of Canada.* Ottawa: James Hope and Sons.

Caribou Tribal Council. 1991. *Faith misplaced: Lasting effects of abuse in a First Nations community.*

Carson, B., and B. D. Postl. 1991. Perinatal infant morbidity and mortality study, NWT follow-up, 1982–83. Pp. 185–97 in *Between two worlds: The report of the NWT perinatal and infant mortality and morbidity study,* ed. B. Carson and B. D. Postl. Edmonton: Canadian Circumpolar Institute.

Cassidy, Frank, and Robert L. Bish. 1989. *Indian government: Its meaning and practice.* Lantzville, BC, and Halifax: Oolichan Books and the Institute for Research on Public Policy.

Cohen, Benita. 1993. Health services development in an Aboriginal community: The case of Peguis First Nation. Final report submitted to the Royal Commission on Aboriginal Peoples, Ottawa.

Connell, G., R. Flett, and P. Stewart. 1990. Implementing primary health care through community control: The experience of the Swampy Cree Tribal Council. In *Circumpolar health 90,* ed. B. Postl et al. Winnipeg: University of Manitoba Press.

Department of Health and Welfare. 1979. *Indian health discussion paper.* Ottawa: Department of Health and Welfare.

Department of National Health and Welfare. 1981. *Discussion paper: Transfer of health services to Indian communities.* Ottawa: Department of National Health and Welfare.

Dion-Stout, M. 1991. The role of participation in First Nations health development: Is transfer an empowering process? *Synergy* 3(3):1–2.

Dufour, R., and F. Therien. 1990. Otitis media and the patterns of child morbidity in Kuujjuarapik. Pp. 650–51 in *Circumpolar health 90,* ed. B. Postl et al. Winnipeg: University of Manitoba Press.

Femmes Autochthones du Québec. 1991. *Domestic violence in Aboriginal communities: Reference manual.* Quebec: Government of Quebec.

Four Worlds Development Project. 1990. Survival secrets of NNADAP workers. *Four Worlds Exchange* 2(1):24–39.

Fumoleau, R. 1973. *As long as the land shall last.* Toronto: McClelland and Stewart.

Garro, L. C. 1988. Resort to traditional healers in a Manitoba Ojibwa community. *Arctic Medical Research* 47(Suppl. 1):317–20.

Garro, L. C., J. Roulette, and R. Whitmore. 1986. Community control of health care delivery: The Sandy Bay experience. *Canadian Journal of Public Health* 77 (July/August):281–84.

Gibbins, Roger, and J. Rick Ponting. 1986. Historical overview and background. Pp. 18–57 in *Arduous journey: Canadian Indians and decolonization,* ed. J. R. Ponting. Toronto: McClelland and Stewart.

Gibbons, Adrian, and Associates. 1992. *Short-term evaluation of Indian health transfer.* Ottawa: National Health and Welfare Canada.

Graham-Cumming, G. 1967. Health of the original Canadians, 1867–1967. *Medical Services Journal of Canada* 23:115–66.

Gregory, David. 1988. An exploration of the contact between nurses and Indian elders/traditional healers on Indian reserves and health centres in Manitoba. Pp. 39–43 in *Health care issues in the Canadian north,* ed. D. Young. Edmonton: Boreal Institute for Northern Studies.

Gregory, D., C. Russell, J. Hurd, J. Tyance, and J. Sloan. 1992. Canada's Indian health transfer policy: The Gull Lake Band experience. *Human Organization* 51(3):214–22.

Hagey, R. 1984. The phenomenon, the explanations, and the responses: Metaphors surrounding diabetes in urban Canadian Indians. *Social Science and Medicine* 18(3):265–72.

Hagey, N. J., G. Larocque, and C. McBride. 1989. *Highlights of Aboriginal conditions 1981–2001.* Ottawa: Indian and Northern Affairs Canada.

Hawkes, David C., ed. 1989. *Aboriginal Peoples and government responsibility: Exploring federal and provincial roles.* Ottawa:Carleton University Press.

Health Advisory Network. 1992. *Manitoba northern health services task force, final report.* Winnipeg: Government of Manitoba.

Health and Welfare Canada. 1991. *Health status of Canadian Indians and Inuit— 1990.* Ottawa: Minister of Supply and Services.

Hoffman, W. J. 1981. *The Midewiwin or 'Grand Medicine Society' of the Ojibwa.* Washington: U.S. Government Printing Office.

Indian Management Systems. 1985. *CHDP evaluation report.* Regina: Indian Management Systems.

International Conference on Health Promotion. 1986. Ottawa charter. Paper presented at the International Conference on Health Promotion, Ottawa.

Jilek, W. 1982. *Indian healing: Shamanistic ceremonialism in the Pacific Northwest today.* Surrey, BC: Hancock House.

Jilek, W., and N. Todd. 1974. Witchdoctors succeed where doctors fail: Psychotherapy among coast Salish Indians. *Canadian Psychiatric Association Journal* 19:351–55.

Johnston, V. 1990. Health: Yesteryear and today. In *Multiculturalism and health care: Realities and needs,* ed. R. Masi. Ontario: Canadian Council on Multicultural Health.

Kaufert, J. M., and W. W. Koolage. 1984. Role conflict among 'culture brokers': The experience of Native Canadian medical interpreters. *Social Science Medicine* 18(3):183–286.

Kaufert, J. M., and J. O'Neil. 1990. Biomedical rituals and informed consent: Native Canadians and the negotiation of clinical trust. In *Social science perspectives on medical ethics*, ed. G. Weisz. Dordrecht: Kluwer Academic Publishers.

Little Bear, Leroy., Menno Boldt, and J. Anthony Long, eds. 1984. *Pathways to self-determination: Canadian Indians and the Canadian state*. Toronto: University of Toronto Press.

Macaulay, A. C. 1988. The history of a successful community-oriented health service in Kahnawake, Quebec. *Canadian Family Physician* 34:2167–69.

McClure, L., M. Boulanger, J. Kaufert, and S. Forsyth. 1992. *First Nations urban health bibliography: A review of the literature and exploration of strategies*. Winnipeg: Northern Health Research Unit.

Martin, Fred V. 1991. Federal and provincial responsibility in the Metis settlements of Alberta. Pp. 243–97 in *Aboriginal peoples and government responsibility: Exploring federal and provincial roles*, ed. D. C. Hawkes and Allan Maslove. Ottawa: Carleton University Press.

Mayhurst Consulting Group Inc. 1993. *Department of National Health and Welfare submission to the Royal Commission on Aboriginal Peoples*. Ottawa: Mayhurst Consulting Group Inc.

Miller, J. 1989. *Skyscrapers hide the heavens*. Toronto: University of Toronto Press.

Moffatt, M. E. K. 1991. Nutritional deficiencies and Native infants. *Canadian Journal of Paediatrics* December:20–25.

Moore, M., H. Forbes, and L. Henderson. 1990. The provision of primary health care services under band control: The Montreal Lake case. *Native Studies Review* 6(1):153–64.

Morris, A. [1880] 1979. *The treaties of Canada with the Indians*. Reprint, Toronto: Coles.

Nandy, Ashis. 1983. *The intimate enemy: Loss and recovery of self under colonialism*. Delhi: Oxford University Press.

Norris, M. J. 1990. The demography of Aboriginal people in Canada. In *Ethnic demography: Canadian immigrant, racial and cultural variations*, ed. S. S. Halli, F. Travato, and L. Dreidger. Ottawa: Carleton University Press.

Nuttall, R. N. 1982. The development of Indian boards of health in Alberta. *Canadian Journal of Public Health* 73(5):300–03.

Obomsawin, R. 1980. Traditional Indian health and nutrition: Forgotten keys to survival into the 21st century. Pp. 43–55 in *Selected readings in support of Indian and Inuit consultation* (vol. 1), Health and Welfare Canada. Ottawa: Health and Welfare Canada.

O'Neil, J. D. 1991. Democratizing health services in the Northwest Territories: Is devolution having an impact? *Northern Review* 5:60–82.

———. 1990. The impact of devolution on health services in the Baffin region, NWT: A case study. In *Devolution and constitutional development in the Canadian north*, ed. G. Dacks. Ottawa: Carleton University Press.

————. 1989. The cultural and political context of patient dissatisfaction: A Canadian Inuit study. *Medical Anthropology Quarterly* 3(4):325–44.

————. 1986. The politics of health in the fourth world: A northern Canadian example. *Human Organization* 45(2):119–28.

————. 1981. Health care in the central Canadian Arctic: Continuities and change. In *Health and Canadian society: Sociological perspectives*, ed. D. Coburn et al. Toronto: Fitzhenry and Whiteside.

O'Neil, J. D., and P. Kaufert. Forthcoming. Irniktakpunga: Sex determination and the Inuit struggle for birthing rights in northern Canada. In *Conceiving the new world order: Global and local intersections in the politics of reproduction*, ed. F. Ginsberg and R. Rapp. Los Angeles: University of California Press.

Peters, Evelyn J. 1989. Federal and provincial responsibilities for the Cree, Naskapi, and Inuit under the James Bay and northern Quebec, and northeastern Quebec agreements. Pp. 173–243 in *Aboriginal peoples and government responsibility: Exploring federal and provincial roles*, ed. David C. Hawkes and Allan Maslove. Ottawa: Carleton University Press.

Ponting, J. Rick, and Roger Gibbins. 1980. *Out of irrelevance: A socio-political introduction to Indian affairs in Canada*. Toronto: Butterworths.

Postl, B. D. 1986. Native health—A continuing concern. *Canadian Journal of Public Health* 77(4):253–54.

Royal Commission on Aboriginal Peoples. 1993. *Aboriginal peoples in urban centres*. Ottawa: Minister of Supply and Services.

Salisbury, R. F. 1986. *A homeland for the Cree: Regional development in James Bay—1971–1981*. Montreal: McGill-Queen's University Press.

Shah, C. P. 1988. A national overview of the health of Native peoples living in Canadian cities. In *Inner city health—the needs of urban Natives*, ed. Y. Yacoub. Edmonton: University of Alberta.

Speck, Dara Culhane. 1989. The Indian health transfer policy: A step in the right direction or revenge of the hidden agenda? *Native Studies Review* 5(1):187–213.

————. 1987. *An error in judgement: The politics of medical care in an Indian/white community*. Vancouver: Talon Books.

Stanley, G. F. 1983. As long as the sun shines and the river flows: An historical comment. In *As long as the sun shines and the river flows: A reader in Canadian Native studies,* ed. A. L. Getty and A. Lussier. Vancouver: University of British Columbia Press.

Thorton, R. 1985. *American Indian holocaust and survival: A population history since 1492*. Norman, OK: University of Oklahoma Press.

Titely, R. 1989. *A narrow vision*. Toronto: University of Toronto Press.

Union of Ontario Indians and Assembly of First Nations. 1991. *First Nations health transfer forum*. Ontario: Union of Ontario Indians.

Vanast, W. 1991a. Hastening the day of extinction: Canada, Quebec, and the medical care of Ungava's Inuit, 1867–1967. *Etudes/Inuit/Studies* 15(2):55–84.

———. 1991b. The death of Jennie Kanajuq: Tuberculosis, religious competition, and cultural conflict in Coppermine, 1929–31. *Etudes/Inuit/Studies* 15(1):75–104.

Voices of Aboriginal Women. 1989. *Aboriginal women speak out about violence*. Ottawa: Canadian Council on Social Development.

Weaver, S. 1990. Self-government policy for Indians 1980–1990: Political transformation or symbolic gestures. Paper presented at the 1989 UNESCO conference on migration and the transformation of cultures, Calgary, October 1989.

Waldram, J. 1989. *Health care in Saskatoon's inner city: A comparative study of Native and non-Native utilization patterns*. Winnipeg: Institute of Urban Studies.

Whitehead, M. 1992. The concepts and principles of equity and health. *International Journal of Health Services* 22(3):429–45.

Young, D., G. Ingram, and L. Swartz. 1989. *Cry of the eagle: Encounters with a Cree healer*. Toronto: University of Toronto Press.

Young, D., and L. Smith. 1992. *The involvement of Canadian Native communities in their health care programs: A review of literature since the 1970's*. Edmonton: Canadian Circumpolar Institute.

Young, T. K. 1988a. *Health care and cultural change: The Indian experience in the central subarctic*. Toronto: University of Toronto Press.

———. 1988b. Are subarctic Indians undergoing the epidemiologic transition? *Social Science and Medicine* 26(6):659–71.

———. 1984. Indian health services in Canada: A sociohistorical perspective. *Social Science and Medicine* 18:257–64.

———. 1983. Cancer surveillance in a remote Indian population in northwestern Ontario. *American Journal of Public Health* 73:515–520.

CHAPTER 5

EDUCATION FOR SELF-DETERMINATION[1]

EBER HAMPTON AND STEVEN WOLFSON
SASKATCHEWAN INDIAN FEDERATED COLLEGE

In this chapter, we examine the assimilationist, integrated, federated, and independent models of First Nations education as possible approaches to a national Aboriginal education strategy. We argue that a combination of the independent and federated models is the most consistent with the principles of self-determination and is also the one most likely to succeed in improving educational opportunities for the Aboriginal Peoples.

The strategy we favor involves establishing an independent post-secondary educational system that can support continued development of local and regional Aboriginal education and self-government initiatives. Although the focus of the discussion is on post-secondary education, we believe many of the same principles also apply to primary and secondary education for the Aboriginal Peoples. Similarly, while our main interest is in the development of educational opportunities for First Nations Peoples, we believe the strategy we are proposing also applies, albeit with some modifications, to other Aboriginal groups in Canada.

To conclude this chapter, we present the history of the Saskatchewan Indian Federated College as a leading example of the struggle to create and implement an independent, Aboriginally controlled post-secondary educational system in Canada.

CANADA'S TREATY OBLIGATIONS:
EQUAL EDUCATIONAL ATTAINMENT

Eber Hampton, co-author of this chapter, states his personal experiences with the Canadian educational system:

> I didn't understand my own education until my grandfather helped me put it into perspective. In college I took a course in the psychology of human motivation that covered concentration camps, brainwashing, and prisoners of war. When I talked to Grandpa about what we were studying, he said to me: "We are prisoners of peace." When he said that, my own

90

educational experience fell into place. I suddenly understood the love-hate relationship I had with education.

In considering the question of rights to post-secondary education, we must consider education as a human right, as an Aboriginal right, and as a treaty right:

1. As a human right because in our complex world, post-secondary education is becoming so necessary that we must begin to consider it as a prerequisite to survival;
2. As an Aboriginal right because there is an additional obligation to provide education that will help preserve distinctive communities, languages, and cultures; and
3. As a treaty right because the treaties that the Crown entered into with the Aboriginal Peoples go beyond basic human and Aboriginal rights.

In exchange for vast tracts of land, the Crown committed Canada to equally vast educational obligations. The essence of these obligations was a commitment to equal educational attainment for Aboriginal and non-Aboriginal people. The Crown's failure to perform these obligations is often attributed to a lack of will or to a shortage of funding. Even though these problems have been significant, we believe that the Crown's more fundamental failure has been in the model of education it has chosen to adopt.

Education has hurt the Aboriginal Peoples and it has helped us. It is part of the problem and part of the solution. The fire that cooks our food and the fire of napalm are both called fire. In the same way, we can distinguish between many different human activities that are called education (Hampton 1993).

There is a difference between "education for assimilation" and "education for self-determination" (Havighurst 1981; Saskatchewan Indian Federated College 1993). "Education for assimilation" is based on the belief that Aboriginal cultures and languages are inferior and that the Aboriginal Peoples should assimilate to the "better" ways of the racially and culturally superior dominant society (Haig-Brown 1988).

The assimilationist model of education is most clearly seen in the residential schools. In these schools, Aboriginal children were removed from their communities; they were required to learn the customs and traditions of the dominant society; they were punished for practicing their language or culture; and they were subjected to all manner of physical and psychological abuse. In the process, Aboriginal education was undermined.

91

While residential schools are an extreme example, vestiges of this approach remain to this day. For several generations, Aboriginal individuals, families, and communities have experienced something called education based on this false premise. The effects of this perversion of education have been devastating to all concerned.

Education for self-determination, on the other hand, was what our chiefs and elders had in mind when they negotiated the treaties. Our ancestors made treaties to share this beautiful country. They looked ahead with love and wisdom, and they saw a changing world. To the people newly arrived from Europe they said: let us put our minds together and see what kind of world we will make for our children; we will share the land with you; you will share schools, medicine, and the tools for making a living in this changing world with us. Both Aboriginal and non-Aboriginal treaty makers shared a vision of a future in which Aboriginal people would be as well educated as non-Aboriginal people. In the words of Alexander Morris (1880, p. 213), the Queen's representative: "Your children will be taught, and then they will be as able to take care of themselves as the whites around them." The brainwashing model of education cannot succeed. Rather, it is only in partnership with Aboriginally controlled institutions that Canada can fulfill its treaty obligations of equal educational attainment.

FOUR MODELS OF INDIGENOUS EDUCATION

Barnhardt (1991) has completed an analysis of over one hundred Indigenous higher education programs and institutions. He grouped programs into three categories—independent, affiliated, or integrated—according to the degree of organizational autonomy they exhibited. Barnhardt correctly included only those programs or institutions that were "controlled or guided by indigenous people," and that were "intended to address the particular social, cultural, political, and economic interests" of the Aboriginal population they served. Thus, he excludes as unworthy of consideration a fourth model—the assimilationist model—even though it is the most common. For the purposes of our analysis, however, we would like to briefly discuss all four models of Indigenous higher education.

1. THE ASSIMILATIONIST MODEL OF INDIGENOUS HIGHER EDUCATION: DISCREDITED BUT POPULAR

The assimilationist model assumes that the non-Indigenous, Euro-centric university is a universal institution. The racism of North American universities is ignored, or it is understood only in so far as it is sometimes recognized that Indigenous students are denied access to these institutions. The effects of racism on universities' knowledge base, governance, teaching, and service, however, is not widely understood and is, therefore, not addressed.

The assimilationist model denies the legitimate contributions and decision-making roles of the Aboriginal Peoples in higher education. The task of Indigenous education, according to the assimilationist model, is to create access to the benefits of a university education by providing funding and support to Aboriginal students so that they can attend these institutions. Indigenous students will then be able to attain "university standards."

A recent review of university education in Saskatchewan (Johnson 1993) provides an example of an approach to Aboriginal education guided by the assimilationist model. In this report, Johnson recommends so-called access programs as a temporary measure to help Aboriginal students meet university standards. Once these standards are attained, however, it is proposed that Aboriginal students be fully assimilated into the university system. The report mistakenly concludes that, once access is achieved, the need for Aboriginal programs and institutions will fade away to a narrow cultural and artistic focus.

The Indian student support program funded by the Department of Indian Affairs and Northern Development (DIAND) is another example of the assimilationist model in action. It provides a marginally higher standard of living than social assistance for some Aboriginal students who qualify for the program. However support is only available as long as Aboriginal students are able and willing to maintain student status in universities that are structurally, epistemologically, and instructionally biased against them (TeHennepe 1993).

There is nothing new about the assimilationist model of Aboriginal education. The first higher education institution in North America, Harvard College, was established to educate the Aboriginal and non-Aboriginal youth of the colonies. Thus, there is over three hundred years of experience on which the assimilation model of education can be judged. Education for assimilation has left the Aboriginal Peoples with the lowest educational attainment of any group in Canada. It has been an expensive failure. But the results are far worse than that. Aboriginal individuals and communities have been repeatedly branded as failures, the racism of universities and society has been perpetuated, and avenues for Aboriginal contributions to world knowledge have been denied.

The assimilationist model creates and maintains a dependence on systemic oppression, and it amounts to a form of cultural genocide. Resources devoted to it create more problems than solutions. There are, however, other approaches that provide opportunities to create and implement education for self-determination. These involve increasing degrees of Aboriginal control over Aboriginal education.

2. THE INTEGRATED MODEL OF INDIGENOUS HIGHER EDUCATION: SUCCESSFUL IN RARE CIRCUMSTANCES

Integrated models of Aboriginal education include "programs and units contained wholly within and administered by existing mainstream institutions" (Barnhardt 1991, p. 216). Within the integrated model, there is a continuum of practices that provide for varying levels of Aboriginal control and guidance. At one end of the continuum, isolated students and faculty members may exert (sometimes considerable) influence on the assimilationist model. At the other end of the continuum, there may be formalized Aboriginal advisory boards and designated program staff. The integrated model is the second most common model and, after the assimilationist approach, the second most likely model to be supported by non-Aboriginal educators and policy makers. Like the assimilationist model, it does not directly challenge non-Aboriginal control of Aboriginal education.

Despite its failure to address underlying issues of power and control, there are some rare examples of integrated approaches that have had some limited success in promoting Aboriginal self-determination. The First Nations House of Learning at the University of British Columbia is one example of a successful integrated program. An unusual combination of heroic First Nations' leadership, continual struggle, active support from top university administrators, gifted staff, and strong community involvement was necessary to ensure the success of this program. Had one or more of these elements been weak or missing, the structural racism of the university would likely have pushed the program toward an assimilationist model.

3. THE INDEPENDENT MODEL: LIMITED BY SIZE AND ISOLATION

Tribal and regional colleges that are controlled by Aboriginal communities are examples of the independent model of Aboriginal education. Because they are usually controlled by Aboriginal organizations and have close contacts with the local community, they can design programs that are well suited to meet the needs of the people they serve. There are twenty-four of these colleges in the United States and several in the early stages of development in Canada. Canadian examples include the Red Crow Community College, the Nicola Valley Institute of Technology, and Yellow Quill College.

The main limitation of these colleges is their size. They have limited resources and, therefore, they are generally unable to develop university degree and graduate programs that are nationally and internationally recognized. They are also limited in the number of faculty and students they can draw from local communities.

We believe the independent model can only achieve its potential through the development of a strong mutual support network. This must include the creation of national institutions that would be responsible for implementing a national Aboriginal education strategy.

4. THE FEDERATED MODEL: A SOLID FOUNDATION FOR THE NEXT STEPS IN ABORIGINAL EDUCATION

In a few cases, non-Aboriginal universities have been willing to negotiate mutually beneficial partnerships with Aboriginal institutions. As Barnhardt (1991, p. 211) has said, these are arrangements:

> ... whereby educational services for indigenous people are administered by an indigenous-run institution under the academic purview and accreditation umbrella of the cooperating institution. These arrangements are often formalized through a contractual arrangement, including shared responsibility for curricula, personnel, and resources.

This model has a number of advantages and some limitations. Because of its potential to grow into an independent post-secondary educational system for Aboriginal people, however, the federated model warrants a more in-depth examination.

THE SASKATCHEWAN INDIAN FEDERATED COLLEGE: THE FEDERATED MODEL IN PRACTICE

The Saskatchewan Indian Federated College (SIFC), federated with the University of Regina, is the largest and oldest example of the federated model of Aboriginal education in Canada.

1. BRIEF HISTORY AND OVERVIEW OF SIFC

SIFC was established in 1976. It is the only Aboriginally controlled university college federated with an accredited degree-granting university in Canada. It was established by the SIFC Act, which was passed by the Assembly of Chiefs of the Federation of Saskatchewan Indian Nations. Its board of governors includes representatives from each tribal council in Saskatchewan, as well as representatives from the University of Saskatchewan, the University of Regina, DIAND, the provincial education department, and SIFC faculty and students.

SIFC is academically federated with the University of Regina. This ensures that all regulations respecting admissions, hiring of faculty, and academic programs meet University of Regina degree standards. The academic programs of SIFC are designed to complement those of the University of Regina, not duplicate them. In addition, SIFC adopts other measures to improve the success rate of Aboriginal students while at university.

Initially, the college focused on developing programs in Indian Studies, Indian Art, Indian Languages, Indian Teacher Education, and Indian Social Work. Programs in Indian Management and Administration, Indian Communications Arts, and Indian Health Careers followed in the early 1980s. More recently, in response to the needs of Aboriginal communities, SIFC established a Department of Science to encourage more Indian students to enter science-based professions such as the health professions, engineering, and agriculture. A School of Business and Public Administration has also been established.

To provide student and program support, the college has over fifty full-time academic faculty members. As well, there are five elders, nineteen student support and administrative staff, and nineteen support staff.

Approximately 56 percent of the 1,100 students at the college are taught on the Regina campus, 26 percent at the college's Saskatoon campus, and 18 percent through the college's extension program. The extension program operates at six off-campus locations from La Ronge in northern Saskatchewan, to the Cowessess Reserve in the south. About 20 percent of SIFC's students are from out of province.

2. Highlights of Activities and Accomplishments

Aboriginal control of Aboriginal education succeeds. In the words of the Smith report on Canadian universities (Smith 1991, p. 98), "The results of the SIFC experiment justify its continued support." The SIFC has been extraordinarily successful in encouraging more Aboriginal people to seek a university education, and it has been more successful than non-Aboriginal institutions in ensuring that the students who do come to university succeed. The success of SIFC is directly attributable to the support provided by Indian governments and legislation these governments have passed. Thus, SIFC is both an expression of and a tool for the development of self-government.

From fewer than a dozen students in 1976, SIFC's enrollment has grown to over 1,100 students in 1993. It has graduated 780 students over the sixteen years of its existence. What is more important, it graduated over 140 students in 1993, indicating that the return on the investment in this institution is just beginning.

While the number of students enrolled in SIFC programs and the number of graduates are important measures of success, an exclusive focus on these indicators could easily obscure other significant spin-off effects directly attributable to Aboriginally controlled institutions. In measuring the result of any exercise in self-government, these other factors must also be taken into account.

In the case of SIFC, in addition to the wide variety of courses offered and the growing student population, there are a number of other academic and cultural activities that make up an important part of the college's success:

1. SIFC participates in a range of publishing activities that contribute to the development of an Aboriginal knowledge base. For example, *The First Ones: Readings in Indian/Native Studies* was published in September 1992 by SIFC Press, with the assistance of the Saskatchewan Communications Network. The text will be used in the Introduction to Indian/Native Studies course offered on public television, as well as in introductory Indian Studies courses at SIFC. It has also been adopted for use in Indian Studies courses at several other North American universities;

2. SIFC attracts outstanding Aboriginal faculty and, thereby, promotes academic excellence among Aboriginal students and faculty;

3. SIFC promotes Aboriginal education and Aboriginal self-government at the local, regional, and national levels. For example, professors in SIFC's School of Business and Public Administration played a major role in the formation of a national working group on Indian/Aboriginal Management and Economic Development. Moreover, SIFC's activities are not confined to Saskatchewan. Yukon College is working with SIFC to create a Yukon Northern Human Service Worker Bachelor of Social Work program modeled on SIFC's Bachelor of Indian Social Work program. Academic programs have been offered jointly with Aboriginal institutions in British Columbia, Alberta, and Manitoba;

4. SIFC has reached out to Aboriginal people around the world through its Centre of International Indigenous Studies and Development (CIISD), which is supported by the Canadian International Development Agency (CIDA). Since its inception in 1986, the CIISD has entered into eight international agreements. It has hosted and exchanged students and

visiting scholars from the People's Republic of China, Mongolia, Australia, Norway, New Zealand, Tanzania, South Africa, Papua New Guinea, and several countries in the Caribbean, South America, and Central America. It has initiated links between Aboriginal communities in Canada, the Caribbean, and South and Central America. The center is currently negotiating with the United Nations to develop a program with the United Nations University of Peace in Costa Rica. This joint international Indigenous program will allow students to spend one-half of their time in Costa Rica and the other half at SIFC. The center offers a one-year certificate in Administration with a specialization in Indian Management. The program has had thirty-nine graduates from twenty countries, and nineteen Aboriginal groups;

5. SIFC promotes the development of Aboriginal secondary education as another of its priorities. During the summer of 1993, for example, the Department of Science held its second math/science camp for Indian high school students. The camp is intended to encourage students to pursue science or health-related careers;

6. SIFC provides innovative educational programs that equip Aboriginal students to compete in a competitive labor force. For example, a co-op work/study program last year placed students in a wide variety of work placements; and

7. SIFC believes promoting traditional Aboriginal cultural practices is also important. Elders conduct pipe ceremonies on the second Thursday of each month for students and staff of the college. In addition, elders regularly provide cultural and spiritual counselling to students and staff, and serve on the senior management team of the college. The SIFC powwow has been an annual event for fifteen years. The powwow has grown to include more than five hundred dancers and twenty drums. In 1993 more than thirty thousand people attended over the two days of the event.

In addition to these activities, many of which are unique to SIFC, the college participates in the full range of scholarly activities that would normally be associated with institutions of higher learning. These activities promote faculty and student involvement in nationally and internationally recognized research and publishing activity, and the development of academic and professional networks and organizations. Like other institutions, SIFC also sponsors an extensive athletics program.

We mention these accomplishments, not so much to brag about SIFC, although we are very proud of the college's accomplishments, as to illustrate the multifaceted dividends associated with investments in Aboriginal institutions. SIFC is an expression of the spirit and intent of the treaties. It is an example of an educational institution that is creating and implementing self-determination, sometimes in partnership with the non-Indigenous university system but often constrained by its very ties to this system.

3. STRENGTHS AND WEAKNESSES OF THE FEDERATED MODEL

As an example of the federated model, SIFC inherits the strengths and weaknesses of that model. On the one hand, it enjoys academic credibility from its federation with the University of Regina, it is able to share library and other resources, its students can easily take other courses at the university, and it rents space on favorable terms. On the other hand, SIFC has no permanent facilities, it is not a priority for university space allocation—even though it contributes about half a million dollars annually to the university in addition to space rental—it is outnumbered in academic governance committees, and it must submit all faculty appointments to the university for approval, even in the areas—such as linguistics and Indian Studies—where the university has no academic expertise.

OPTIONS FOR THE DEVELOPMENT OF ABORIGINAL POST-SECONDARY EDUCATION IN CANADA

There is a growing demand for Aboriginal post-secondary education in Canada. If these needs are to be addressed, serious consideration will have to be given to the nature and extent of current demands, as well as to expected future demands. In addition, there are a number of options for addressing these educational needs that grow directly out of the four models of Aboriginal education discussed earlier. Which approach will be best for the Aboriginal Peoples and for Canada?

1. CURRENT AND FUTURE NEEDS FOR ABORIGINAL POST-SECONDARY EDUCATION

Existing needs for Aboriginal post-secondary education are not currently being met in Canada, and there is every reason to believe that these needs will continue to grow in the future. The ever-increasing demands on Aboriginal post-secondary institutions to expand existing programs and develop new ones arise from several sources:

1. The increasing number of Aboriginal students seeking a university education;
2. The increasingly wide-ranging educational interests of the Aboriginal students who enroll in post-secondary programs;
3. The fact that success itself increases demands—as more Aboriginal students succeed in university, the number of students interested in moving beyond basic studies into advanced studies also increases; and
4. The speed at which many Aboriginal communities are moving toward self-government places a heavy burden on the few educational institutions that are able to assist Aboriginal people in managing their own affairs.

There are major costs associated with the development of educational programs to meet these demands; however, the price of not moving ahead is even greater for individuals, communities, and governments. This price includes both lost human potential and wasted resources because of inadequate human resources. In Aboriginal terms, post-secondary education is part of the circle of community development and, if this part of the circle is not developed, the health of the entire community will continue to suffer.

Moreover, the post-secondary educational institutions of the future, including those that are Aboriginally controlled, will face new challenges. It is important to begin planning now to meet these current and emerging needs. Some examples include:

1. DISTANCE EDUCATION. As Aboriginal communities take control of their education, more and more students will be able to get their primary and secondary education in community schools. However, students that want to go on to university must currently travel to a larger center. There they have the advantage of a wide range of resources, but they lose the support of their family and community. The goal of distance education is to deliver university courses in or near a student's home community and to make each community part of the university campus;
2. ADVANCED TECHNOLOGY. Increasingly, post-secondary institutions are being called upon to develop and use methods of course delivery that rely on the latest technology. These technologies involve advanced systems of communication, the storing and retrieving of vast quantities of information, and the use of computers. For example, communications technology is now being used to facilitate distance education, self-paced systems of learning are being developed for use in interactive computers, computer networks are providing access to huge data bases,

and information can be stored and distributed using CD-ROMs and a variety of other formats. In order to meet the needs of Aboriginal communities and nations, Aboriginal post-secondary educational institutions must also make use of these technologies;

3. UNIVERSITY ENTRANCE PROGRAMS (UEPs). These programs allow students the opportunity to prepare for university level courses. They are particularly important for providing access to university for mature students and to others who may not be entering university directly from high school. UEPs have been successful; however, they will increasingly have to be tailored to the individual needs of students. Moreover, while UEP programs are ideal programs to be delivered using a distance education approach, considerable resources would be required to modify existing programs and create the necessary support materials to respond to the educational needs of Aboriginal students. Once completed, however, the potential for providing a Canada-wide UEP program through distance education would be immense; and

4. GRADUATE STUDIES. Obtaining a university degree is a dream that is coming true for more and more Aboriginal people in Canada each year, but there is also a need to provide capable and motivated graduates with an opportunity to participate in advanced studies leading to masters and doctoral level degrees. Whereas some of these students will be able to go to non-Aboriginal universities, many, if given the choice, would prefer to work in areas of study not offered at non-Aboriginal universities—Aboriginal studies, Aboriginal linguistics, Indian health, and other fields.

Creating educational opportunities for Aboriginal students has benefits for the larger Aboriginal community and Canadian society. These opportunities prepare Aboriginal people to assume key leadership roles in their communities, in Aboriginal governments, and in provincial and federal government agencies. They also prepare Aboriginal people to take on important roles in the Aboriginal education system, including vital roles as educators.

Having outlined these present and future needs, we now wish to consider some of the options available to meet these needs.

2. ASSIMILATION AND INTEGRATED APPROACHES

All resources for Aboriginal post-secondary education could be devoted to placing Aboriginal students in established non-Aboriginal post-secondary institutions. This is a continuation of the assimilationist model, although depending on the precise manner of implementation, this strategy could also be based on the integrated model discussed above. There would be several advantages, and a number of important disadvantages, to such an approach.

This option appears to be the lowest cost option. Even considering that some funds would have to be allocated for the development of special initiatives to create Aboriginal programs in non-Aboriginal institutions, the institutions themselves are already established. Therefore, costs would likely be less than those associated with developing or expanding existing Aboriginally controlled institutions. In addition, existing universities offer students and faculty the advantages of a large educational resource base.

Despite these advantages, over three hundred years of experience has proved that non-Aboriginal institutions are not effective in educating Aboriginal people. Moreover, an education system that aims to assimilate or integrate Aboriginal people into mainstream programs is not acceptable to Aboriginal people. Furthermore, such an approach to Aboriginal education will not provide the support that Aboriginal communities need to deal effectively with the challenges of self-government and other emerging needs.

3. THE FEDERATED APPROACH

Resources could be dedicated to the development of a number of Aboriginal colleges that are federated with non-Aboriginal universities. These relationships would be similar to the current relationship between the SIFC and the University of Regina. This approach would also have advantages and disadvantages.

Aboriginal colleges provide for a significant level of Aboriginal control. Moreover, students and faculty have access to the resources of the university. Therefore, there would be areas that the Aboriginal college would not have to develop (for example, library services, support services, etc.). The non-Aboriginal university may also lend apparent credibility to the Aboriginal college, its courses, and its graduates.

This model, however, also has a number of disadvantages. Aboriginal colleges remain dependent on their host university for degree-granting status. This means that there are significant restrictions on how programs can be designed. In addition, dealing with the university's internal political system can make progress frustrating and inordinately slow. Furthermore, tying an Aboriginal college's credibility to a university may perpetuate a stereotype of Aboriginal institutions being unable to provide education that is up to "standard."

There are also other problems with this model. Funding agencies may use the availability of university resources as a justification for limiting the resources that are made available to the Aboriginal college. And because of power differentials, Aboriginal resources are inevitably "siphoned off" to benefit the non-Aboriginal university.

4. THE INDEPENDENT APPROACH

Resources could be directed to the establishment of a system of independent, Aboriginally controlled tribal colleges. These colleges would be able to develop programs that are specifically designed for the Aboriginal Peoples. Many students would be able to study close to home and, consequently, would enjoy higher levels of community and family support. Aboriginal communities would also have the opportunity to be more closely involved in the planning and operation of these colleges.

Providing local Aboriginal colleges that were able to meet the present and future needs of Aboriginal communities would be a very costly undertaking. Moreover, there are not enough Aboriginal faculty members to provide the necessary critical mass of Aboriginal faculty at multiple institutions.

5. THE PREFERRED APPROACH: A NATIONAL FIRST NATIONS UNIVERSITY

We believe the preferred strategy is one that develops elements of the federated and independent models.

We believe that a national First Nations university should be established.[2] This university would be established by Aboriginal government legislation, and have independent degree-granting status. It would provide courses of study that are nationally and internationally recognized. This university would also have formal relationships with non-Aboriginal post-secondary institutions to facilitate the sharing of resources (for example, libraries), access to certain courses of study, and the undertaking of joint research and development projects.

Besides the development of this national institution, we also envision that there would be a number of local and regional initiatives in Aboriginal post-secondary education. These would include tribal colleges and federated colleges that would be affiliated with the national university. Over time, one or more of these initiatives might evolve into other Aboriginally controlled universities.

The model we are proposing would have other advantages. Through affiliation with local colleges and the development of distance education programs, a significant portion of post-secondary education could be delivered in or near the home communities of Aboriginal students. Aboriginal communities would also have the opportunity to have direct involvement in the design and delivery of Aboriginal post-secondary education. This approach could also be adapted to recognize the mosaic of Aboriginal communities in Canada and the fact that different Aboriginal communities will identify the need for different approaches to post-secondary education.

The work of the university should reach far beyond the boundaries and buildings of a single campus. In partnership with communities, and in conjunction with other Aboriginal and non-Aboriginal educational institutions, it should deliver programs in rural and urban Aboriginal communities across Canada. It should also reach far beyond the borders of Canada and be recognized around the world as a center of excellence in Aboriginal education, research, and community development. It should be sought out by those persons inside and outside Canada who are seeking knowledge and guidance in these areas. It should also form links with Aboriginal communities and educational institutions in other parts of the world that have similar aspirations. Like other great Canadian universities, it should have internationally recognized education and research programs, and offer both undergraduate and graduate degrees in a wide range of subject areas.

Unlike other Canadian universities, however, the National First Nations University would be designed to foster the success of Aboriginal students and the development of Aboriginal communities. It would incorporate into its courses and programs a holistic view of education aimed at the development of the spiritual, emotional, physical, and intellectual aspects of its students. At the National First Nations University, elders would always have a role to play—their knowledge and spiritual guidance would provide a secure foundation for the curriculum, governance, research, and services of the university.

This university would build into its programs the necessary support services to ensure the success of Aboriginal students—a university entrance program; a flexible admissions policy; an extended instructional period; and a committed, competent, caring staff devoted to excellence in teaching. The environment would seek to eliminate ethnic isolation and would foster collaborative learning. Instituting work-study opportunities would also be an important part of the university's programming.

The celebration of Aboriginal culture would also be an objective of such an institution. Adequate and appropriate support services would be provided, including access to elders. Cultural activities would be organized, and programs would be developed to help students maintain strong links with their communities and families.

The development of such a national institution would be an ambitious undertaking requiring significant investments in human and financial resources. In addition, there would be many interested parties and, therefore, the process of developing this institution would be more complex and time consuming than a centralized approach. However, there would be a great deal to gain from the development of Canada's first Aboriginally controlled university, and some of the important building blocks for such an institution are already in place.[3]

Canada would have the prestige of being the home of an internationally recognized center of excellence in education. The university would help to facilitate the development of Aboriginal people and Aboriginal communities throughout Canada. But there are even more pragmatic reasons for moving ahead with a national Aboriginal post-secondary education strategy.

The Canadian Council for Aboriginal Business (1993), in their brief to the Royal Commission on Aboriginal Peoples, pointed out that the private sector "must recognize that long-term economic growth and productivity in Canada hinges on the full employment and participation of the Aboriginal population." Their brief makes it clear that it is not just Aboriginal communities that benefit from economic development, but the entire Canadian economy.

In today's world, a sound education is a prerequisite to employment, and it is an important ingredient of success in creating and sustaining successful businesses. By enhancing post-secondary educational opportunities for the Aboriginal Peoples, increasing numbers will move from welfare to productive employment, and they will create new businesses. Even a small increase in the economic output of Aboriginal communities will return to the Canadian economy many more dollars than the cost of even a generous investment in such an institution.

CONCLUSION

The importance of university education for individual Aboriginal people and for Aboriginal communities, and the reasons that Aboriginally controlled education is more successful than other models, have been well documented in many studies and briefs. The time has come to put theory into practice. This involves a national strategy for Aboriginal post-secondary education.

We believe the creation of a national institution would provide the infrastructure to effectively support Aboriginal post-secondary education at all levels. Not only would it represent a high level of achievement in

Aboriginally controlled education, it would provide Aboriginal people with an opportunity to pursue advanced courses of studies in areas, and in a manner, that otherwise would not be available to them. In this way the institution would make an important contribution to the development of Aboriginal leaders who could contribute to the implementation of self-government and address other important issues in Aboriginal communities and Canadian society.

Aboriginal control of education is a vital part of the move to self-determination and self-sufficiency. These words imply much more than just providing Aboriginal people with access to education. They imply that education in Canada will change from an exclusive Euro-centered system to one that includes First Nations institutions. This is a difficult goal to achieve, but one that Canada committed itself to long ago. To meet its needs in the twenty-first century, Canada must develop a fully funded Aboriginal post-secondary system.

NOTES

1   This paper is based on a brief prepared for the Royal Commission on Aboriginal Peoples by the Saskatchewan Indian Federated College.
2   Similar institutions might also be developed for the Métis and Inuit.
3   It is beyond the scope of this paper to discuss the specific steps that would be required to bring about the creation of a national First Nations university; however, we have discussed this more detailed plan elsewhere. One option, and the one we favor, is to develop the existing SIFC program into this national institution. For a further discussion, see Saskatchewan Indian Federated College (1993).

REFERENCES

Barnhardt, R. 1991. Higher education in the fourth world: Indigenous people take control. *Canadian Journal of Native Education* 18(2):199–231.

Canadian Council for Aboriginal Business. 1993. *Brief to the Royal Commission on Aboriginal Peoples*. Ottawa: Canadian Council for Aboriginal Business.

Haig-Brown, Celia. 1988. *Resistance and renewal: Surviving the Indian residential school*. Vancouver: Tillacum Library.

Hampton, E. 1993. Toward a redefinition of American Indian/Alaskan native education. *Canadian Journal of Native Education* 20(2):261–309.

Havighurst, R. 1981. Indian education: Accomplishments of the last decade. *Phi Delta Kappan* 62:329–31.

Johnson, Albert. 1993. *Looking at Saskatchewan universities: Programs, governance, and goals*. Regina: Saskatchewan Department of Education.

Morris, A. 1880 [1979]. *The treaties of Canada with the Indians.* Reprint, Toronto: Coles.

Saskatchewan Indian Federated College. 1993. *Brief to the Royal Commission on Aboriginal Peoples.* Regina: Saskatchewan Indian Federated College.

Smith, Stuart. 1991. *Report of the commission of inquiry on Canadian university education.* Ottawa: Association of Universities and Colleges of Canada.

TeHennepe, S. 1993. Issues of respect: Reflections of First Nations students' experiences in post-secondary anthropology classrooms. *Canadian Journal of Native Education* 20(2):193–260.

CHAPTER 6

SELF-GOVERNMENT AND CRIMINAL JUSTICE: ISSUES AND REALITIES

CAROL LA PRAIRIE,[1] DEPARTMENT OF JUSTICE, CANADA

This chapter is primarily based on research projects that were carried out from 1990 to 1992 in James Bay, Quebec, and the Yukon. The research explored several dimensions of crime and disorder, particularly the role of the criminal justice system and the desire of local communities to exercise greater control over criminal, civil, and family justice matters. This chapter focuses on the most relevant issues, concerns, and conclusions that arise from this research. My objective is to provide both Aboriginal and non-Aboriginal leaders with information that may prove helpful in finding more appropriate and effective approaches to dealing with justice issues in Aboriginal communities. Unlike the four recent provincial inquiries into Aboriginal justice issues and the work of the Royal Commission on Aboriginal Peoples, which have examined the broader issues,[2] this paper focuses on findings from research in specific communities.

PROBLEMS WITH THE EXISTING CRIMINAL JUSTICE SYSTEM

Aboriginal people have high expectations of the criminal justice system. They believe that it should prevent crime, resolve disputes between members of the community, and rehabilitate offenders. Just like people in other communities, Aboriginal people also want to be protected from disorder and disruption, and they want members of their community, whether offenders or victims, treated appropriately by the authorities.

Throughout Canada, the prevailing view among Aboriginal people is that the criminal justice system has "failed." The system is frequently viewed as unwilling or unable to understand local conditions and cultures, to meet local needs, or to reform offenders. The failure of the system is perceived to be linked to the overrepresentation of Aboriginal offenders in correctional institutions, and many believe that this disproportionate representation results from discriminatory treatment.

When Aboriginal communities are not protected from crime, they question the effectiveness of the justice system. Relations get complicated when "the system" does not recognize the concerns of the local community or treats these concerns as if they are not important or legitimate.

Strained relations between the police and many Aboriginal communities illustrate the types of problems that frequently occur. The lack of clearly defined and accepted rules and understandings between the police and many Aboriginal communities often leads to frustration on both sides. The police may have difficulty responding to some requests because their mandate is limited or because they lack the necessary training. Yet, Aboriginal communities want services, and they believe the police are failing them when these services are not provided. In other words, the needs and desires of the community to deal with certain kinds of disorders are ignored because they do not fit into the prevailing mandate of the criminal justice system.

Aboriginal communities see many of their members going through the court process. They also know that, in many instances, this processing does not change the behavior of offenders (La Prairie 1991). Rightly or wrongly, they expect judges to influence behavior. When this does not happen, it only adds to the growing cynicism about the system.

Even the written law has serious limitations. It is more conducive to regulating relations among strangers than to resolving disputes among those who are familiar and living in proximity with one another. Thus, the law itself often falls short of community expectations (La Prairie 1991).

ABORIGINAL JUSTICE:
AN OVERVIEW OF VISIONS AND REALITIES

Because of the widespread and long-standing concerns about the Canadian criminal justice system, there is little doubt that, in one way or another, many Aboriginal communities in Canada want to have greater control over family, civil, and criminal justice matters. This does not mean that every community wants extensive jurisdiction, or total control, over justice, but it does mean that most communities want significant changes in the way laws are made and enforced, in the way alleged transgressions are adjudicated, and in the way offenders are treated.

The desire for autonomy reflects concerns about the effectiveness of the current system, but it also results from the broader movement toward self-determination in Aboriginal communities across Canada; Aboriginal communities want to replace the control of external institutions with local community control. For Aboriginal communities, greater control over justice matters is an important symbol and reality of self-determination.

There is an abyss between what Aboriginal communities want and need and what the criminal justice system provides, even though various strategies have been tried to address Aboriginal needs within the current system. Notwithstanding these attempts, the community and officials in the criminal justice system are dissatisfied. It is possible that the only viable way of redressing the problem is for Aboriginal Peoples to have greater control over defining and dispensing "justice." Indeed, the conclusion reached by many Aboriginal people, and other observers, is that there is an urgent need for Aboriginal participation in, and control over, institutions that affect the lives of Aboriginal people.

Beyond wanting change, there must be practical and realistic approaches to Aboriginal justice matters. Yet, for many Aboriginal leaders and communities, a discussion of control over the administration of justice becomes a discussion of structures patterned on the complex systems with which we are all too familiar. Invariably these discussions include references to police, prosecutors, lawyers, probation services, judges, and appellate courts. Whether these are well understood, or workable in a particular community context, may seem unimportant. To many, an Aboriginal justice system can only be "real," if it has all the conventional components.

This inclination to want to replicate the current system must be resisted. What Aboriginal communities often want when they consider local justice initiatives is someone to stop the noise at night, someone to respond to disturbances, and someone to resolve community conflicts. Developing an elaborate justice system may create a system that is too complex and unmanageable. Such a system could even become the major employer in small communities. It needs to be borne in mind that the less cumbersome the system, the more likely it will reflect community needs, and the more likely the community will sustain it.

There is another reason to avoid complex systems. There is a limit to the quantity and quality of human resources in most Aboriginal communities, and for some justice issues may not be the top priority. Therefore, it will be essential for Aboriginal communities to tailor their justice approaches to meet community needs and realities. Whatever the approach, Aboriginal initiatives must recognize that community members live in proximity to one another, that the community has limited resources, and that there are many interrelated social problems beyond the problem of crime.

Because Aboriginal communities will have neither the interest nor the resources to "do it all," there will be a requirement for partnership arrangements. Most communities, for example, do not want to deal with serious offenses or chronic offenders. These communities would be prepared to leave some offenses, and some offenders, to an external non-Aboriginal system. In fact, in some communities there is more clarity about what the community does not want to deal with than about what it does want to deal with.

Every community is unique, and the approach to criminal justice problems should be dictated by local community circumstances. The selection of approaches should depend on the nature and extent of crime and disorder in the community. It should also depend on the level of satisfaction (or the degree of dissatisfaction) with the existing system, and the availability of human and other community resources. The priority the community is prepared to give to justice issues, relative to the many other issues that also require attention in Aboriginal communities, should also be an important consideration. There is an unfortunate necessity for communities to redefine their problems as "justice" problems in order to be eligible for funding under some new government initiatives.

Some communities may decide to focus on changing the existing criminal justice system. For others, the priority may be to develop Aboriginal programs. In still others, communities will identify a need for a combination of approaches. Each option brings its own implications. Instituting reforms in the existing justice system, for example, will require a different level of involvement, and a different level of resources, than will developing parallel Aboriginal laws, policies, and programs.

Much can be accomplished without complex systems or extensive resources. For example, using customary practices, modified to reflect contemporary realities in Aboriginal communities, can yield significant opportunities for communities to exercise more effective and more culturally appropriate forms of social control.

Having provided this brief overview of the key issues, I would now like to turn to the practical implications of establishing Aboriginal justice initiatives.

ABORIGINAL JUSTICE SYSTEMS: THE CHALLENGES

There are many practical issues Aboriginal communities must consider in their deliberations about local justice initiatives. The following list is not exhaustive, but it does attempt to identify the most important issues.

1. DEFINING THE PROBLEM

An understanding of the root problems experienced in Aboriginal communities will be essential to finding effective solutions. It is often difficult to separate symptoms from problems. Underlying causes are not always immediately apparent.

Chronic disruption in the community due to crime and disorder may point to a breakdown in the community's traditional mechanisms of social control. In other words, it is often a symptom of deeper problems. Perhaps the "real" issue is the absence of productive alternatives for large numbers of Aboriginal youth, who often have limited employment and education prospects. Similarly, a heavy reliance on the use of incarceration outside the community may point to an absence of community-based alternatives. High rates of recidivism may suggest the need for something to "break the cycle." The interrelatedness of justice problems and other social and economic problems may suggest a need for a holistic approach to finding solutions.

The cost of delivering criminal justice programs is prohibitive, but the resources are misplaced. Criminal justice programs seem to provide remarkably little assistance to communities in resolving many of their most pressing problems. In the broader context, there is no real "payback" for communities to concentrate their energies solely on policing, courts, and corrections.

The real problems facing Aboriginal communities often have to do with socialization, parenting, education, economic conditions, employment, and rapid change influenced by mass communication and other forces. Early identification and the provision of assistance to individuals and families most liable to present problems to the criminal justice and child welfare systems may achieve some results.[3] However, the most critical policy issue is the recognition of the interconnectedness of justice and social and economic conditions. Thus, policing cannot be considered separately from crime prevention, dispositions from community resources, treatment from aftercare, or community needs from community development.

2. THE MEANING OF CRIME

Important tasks facing Aboriginal communities are to clarify the meaning of "justice" and to decide what crime is. Little work has been done on conceptions of crime in most Aboriginal communities, and the criminal justice system has proceeded as if the Aboriginal and non-Aboriginal definitions of crime and order were the same. Available research reveals, however, that the types and amounts of disorder differ among Aboriginal and non-Aboriginal communities. Moreover, when it comes to perceptions about the seriousness of behavior, communities differ in the way they assess similar acts (Brodeur 1991; La Prairie 1991). Communities must ultimately decide, within guidelines that have yet to be determined, what behavior deserves the designation of "crime," the degree of seriousness that will be accorded to particular acts, and the most appropriate community response.

3. TRADITIONAL OR CONTEMPORARY?

Aboriginal communities face the challenge of modifying traditional practices of social control to address the contemporary realities of Aboriginal communities. Some communities, and some community members, will feel caught in a conflict between traditional and modern approaches. A return to customary practices will be seen as logical to some, but others will want new approaches.

Although the discussion about local justice systems often proceeds as if a choice must be made between the old and the new, in reality, a combination of different approaches may be warranted.[4] It is important, however, that there be community consensus about the role that leaders and other members of the community will play in the community's system of social control.

In the absence of accepted rules and practices, familiarity between residents of the community and extended family relationships may present some difficulties in developing and operating justice systems, particularly in small communities.[5]

4. WHOSE VALUES?

There is potential for conflicts in values in Aboriginal communities, as there is in non-Aboriginal communities. Not everyone will agree on what the rules should be or on how to handle transgressions. This is particularly likely to be the case where justice hearings, decision-making, and dispositions are involved. After all, these are all areas where considerable controversy may be engendered because important decisions are being made.

The desire in many Aboriginal communities to involve elders in the administration of justice may give rise to specific instances of conflicts in values. The segment of the community that holds elders in the highest esteem may be the least likely to become involved in the criminal justice system. On the other hand, some young people, who are more likely than the older generation to come into conflict with the law, have lost touch with their culture and traditions. They may not hold elders in high esteem, and they may reject traditional practices.

Few communities are untouched by events of the past two decades, during which women's issues, victims' rights, and alternate lifestyles have gained recognition. The social changes evolving from these events often gain more acceptance in some segments of the community than in others. Aboriginal women, for example, may feel very strongly about the treatment of perpetrators of family violence. These views, however, may not be shared by all segments of the community. Therefore, in selecting community members to serve important roles in the local justice system, it will be important to consider balanced representation that reflects the diversity of the community. To deflect accusations of favoritism, it is also important that members are evenly selected from all major family groupings (Clairmont 1993).

5. RESOURCE REALITIES

Local systems of justice will bring new responsibilities, many of which were formerly assumed by the non-Aboriginal justice system. However, the range of criminal justice responsibilities that Aboriginal communities want to assume is often articulated before there has been sufficient opportunity to consider the human and other resource implications.

Aboriginal leaders have many pressures placed upon them and band administrators are typically overworked. Land claims, self-government, economic development, job creation, and other priorities may keep leaders otherwise occupied, and away from communities, for long periods of time. This severely depletes the available human resources. Communities may simply have too few resources to proceed with changes as quickly as some might like.

There is a danger in attempting to set up and sustain structures requiring resources far beyond the ability of communities to provide. These constraints must be carefully considered. Maintaining structures and community interest over the long term may be one of the greatest challenges facing many Aboriginal communities.

Specialized programs and services will also have extensive resource implications. Provincial governments and large municipalities, jurisdictions with many more resources than most Aboriginal communities, must sometimes rely on outside help to deal with highly complex issues. Examples include complex investigations, decisions about fitness to stand trial, and cases involving specialized medical care for offenders—for instance, offenders with AIDS, substance abuse problems, mental handicaps, mental illness, or other disorders. Trying to provide all these services would bankrupt even the most wealthy community.

The prevalence of Fetal Alcohol Syndrome (FAS) is a challenge for all communities. Despite a move to sobriety in Aboriginal communities, those who continue to drink are often heavy drinkers and many of these are women of child-bearing age. In time the problem will abate, but those presently coming to the attention of the criminal justice system have a high probability of being affected. The dilemma for any justice system, Aboriginal and non-Aboriginal alike, will be how to respond, given the behavioral problems this group presents. The real dilemma for resource-starved Aboriginal communities that are themselves struggling toward health is how to respond effectively to this group.

6. JURISDICTIONAL ISSUES AND RELATIONS WITH THE EXTERNAL SYSTEM

Jurisdictional issues must be considered. Some of these include:

1. Whether Aboriginal people living off reserve or settlement lands will be dealt with by Aboriginal justice systems, even if they commit offenses in other communities;
2. If so, whether there will be some mechanism (perhaps akin to extradition) to return Aboriginal offenders to their own communities;
3. Whether the authority of the local Aboriginal justice system will extend to transients, or others, who commit offenses on, but are not residents of, reserve or settlement lands; and
4. Whether sentencing options available to local Aboriginal justice systems will be restricted to those offenses carried out on reserve or settlement lands, or whether local systems will be able to impose (and perhaps supervise) sentences in non-reserve communities.

Depending on the answers to these and related questions, the resources required by Aboriginal justice systems will vary. It is not difficult to imagine resources being stretched to the limit if local systems try to meet the obligations implied in extending jurisdiction beyond the immediate community. If adequate resources are not available, there is a danger that a watered-down, ineffective system could result. Some form of partnership with the external system seems inevitable, and there are indications that this would be acceptable to at least some Aboriginal communities.

Despite many complaints about the existing justice system, research in James Bay and the Yukon has revealed that there is a willingness to use that system if:

1. An offense is serious (for example, homicides and serious assaults);
2. An offender did not comply with conditions stipulated under local systems; or
3. The offending is chronic and the offender continues to re-offend.

While these communities want their own justice system, they are quite prepared to relinquish jurisdiction for more difficult problems to the existing system.

Most Aboriginal offenders who come to the attention of the criminal justice system are repeaters. Therefore, the exclusion of this group from the jurisdiction of local Aboriginal systems could significantly limit the self-sufficiency of these systems. It seems obvious that there will be a need for precise definitions and partnership arrangements with the external system.

A word about banishment is also in order. While banishment is frequently put forward as a solution for dealing with serious or repeat offenders, it may be unreasonable to assume there will always be external solutions available. Moreover, banishment today has a very different impact than in years gone by. In addition to Charter of Rights issues, other realities include the tolerance levels of other communities and the potential to create serious divisions in communities over decisions to banish.

7. DEALING WITH OFFENDERS

Aboriginal communities interested in assuming greater control over criminal justice matters must confront the problem of responding to offenders. It will be a challenge for local justice systems to fashion and carry out sanctions that are more effective and appropriate than those imposed by the current system. Although initiatives have been developed in the past few years and there have been several major reports on Aboriginal justice, there is still very little information about the effectiveness of various program alternatives. Therefore, developing effective sanctions will be a learning experience for most communities.

There is strong support in many Aboriginal communities for new approaches to justice problems. Initiatives such as the involvement of clan leaders in sentencing at Teslin and the use of elders' councils in Attawapiskat, Sandy Bay, and Pelly Crossing reflect a desire for more effective local responses to crime and disorder. Leaders often speak about the need for a new philosophy based on diversion and alternatives to incarceration. Generally, there is a reluctance to see offenders incarcerated, but there is also a recognition that there are few local resources to support community-based sentences.

Beyond philosophy, there is the practical matter of deciding on specific community responses to individual offenders. From the perspective of any justice system, whether Aboriginal or non-Aboriginal, it is important to consider the unique characteristics of offenders and offenses before deciding upon an appropriate community response. These characteristics may include age, sex, education, criminal background, the circumstances of the offense, and a host of other factors.

The community also has an obligation to assess the kind of relationship it wants to have with offenders. Too often, there is a tendency to perceive offenders as "outsiders," as members of an isolated group that deserves to be rejected by the community. It is more difficult to see offenders as reflecting certain power, social, and other arrangements within communities and to recognize that, for various reasons, some individuals and groups are more vulnerable than others to criminal justice processing.

8. CREDIBILITY AND LEGITIMACY OF LOCAL ABORIGINAL JUSTICE SYSTEMS

A major challenge facing Aboriginal justice systems is to develop credibility and legitimacy in the local community. One of the central findings from the James Bay Cree community interviews, for example, was that community residents did not want local justice systems to be mere extensions of community power structures. There was an insistence on fairness and objectivity.

Family and kinship relationships and the general closeness of residents living in small, isolated communities means that serious attention must be paid to ensuring both the reality, and the perception, of fairness. To a significant degree, credibility will depend on the individuals who are given responsibility for making decisions. If they are credible in the community, the system is more likely to be perceived as legitimate.

It will also be necessary to consider the perceptions of the larger surrounding community. If it is perceived that preferential treatment is accorded either by the local system or by the larger, non-Aboriginal system, efforts to avoid the jurisdiction of one set of authorities—to be dealt with by the other system—can be expected. Will this be allowed? Will there be instances where an accused person gets to choose which system will deal with the case? These possibilities have extensive resource and jurisdictional implications.

OPTIONS FOR THE DEVELOPMENT OF ABORIGINAL JUSTICE INITIATIVES

Having reviewed key issues, problems, and dilemmas that Aboriginal communities are facing, and will continue to face, in implementing local justice programs, I will now turn to the criminological literature. While much of this literature is based on research in non-Aboriginal settings, there are, nonetheless, findings that are relevant to the pursuit of justice in

Aboriginal communities. The literature discusses several approaches. Aboriginal communities may wish to consider how these approaches can be integrated with customary practices to respond to their unique circumstances.

Set out below are three ways of considering "justice" and justice approaches, which incorporate varying degrees of formal (external) and informal (internal) control. These approaches, or models, are:

1. The broad-based crime prevention approach;
2. The community justice development approach; and
3. The community-based alternatives to formal processing approach.

1. THE CRIME PREVENTION APPROACH[6]

Increasingly, criminologists and government agencies with justice mandates have been arguing the futility of focusing exclusively on the "back end" of the criminal justice system to solve community problems, despite the reality that most resources are funneled in that direction. Family stress, marital discord, unemployment, poverty, child-rearing practices, and various forms of physical and sexual abuse are increasingly being recognized as causes of crime and delinquency. As Skogan (1991, p. 10) notes:

> Many of the factors that predict later misfortune are school or family related. They include poverty and child abuse. Parental factors are very important; later criminality is related to neglect and lack of parental supervision, poor nurturing, family disruption and marital discord, and having criminal parents. Doing badly and misbehaving in school is also symptomatic of later difficulties.

Similarly, recent cross-cultural comparisons of the self-concepts of confined young offenders in the U.S. and England (Evans et al. 1992) examined the impact of parenting on self-esteem and subsequent delinquent behavior. The researchers found that parents play an important role in shaping healthy self-esteem in their children, and that delinquents had lower self-esteem than non-delinquents. Black delinquents had even lower perceptions of themselves than their white delinquent counterparts. Furthermore, differences in self-concept were more likely to be the product of cultural rather than genetic differences. Differences were not found to result from the justice system negatively labeling delinquents, since self-concept formed before involvement with the justice system began (Evans et al. 1992).

Recurrent findings similar to those reported in the Evans et al. study have generated much interest in the development of comprehensive crime prevention programs. For example, Skogan (1991, p. 10) has commented:

> The policy implications of these findings are both fairly clear and untested. All of them call for an emphasis on primary prevention rather than later intervention by the criminal justice system. An incomes policy aimed at ensuring a basic level of support for children's families could alleviate some of the risk factors. It would be especially important to combine this with parenthood education programs targeted at families with poor child rearing skills. Likewise, special schooling programs aimed at large groups of high risk youths . . . without seemingly selecting for special attention "the criminally inclined" . . . would have positive benefits.

Similarly, Bottoms (1990, p. 14), in considering the implications of the findings about the causes of delinquency, notes that:

> Farrington has recently made some interesting suggestions—on the basis of up-to-date research—these suggestions include behaviourial parent training, Head Start educational programs, increased economic resources for deprived families, and techniques to help children avoid peer-group pressures. . . . If the persistent offenders could be identified at an early age, then one form of crime prevention worth attempting would be to work with them in a range of voluntary prevention programs; the indications are that early identification, on the basis of troublesome behaviour and other data available at age 10, is possible.

He suggests that future crime prevention strategies include a "balanced strategy embracing the situational, the social and the developmental" (Bottoms 1990, p. 15). For Bottoms, the "situational" refers to cocoon-type neighborhood watch schemes, whereby the opportunity to commit crimes is reduced through increased neighborhood vigilance, and there is an attempt to develop stronger social networks and social cohesion in the neighborhood. The "social" refers to a focus on drugs, alcohol, unemployment, and debt, since these problems are often evident in interviews with offenders. The "developmental" strategy incorporates the types of initiatives that Skogan (1991) has identified—income, education, and training programs, for children and parents.[7]

Evaluation research that has assessed the effectiveness of programs designed to prevent specific crimes also has the potential to provide significant direction for programming. In reviewing evaluations of primary drug prevention strategies in the United States, for example, Skogan (1991) examined the effectiveness of social pressures competence programs relative to other approaches. These programs teach participants how to:

1. Evaluate peer and media pressures to become involved in drugs;
2. Build friendship networks of like-minded people;
3. Recognize situations in which they will be expected by peers to use drugs; and
4. Counter social pressures.

In terms of reducing high levels of drug use, Skogan (1991) found that competence programs were more effective than programs focused on providing information about the health and social hazards of drug use. They also worked better than affective education programs that concentrated on improving self-esteem, personal confidence, and knowledge about drug risks.

The implementation of a crime prevention approach in Aboriginal communities might involve setting up the following types of initiatives:

1. Crime prevention councils with a broad-based policy setting function and representation from Aboriginal and other governments;
2. Ongoing community parenting and life-skills courses;
3. Family support and marriage counselling programs;
4. Preschool education programs for children at risk;
5. Social pressures competence programs, as well as "stay in school" and "beat the street" initiatives;
6. Community recreation programs;
7. Job training programs;
8. Community support and assistance programs for those with serious parenting, marital, family, drug abuse, or other problems; and
9. Intensive treatment programs for small groups of offenders aimed at preventing recidivism.

The land claims and self-government processes hold out much promise that the underlying problems leading to crime, delinquency, and victimization in Aboriginal communities can be addressed. These developments will complement the kinds of crime prevention initiatives listed above.

2. THE COMMUNITY JUSTICE DEVELOPMENT APPROACH

The community justice development approach does not exclude the crime prevention approach, it is integral to it. It contributes the "community mobilization" component to crime prevention, and recognizes that the local community is the primary resource in organizing and implementing crime prevention initiatives. Identifying it as a distinct approach highlights the importance of community infrastructures in developing justice initiatives.

In every community, there are the "seeds" for community justice development (Stevenson 1992); however, this potential must be explored and fostered to achieve an organized system of crime prevention and community-based alternatives. Careful preparatory work and active, broad-based community participation are essential components of this approach.

The link between the crime prevention and community justice development approaches is evident in the "safe-neighborhoods" movement. Safe neighborhoods initiatives require both community development and community mobilization, and they are a good example of the community justice development approach.

The philosophy behind safe neighborhoods initiatives is consistent with long-standing principles of community development. For example, in a recent report to the Metropolitan Toronto Housing Authority (MTHA) on their safe neighborhoods initiatives in ten designated communities, Osler (1991) described community development as a process that facilitates, enables, involves, mediates, and coaches, rather than helps, fixes, directs, or takes over. She identified the following community development objectives as central to the work of their coordinating committee:

1. To establish strong partnerships and coordinated efforts with other agencies, including the police, social service, etc., to ensure their responsiveness to identified issues in the community;
2. To assist in organizing resident-based prevention and self-help programs; and
3. To assist communities to initiate innovative programs with youth that will offer them alternatives and choices based on preventive education.

Although the MTHA initiative is based in a large urban center, the goals and objectives of the initiative apply to any community.

The literature suggests that Aboriginal communities may be excellent candidates for the community justice development approach. In assessing crime control and prevention strategies, Skogan (1991) concludes that cultural homogeneity of a society, community, or group is a positive factor in success. Skogan (1991, p. 6) notes that:

> Successful neighbourhood organizations are more common in homogeneous areas—in racially and culturally homogenous areas, residents more readily share a definition of what their problems are and who is responsible for them; they share similar experiences and living conditions, and they have the same broad conception of their public and private responsibilities. The empirical evidence is that in homogeneous areas, residents exercise more informal control and are more likely to intervene when they see problems.

Similarly, Braithwaite (1989) contends that "reintegrative shaming," on which his theory of crime control is based, works best in societies where interdependency, communitarianism, and cultural homogeneity exist.

All three of the approaches described in this section are linked. Henricson (1991, p. 14) makes the connection when he argues that:

> If rehabilitation is to be successful, the communities to which young offenders return have to be reasonably stable and provide opportunities for a legitimate and satisfying livelihood. When this is not the case the success of even the best programs will be limited.

Challenges facing community justice developers include:

1. Creating more appropriate justice service delivery mechanisms;
2. Devising more effective ways for educating communities about the workings of the criminal justice system and about the involvement of Aboriginal people in the system;
3. Developing community consultation protocols;
4. Deciding how information about what works can be made available to communities to assist them in developing their own approaches to crime and disorder;
5. Facilitating and coordinating community justice endeavors in conjunction with communities;
6. Assessing treatment and aftercare approaches most appropriate, useful, and conducive to individual, family, and community needs; and
7. Encouraging, facilitating, and assisting with reviews and evaluations of community-based projects.

The setting up of the community justice development approach in Aboriginal communities might involve the following types of activities:

1. Communities selecting and training community justice facilitators (or community justice development workers). Each facilitator might stimulate and channel the energy and will of the community and allow the community to discover and direct its power in a useful way (Stevenson 1992);

2. Community justice representatives, modeled on the community health representatives active in some communities, might be established to provide justice information and community development skills. They might make connections between community and justice institutions and develop local justice initiatives, such as community-based alternatives to formal justice system processing;

3. Community mobilization initiatives. Examples include:
   i. the citizen patrols developed in the Squamish Nation in British Columbia,
   ii. the demonstrations against bootleggers undertaken in South Island Lake, Manitoba, and
   iii. community-based policing, where police are more visible, meet with school children, and talk with residents of the community, not just the leaders, and thereby become "partners rather than aliens" (Clairmont 1992, p. xviii);

4. The creation of Aboriginal justice councils. These councils, already established in non-Aboriginal communities in Manitoba and British Columbia, might represent Aboriginal communities in developing community-based justice initiatives;

5. Safe neighborhoods initiatives;

6. Family violence projects, where individuals are selected by community justice development workers, or others, for life skills, substance abuse, anger management, or other types of programs;

7. Consultation projects aimed at improving communication and relations between Aboriginal and non-Aboriginal communities;

8. Justice trainee programs, where individuals from the community are trained for positions in the local justice system;

9. Streetworker programs for Aboriginal youth in urban areas, involving mobilization of the urban Aboriginal and non-Aboriginal communities; and

10. Urban-based projects that might involve inner-city Aboriginal people designing and delivering their own services rather than being "serviced."

3. THE COMMUNITY-BASED ALTERNATIVES APPROACH

The term "community-based alternatives" has taken on many meanings, and some perceive it to incorporate virtually any initiative that involves the community. In the context that it is used here, however, it refers to alternatives to formal processing that are intended to prevent offenders from going deeper and deeper into the justice system.

A recognition of the need to reduce the onerous effects of the criminal justice system on individual offenders and communities, and an awareness of the inability of the system to "solve" crime problems, has provided the impetus for community-based alternatives. Common alternatives include:

1. Diversion;
2. Intermediate sanctions that involve some community action, but not the incarceration of the offender;[8] and
3. Alternate dispute-resolution.

To carry out these types of alternatives, community structures such as panels and councils have often emerged.

It should be remembered, that as Henricson (1991, p. 14) has said:

> A key issue influencing the success of a programme is the conditions under which it is delivered. In the right circumstances, results can be favourable even for serious delinquents . . . well-managed, adequately resourced, intensive community-based programmes for offenders are more effective (and far less expensive) than custodial sentences in preventing recidivism amongst persistent, non-violent offenders.

It is also known that treatment cannot be very effective without adequate aftercare. An alcohol counselor in one Yukon community, for example, has claimed that no more than 35 percent of Aboriginal clients going through alcoholism treatment stay sober for any reasonable period. In another community, local staff estimated that 90 percent of those sent out of the community for alcoholism treatment began drinking within a few months after their return. Therefore, local attendance centers where residents receive a variety of services including, for example, group therapy, cognitive skills training, anger management, and life skills warrant consideration as a supplement, or a substitute, for treatment outside the community.

It is well known that communities play a critical role in determining behavior. Both Skogan (1991) and Braithwaite (1992) discuss the importance of communities contributing to the onset of deviance, and in recidivism. Skogan (1991, p. 6) writes:

> Studies of recidivism among individuals paroled early from prison indicate that community ties are among the most important predictors of who gets in trouble again.

Alternate dispute-resolution (ADR) has become the cherished hope of criminal justice reformers seeking to counteract a growing reliance on courts to resolve conflict. Civil and family law, for example, have turned increasingly to ADR techniques to resolve disputes. Mediation, restitution, arbitration, and reconciliation are now commonly used in the criminal justice discourse, and informal control, such as mediation and reconciliation, are at the heart of much of the Aboriginal justice discourse.

There is very little literature describing alternate dispute-resolution in the contemporary Aboriginal community context, and the traditional notions of dispute-resolution, such as mediation, are often the main focus of discussions. Future Aboriginal justice initiatives, however, will undoubtedly be rooted in various forms of alternate dispute-resolution. An important issue is how mediation and reconciliation practices that have been tested in small, nomadic, collective societies can apply in larger, sedentary, more individualistic societies. Recent evaluation research in the U.S., for example, has revealed that involving victims and offenders in restitution decisions resulted in higher completion rates than in cases of court-ordered restitution (Umbreit and Coates 1993). This is an important finding for Aboriginal communities, where achieving completion of court orders for juveniles is particularly difficult (La Prairie 1991).

The implementation of the community-based alternatives approach in Aboriginal communities might involve the following activities:

1. Setting up adult and youth diversion programs;
2. Administering alternate dispute-resolution, adult and juvenile mediation, and victim-offender reconciliation programs;
3. Overseeing the use of intermediate sanctions, such as restitution and community service, as alternatives to incarceration;
4. Developing community-based resources for diversion and alternatives to incarceration, perhaps by training community justice development workers in program design;
5. Initiating day attendance centers where offenders can deal with problems related to lack of skills, illiteracy, personal problems, or

difficulties in the home environment;

6. Instituting apprentice programs to link Aboriginal offenders with businesses; and

7. Creating community-based residential treatment options that could bring Aboriginal offenders into contact with both traditional healers and "professional" advisors without the need to leave the community.

An integrated community-based alternatives approach might include some or all of the following:

1. Expanded law-making powers to deal with a range of community problems;

2. Creation of a community-based peace keeping and enforcement capacity (not police officers) to enforce the laws;

3. Development of community panels for the adjudication of laws; and

4. The creation of community-based sanctions.

CONCLUSION

Aboriginal justice initiatives are already a reality in Canada. However, the continued development of effective and appropriate alternatives to the existing criminal justice system represents a challenge that will require the ongoing cooperation and support of the Aboriginal and non-Aboriginal leadership.

A usual government practice when it comes to funding Aboriginal justice projects is to give money and to make a public announcement about the latest Aboriginal "project." As such projects have come and gone, however, more and more Aboriginal communities, and many officials in the criminal justice system, have come to question the effectiveness of this approach. If federal and provincial governments are to work in partnership with the Aboriginal Peoples, it is important that principles be adopted to guide the relationship.

A number of principles might, for example, be considered in the area of funding:

1. Adequate support should be provided to projects when requested, including, for example, visits, advice, information, and technology;

2. There should be an opportunity for proper developmental work to be completed before the project is set up;

3. Monitoring and evaluation strategies should be included in the design of the project and adequately funded;

4. Appropriate training for community justice personnel should be provided;
5. Resources to support community justice sanctions should be identified and developed;
6. The approach of hiring justice personnel from the local community should be used;
7. Communities should have the opportunity to consult, deliberate, design, and carry out community-based approaches. Governments should not impose their need for "products" on communities; and
8. There should be a recognition that funding of justice projects is not a substitute or panacea for long-term economic development and employment in Aboriginal communities.

There has been progress in the area of Aboriginal justice in Canada over the past decade. Yet, much remains to be learned, and there are many issues that require resolution. By recognizing the failures, and building on the successes, however, increasingly more effective and appropriate alternatives can be developed.

The current justice system can learn from traditional Aboriginal social control practices. At the same time, there are many studies, and many models, that have been developed in non-Aboriginal communities. They can assist Aboriginal communities to address contemporary problems. Partnerships are required—ones built on respect and goodwill on both sides. Such partnerships are a prerequisite to attaining the promise of more effective approaches to justice.

NOTES

1   Any views expressed in this paper are those of the author, and do not necessarily reflect those of Justice Canada, or any other organization. The author would like to thank Justice Canada, the Department of Justice of the Yukon Territorial Government, and the Cree Regional Authority, for permitting the use of the research findings. Parts of this paper are based on La Prairie (1992).

2   Inquiries into the situation of Aboriginal people and the criminal justice system have occurred in the provinces of Nova Scotia, Alberta, Saskatchewan, and Manitoba (Royal Commission 1989; Task Force 1991; Lynn 1991a and 1991b; Hamilton and Sinclair 1991). The work of the Royal Commission on Aboriginal Peoples is still in progress.

3   Criminologist Wesley Skogan (1990, p. 10), notes that: "Special delinquency programs need to be targeted at high-risk populations. . . . If at age 7 or 8, children are asked to rate the aggressiveness of their playmates, those ratings

are highly predictive of later offending; the same holds true for adults conducting concealed observations. Further, later criminality is highly related to poor performance in school. . . . Farrington's London study identified seven variables that at age 10 successfully predicted later heavy criminal involvement."

4   There is a danger that communities will feel pressured by Aboriginal political organizations, governments of the dominant society, or community interest groups, to negotiate justice systems before essential developmental work is completed. Aboriginal communities may lack accurate information about the existing criminal justice system, and about Aboriginal and non-Aboriginal approaches that have been tried elsewhere. The need to ensure that what is implemented is long-lasting and effective in meeting justice needs, cannot be over-emphasized.

5   My analysis in this paper deals mainly with reserve-based and settlement-based communities. When it comes to Aboriginal justice initiatives off reserve or settlement lands, there are many additional complications.

6   The term *crime prevention* is sometimes used to refer to so-called target-hardening approaches that are aimed at discouraging offenders from committing crimes. In this discussion, however, the focus is on the social and psychological variables that influence criminal disposition. This is not to say that target hardening may not also have some application in Aboriginal communities.

7   Interestingly, comprehensive models of crime prevention have also been adopted by some political parties. For example, the British Labour Party produced a criminal justice white paper in 1990. In the period leading up to the 1993 federal election in Canada, crime control was also an issue with a number of national political parties. Generally, however, there appeared to be more interest in "getting tough" than there was on preventing crime.

8   There is a need to explore "means whereby Intermediate Sanctions can become viable and credible with communities, the courts, and offenders" (Parry 1992). Pilot projects in this area are urgently needed. Results of such projects would be of use to many Aboriginal and non-Aboriginal communities across Canada.

REFERENCES

Bottoms, Anthony E. 1990. Crime prevention facing the 1990's. *Policing and Society* 1(1):1–19.

Braithwaite, John. 1992. Reducing the crime problem: A not so dismal criminology. *Australian and New Zealand Journal of Criminology* (March) 25:1–10.
———. 1989. *Crime, shame, and reintegration.* Cambridge, England: Cambridge University Press.

Brodeur, Jean-Paul. 1991. *Policing and alternate dispute resolution: Justice for the Cree.* Nemaska, Quebec: Cree Regional Authority.

Clairmont, Donald. 1993. *Diversion and the Shubenacadie Band: An analysis and interim evaluation*. Ottawa: Justice Canada.

————. 1992. *Native justice in Nova Scotia: Executive summary of a report submitted to the tripartite forum on Native justice*. Halifax: Atlantic Institute of Criminology, Dalhousie University.

Evans, Robert C., Gary Copus, Peter Hodgkinson, and Thomas Sullenberger. 1992. A cross-cultural comparison of the self-concepts of confined youthful offenders by country, residence, and race. Revised version of a paper presented at the American Society of Criminology meetings. San Francisco: unpublished.

Hamilton, A. C., and Murray Sinclair. 1991. *Report of the Aboriginal justice inquiry of Manitoba*. Winnipeg: Government of Manitoba.

Henricson, Clem. 1991. Tackling the causes of crime: Policy for the 1990's. *Labour's Crime Management*. London, England: NARCO.

La Prairie, Carol. 1992. *Exploring the boundaries of justice: Aboriginal justice in the Yukon*. Ottawa: Justice Canada.

————. 1991. *Communities, crime and order: Justice for the Cree*. Nemaska, Quebec: Cree Regional Authority.

Lynn, Patricia. 1991a. *Report of the Indian Justice Review Committee*. Regina: Government of Saskatchewan.

————. 1991b. *Report of the Metis Justice Review Committee*. Regina: Government of Saskatchewan.

Osler, Carol. 1991. *Terms of reference for consultant: Safe neighbourhood initiatives program*. Toronto: Metropolitan Toronto Housing Authority.

Parry, Gordon. 1992. *Memorandum on intermediate sanctions in Whitehorse*. Yukon: Department of Justice.

Royal Commission on the Donald Marshall Junior Prosecution. 1989. *Digest of findings and recommendations*. Halifax: Royal Commission on the Donald Marshall Junior Prosecution.

Royal Commission on Aboriginal Peoples. 1993. *Aboriginal peoples and the justice system*. Ottawa: Royal Commission on Aboriginal Peoples.

Skogan, Wesley. 1991. Recent research on urban safety, drugs, and crime prevention in the United States. Paper presented at the second international conference on urban safety, drugs, and crime prevention.

————. 1990. *Disorder and decline*. New York: The Free Press.

Stevenson, A. 1992. *Community justice development proposal*. Whitehorse, Yukon.

Task Force on the Criminal Justice System. 1991. *Justice on trial: Report of the task force on the criminal justice system and its impact on the Indian and Metis people of Alberta*. Edmonton: Task Force on the Criminal Justice System.

Umbreit, Mark S., and Robert Coates. 1993. Cross-site analysis of victim-offender mediation in four states. *Crime and Delinquency* 39(4):565–85.

CHAPTER 7

PATHWAYS TO SUCCESS: ABORIGINAL DECISION-MAKING IN EMPLOYMENT AND TRAINING

TINA EBERTS, HUMAN RESOURCES DEVELOPMENT CANADA[1]

This is the story of Pathways to Success, an Aboriginal training and employment initiative that puts decisions into the hands of Aboriginal people through community boards. Pathways to Success is a process, not another new program for Aboriginal people. It incorporates Aboriginal decision-making rather than Aboriginal "input."

Employment and Immigration Canada (EIC) did not require a change in legislation to develop the Pathways model, and no mandate has been given to EIC to negotiate self-government arrangements. Rather, the program reflects what can be accomplished within existing structures and mandates if there is vision and a genuine commitment to improve human services programs that affect the Aboriginal Peoples.

The philosophy of Pathways is based on the principle of partnership. The traditional EIC role, focused almost exclusively on direct intervention, has been changed to a partnering approach, where the labor market is developed according to the directions of stakeholders. The Pathways strategy was driven forward by individuals who believed in partnership and who rolled up their sleeves with a shared commitment to work together to make it so.

THE BIRTH OF PATHWAYS TO SUCCESS

1. THE ENVIRONMENT

In 1989, EIC announced the Labour Force Development Strategy (LFDS) (Employment and Immigration Canada 1989). Among other things, this strategy focused on evolving partnerships with key players to develop the labor market. The new direction altered the traditional role of EIC. It required EIC to move from providing full delivery of labor market programs and policy to a role of supporting labor market policy development and interventions through partnerships.

The announcement of the LFDS had significant implications for EIC. The

130

department needed to introduce measures to help EIC staff adapt to the new role. Many EIC employees had been hired and developed to intervene in the labor market through highly regulated programs. Performance had been evaluated on the basis of how well the rules and regulations were enforced. Now, however, they were being asked to share that responsibility. This involved partnering training sessions, change management workshops, and stress seminars. It was, and remains, a massive adjustment in both personal and professional terms. LFDS also required significant changes in departmental organizational structure.

During this same period, economic constraints were increasing, and the program and operating budgets of government departments were being reduced. At EIC, contract negotiations with employees saw a high priority given to job security, and strict limitations were placed on "contracting out." These factors reduced EIC's flexibility in implementing Pathways.

Constitutional discussions began while Pathways was still in its infancy. This had the effect of destabilizing the environment around an initiative that was not yet fully under way. While Pathways was a very significant initiative for EIC, it soon became apparent that, for the Aboriginal Peoples, it paled in comparison to many fundamental issues of Aboriginal rights that were being negotiated at the constitutional table.

Within EIC, the constitutional discussions concerning Aboriginal self-government allowed the department to consider Pathways in the context of a broader vision. It was decided by Aboriginal people not to abandon the development of Pathways, even though it was widely believed at the time that a self-government framework would emerge from the constitutional process. In retrospect, this decision was vital to reforming training and employment initiatives for Aboriginal people.

2. CONSULTATIONS

Consistent with the new focus on partnering, a round of consultations with stakeholders was initiated to discuss the LFDS. These consultations were intended to solicit advice on how the labor market could better respond to emerging Canadian skill needs in the context of growing global economic influences. Much of the discussion was centered on external partners assuming roles and responsibilities that had previously been the exclusive domain of EIC.

Aboriginal representation was overlooked in the early rounds of consultations. When Aboriginal representatives were invited to participate, it became apparent that programs and policies aimed at the wider labor market would not be sufficient to respond to the specific and growing needs

131

and aspirations of Aboriginal Canadians. These concerns were raised by Aboriginal communities across the country.

Aboriginal representatives challenged the consultation process, arguing that it would not mitigate the barriers faced by the Aboriginal Peoples. Rather, they suggested that a separate consultation process, distinct in its focus on Aboriginal concerns, would have to be initiated to bring about meaningful changes. By November 1989, EIC and Aboriginal representatives from across Canada were sitting around the same table with a mandate to propose changes that would remove employment and training barriers for Aboriginal Canadians.

3. CRITICAL DECISIONS

In the early stages of designing Pathways, a number of decisions were made that account for the continuing strength and survival of the process. Most importantly, it was decided that, to the extent possible and within existing legislative parameters, the approach would be built on Aboriginal decision-making and control.

The first action to place the initiative firmly within the purview of Aboriginal control was for EIC to hire an Aboriginal coordinator, with national credibility, to manage the process. This had the effect of bringing a fresh perspective to EIC—an external, non-departmental perspective. During the development of Pathways, this strategy consistently helped the process remain focused on devolving decision-making to Aboriginal groups. Inevitably, at many stages of the process, EIC would slip back to "thinking" in an independent rather than in a partnership style. But the implanting of a non-departmental, Aboriginal perspective required EIC to continually question its assumptions throughout the development and implementation process.

The national coordinator for Pathways ensured that the invitations to Aboriginal representatives to participate in the process included both political and institutional representatives. This was also a significant step in building the program. EIC staff from the national and regional offices, who were in a position to make a senior-level commitment, were also invited to participate in the development of the Pathways strategy.

At the initial meeting, Aboriginal spokespersons made it clear that if the meeting was solely about Aboriginal "input," without actual Aboriginal participation and results, it was not in their interests to participate. This position, and EIC's agreement, constituted a further key factor that contributed to the survival of the "strategy to be." The process would not be an attempt by government to quiet Aboriginal voices. It was a commitment to accomplish results.

Senior-level involvement by EIC was also an important ingredient of success. The associate deputy minister of EIC was a participant in the process as co-chair of what became the National Aboriginal Employment and Training Working Group (AETWG). Despite skepticism and outright disbelief in parts of EIC, the co-chair role of the associate deputy minister, and occasional participation by the deputy minister and minister, provided a clear message to the department that this process would produce an outcome beyond that of past "consultations."

A further contributing factor to the success of the initiative was a decision made by the Aboriginal representatives that political and internal organizational differences would be set aside at the national table. This decision, involving six major national Aboriginal organizations, as well as regional bodies and other Aboriginal organizations, had the effect of precluding unintentional sabotage of the process. For example, issues that would later nearly derail the implementation phase of Pathways at some regional and provincial levels, such as the recognition of the distinct interests of First Nations and Métis peoples, were considered to be outside the mandate of AETWG.

A final critical action was an outgrowth of the decision not to involve AETWG in political differences. Aboriginal representatives insisted on having time to caucus without the participation of EIC. As a result, Aboriginal representatives developed five principles that they agreed could form a mutually acceptable foundation for an Aboriginal training and employment strategy. These principles were subsequently tabled with the minister of Employment and Immigration Canada, and accepted as the basis for preparing an Aboriginal labor force development strategy.

PRINCIPLES, STRUCTURES, AND FUNDING

Having described the environment in which Pathways was developed and the key decisions that have contributed to its ongoing success, I would like to describe the principles, structures, and funding mechanisms that underpin the Pathways program.

1. THE PRINCIPLES

The five principles underlying Pathways to Success were intended to maintain a stable planning environment and a consistent offering of training and employment activities. A detailed discussion of these principles may be found elsewhere (Employment and Immigration Canada 1990a; 1990b), therefore, only a summary is provided here.

1. The first principle of Pathways is that decision-making must be local— as close to community needs as possible. As will be discussed more fully later, geographic catchment areas were delineated across Canada, and each area sent representation to regional and national boards. Thus, from the beginning, the initiative was designed to build from the bottom up.
2. The second principle of Pathways is that there must be funding stability. This is intended to allow for a relatively consistent planning environment from year to year. In addition, the principle is intended to acknowledge that, beyond direct costs associated with the delivery of employment and training programs, adequate funding must be provided for administrative costs associated with planning and decision-making;
3. The third principle of Pathways calls for training and employment programs to be delivered through Aboriginal infrastructures wherever possible. This was particularly important in some regions of the country where there was a good deal of Aboriginal experience in program delivery. In some jurisdictions, for example, there were long-established Aboriginally controlled institutions that had built up a significant track record in the area of training and education programs.

   Delivery of programs through institutions controlled by the Aboriginal Peoples is criticized by some as a duplication of mainstream programs and institutions. Aboriginal groups point out, however, that uniquely Aboriginal programs do not duplicate mainstream programs since the Aboriginal Peoples are generally not effectively served by these programs. A more sensitized and responsive environment can be provided through institutions under Aboriginal control. The importance of this supportive environment is demonstrated in the success rates of Aboriginal institutions;
4. The fourth principle of Pathways is a commitment to proactive approaches to employment equity. This reflects the concern that programs of employment equity historically have had little impact on altering the employment prospects for the Aboriginal Peoples; and
5. The fifth and final principle of Pathways calls on EIC to assess employment and training programs for barriers to Aboriginal participation. This principle lays the foundation for the planning process to remain dynamic and open to changing needs. It also legitimizes an important role for Aboriginal participation in the ongoing development

of policies and programs by insisting that the results of planning have a favorable impact on the Aboriginal Peoples.

2. THE STRUCTURES

Through an extensive series of consultations, a generic Pathways model was developed and published by Employment and Immigration Canada (1990b). Although it was not intended to be fully prescriptive, the document became useful in ensuring that commitments were not reneged on because of disputes over interpretations of what Pathways was supposed to be.

The model was based on a number of local boards being established across Canada, each comprised of community members from a specified geographic area. Each local board provided a representative for regional boards, and, in turn, the regional boards appointed two representatives to the national board. Community consultations determined how board members at the local, regional, and national levels were selected.

Pathways was designed with a recognition that local boards would develop and assume responsibilities at their own pace. They could determine the mix of programming for their geographic area and decide which training proposals would be approved. If desired, they could elect to use some of the training funds allocated to them to establish Aboriginal training and employment centers aimed at improving services to Aboriginal clients.

3. THE FUNDING

Historically, EIC had control of the budgets and made all the decisions about which training initiatives would be approved. Under Pathways, most of the decision-making now rests with Pathways boards, while EIC continues to administer the contracts according to its legal authority.

Pathways provided a national budget of $200 million a year for five years. While a finite allocation, the five-year commitment provided some stability in an environment of significant economic constraint.

Initially, a comparatively simple model was used to allocate the national budget to the regions, based on historical expenditures and negotiations with the Pathways partners. In the initial phases, this approach was adequate. However, in an environment of declining resources, those areas of Canada that historically had expended large amounts for Aboriginal training soon began to call for a more sophisticated allocation methodology. An allocation model that recognizes regional differences in Aboriginal labor market structure is expected to be a contentious item of discussion in 1994 and beyond.

Within regions, decisions also had to be made about the level of funding that would be under the control of each local Pathways board. A variety of approaches were used across the country to determine the method of allocation. In some instances, a population-based formula was used; in others, the formula was based on historical funding levels. In still other instances, equal amounts were provided to boards covering geographic catchment areas of similar size.

Beyond the resources allocated to the Pathways boards, some resources were retained by EIC to support individual access by Aboriginal clients to programming provided through EIC's delivery system (for example, through Canada Employment centers). It was understandable that Aboriginal organizations wanted to maximize the amounts allocated to programs delivered through Aboriginal infrastructures, and the organizations worked closely together to achieve this goal. As a result, within two years of implementation, approximately 75 percent of regional client-based funding was committed for decision-making by local and regional Pathways boards.

The administration of training and employment programs for the Aboriginal Peoples requires a close partnership at the local level. Pathways boards and Canada Employment centers (CEC) must work together to manage funds and programs. However, the CEC offices no longer make the decisions about Aboriginal training and employment needs. Rather, their role is to provide technical advice, and to screen training proposals for compliance with EIC program and financial authorities. The full responsibility for deciding what training is offered, and who is selected to participate, rests with the Pathways boards and their staff.

THE SASKATCHEWAN CASE

It is useful to examine the Saskatchewan case because it illustrates how the process of developing Pathways proceeded. As well, Saskatchewan is an interesting case, because there were some noteworthy departures from the model for Pathways that evolved elsewhere in Canada.

1. SEPARATE INDIAN AND MÉTIS DECISION-MAKING STRUCTURES IN SASKATCHEWAN

Saskatchewan Aboriginal representatives on the AETWG insisted that local and regional political distinctiveness be respected. They pointed out that, on the prairies, there are strong historical and current political foundations supporting the separate identities of their peoples. While the Métis Society of Saskatchewan (MSS) supported this idea, it was the treaty Indian position that drove the issue. As Pathways moved from a national theory to practical implementation, the recognition of separate Indian and Métis decision-making structures would prove to have important, and contentious, ramifications.

Although it was well known that the Federation of Saskatchewan Indian Nations (FSIN) and the MSS were separate organizations, EIC had proceeded on the basis of a national model where all Aboriginal groups (political and service, affiliated and not affiliated) would work together on joint boards at the local, regional, and national levels. This model failed to recognize that the strength of Saskatchewan's Aboriginal community had always been in the separate, cohesive, and sophisticated institutional development that had taken place within the groups themselves. Had adjustments not been made, the failure to recognize the distinct interests of the partners in Saskatchewan could have jeopardized the Pathways process.

Although maintaining the distinctness of different Aboriginal groups was not consistent with the national vision for Pathways, it was possible to find creative alternatives. The MSS and the FSIN agreed to come together on non-financial issues of common interest. Had a pan-Aboriginal approach been imposed, however, both rights and culture would have been compromised. The time is long past where it is acceptable to put administrative simplicity ahead of respect for legal, cultural, and political differences, and, fortunately, the Pathways model provided enough flexibility to respect these differences.

A partnership has to mean more than simply recognizing and respecting differences between partners. The FSIN and the MSS insisted that they be recognized as the only legitimate representatives of the First Nations and Métis peoples in Saskatchewan. Pathways would not proceed in Saskatchewan except through separate board systems under their authorities. Respecting and valuing the separate identities of the Indian and Métis peoples was the beginning of a long and challenging implementation process in Saskatchewan.

Some off-reserve Indians—Bill C-31 Indians who regained their status as a result of changes to the Indian Act—and Métis not affiliated with MSS raised questions about the ability of FSIN and MSS to fully represent their interests in the Pathways process. Many of these individuals have elected to access mainstream services. This concern is, of course, not specific to Pathways. It arises whenever an initiative involving parallel Aboriginal and mainstream structures is being developed, and where control of resources is at issue. In Pathways, the issue was dealt with by commitments from MSS and FSIN that they would provide services to all Aboriginal people within Saskatchewan. In addition, having EIC retain a portion of resources for delivery of services to Aboriginal people through mainstream institutions provided a limited safety net while the two Aboriginal organizations refined their service delivery structures.

EIC adapted to the political position of the FSIN and MSS, even though a broader base of organizations had historically sponsored Aboriginal training initiatives in Saskatchewan. This placed a significant onus of accountability on the two Aboriginal delivery structures to address the needs of all Aboriginal individuals, not only those who were politically affiliated with one or other of the organizations. Although there have been accusations of preferential treatment and denial of service from time to time, the problems have not been widespread. Some boards have begun articulating inclusive policies that require non-discriminatory selection practices.

The Saskatchewan region came under a great deal of scrutiny for its support of separate Indian and Métis local board systems. Opinions vary as to whether or not the Saskatchewan arrangements are setting a precedent. On the one hand, it is clear that the Saskatchewan approach is influencing developments elsewhere.[2] Some feel that Pathways has established ground rules for other important initiatives, including more formalized self-governing arrangements. On the other hand, observers point out that a variety of tripartite and other relationships involving federal and provincial governments have respected the separateness between Indian and Métis organizations for over two decades. They argue that Pathways arrangements simply reflect long-standing practices in the region.

2. FUNDING

In Saskatchewan, the allocation of funds to the separate board systems established by FSIN and MSS added a complication unique to the region, and one that proved to be a divisive issue for all parties. Had the key players not kept coming to the table, trusting the commitment and integrity of all partners, it is questionable whether the process would have moved forward.

The FSIN and MSS consistently declined to discuss how funding would be divided between them because they were concerned this would compromise the positions that chiefs and Métis communities had mandated them to carry forward. Therefore, after discussion with both groups, EIC made an independent decision to allocate 60 percent of the funds to treaty Indian boards, and 40 percent to Métis boards. The decision was based largely on historical levels of funding, and on limited demographic information available from the 1986 census. The allocation was eventually accepted on a "without prejudice" basis by both groups, but only for a one-year period, with the understanding that further changes would be made in subsequent years. In Saskatchewan, and nationally, it is now being proposed that allocations be calculated using the 1991 census that relied on a more sophisticated methodology for assessing the numbers and characteristics of the Aboriginal population.

After the funding is negotiated for each fiscal year, and the Métis and Indian allocations are determined, EIC plays very little role in decision-making. EIC does insist that an adequate funding level be provided for urban centers, and it requires assurance that all Aboriginal people will be able to access programming on an equitable basis. However, it takes no part in determining the allocation for the eleven Indian and six Métis local management boards that have been set up to implement the Pathways program.

Band and tribal council structures have been working with population-based funding models for years, and, as a result, a formula for distributing employment and training monies was quite easily developed among the Indian Pathways boards in Saskatchewan. The challenge for the treaty Indian boards was to consider how service delivery would be extended beyond the band membership to Aboriginal people residing in geographic areas for which the boards were responsible.

The Métis, lacking comprehensive information about the Métis population, divided their allocation equally among six local boards. Some minor adjustments were then made to provide equitable access.

Both the Indian and Métis approaches worked well. Interestingly, the distribution of funding was not dissimilar from what had previously occurred through EIC's hierarchical decision-making process.

3. ISSUES

One of the problems in the implementation of Pathways in Saskatchewan was the myriad of interpretations of the Pathways to Success strategy (Employment and Immigration Canada 1990a; 1990b). This became evident only as implementation proceeded. Presentations of the strategy, and consultations at various levels within EIC, FSIN, and MSS, had been conducted separately. As a result, different understandings developed.

Some interpreted Pathways as full self-government, while others believed that Pathways boards would be mere advisory bodies to local Canada Employment centers. In some areas, confusion still exists, and it has proved difficult to correct misunderstandings and misinterpretations that were introduced early in implementation. The Policy and Implementation paper (Employment and Immigration Canada 1990b) proved to be a crucial document for maintaining accuracy and direction. Nonetheless, greater Aboriginal involvement in the consultations and in the development of the Pathways strategy would have minimized the problems.

It has been suggested that the policy and implementation document (Employment and Immigration Canada 1990b) should have been more comprehensive, and that the practical aspects of implementing Pathways should have been described in greater detail. Although some problems might have been avoided if more prescriptive information had been included, the lack of specific instructions ensured there was latitude in implementing the model, and this encouraged a discussion of alternative approaches at local and regional levels. This open style had the effect of precluding arbitrary limitations that might have restricted, rather than enabled, the process.

Canada Employment Centre staff have often cited Pathways as an example of a pseudo-partnership. Some felt they had very little opportunity to contribute to the process because important decisions and management functions were the responsibility of the Pathways boards. In many respects this is an accurate observation.

Partnership implies full and equal power in decision-making, yet, in some regions, including Saskatchewan, EIC has taken a low profile with respect to most program and service issues. Although it could well have adopted an active role, it has tended to advise and support the Pathways boards. Implicit in this strategy has been a recognition that the boards must be fully responsible and accountable for training decisions, administrative matters, and productive use of funds.

Although some staff anticipated resource savings as a result of the new structure of Pathways boards, the opposite has been the case. An increased time investment has been required on the part of EIC to participate in and manage the partnership process.

One of the outstanding issues relates to funding the administrative infrastructure that is required by Pathways. Within an environment of downsizing, governments are hard pressed to justify administrative costs. Indian local management boards have been able to cope by using existing band and tribal council infrastructures. Pathways responsibilities have become part of an existing staff member's responsibilities. The Métis community, however, lacking comparable resources, has used Pathways funding to try to build an infrastructure.

The debate continues about whether the process has moved ahead quickly enough. Aboriginal groups are pressing for accelerated development; however, there are cost implications. Saskatchewan has certainly moved ahead more quickly than other regions, in part, because of the level of Aboriginal institutional development. In particular, First Nations infrastructures and institutional development are sophisticated, and could effectively assume more employment and training responsibilities. The Métis infrastructure, however, while moving forward, has not yet fully realized its potential.

A major difficulty in implementing Pathways in Saskatchewan is that the process has been so local in focus that it has overshadowed the need for more strategic thinking and direction. A broader perspective and long-term vision have been lacking. While immediate needs will often dominate—and, perhaps, must dominate—at the local level, steps must be taken to ensure a planning process that will help the Aboriginal Peoples respond to economic influences and technological change that are being felt throughout the world. The ability to be self-sufficient in the future will depend on a proactive continuum of economic development, employment, and education strategies.

THE FUTURE OF PATHWAYS

Despite some flaws, the Pathways to Success model has moved beyond early expectations, particularly for EIC. Yet, because of the level of Aboriginal infrastructure and institutional development in parts of the country, it has been viewed by some Aboriginal groups as too limited. In Saskatchewan, for example, three Aboriginally controlled post-secondary training institutions have been operating for over fifteen years.

Pathways has not altered the structure of EIC programming, nor have the contracting or administration procedures been changed. Pathways has only moved decision-making from government to the community for a few parts of a service in a complex array of programs.

In order to devolve more responsibility to Aboriginal organizations, a "One Agreement Model" has been proposed. This approach uses a single agreement with the federal department to enable Pathways boards to deliver the full range of programs and services to the Aboriginal people that would usually be provided by EIC offices. Yet, even this approach has limitations, since only EIC programs are involved. This segmented approach to the development and delivery of programs has been strongly criticized by the Aboriginal leadership.

The early hopes for One Agreement Models have not been realized. The Aboriginal community has shown little interest in being accountable for the administration of programs that are limited in scope, and restrictive in criteria and intent. The only way to accommodate these concerns is to go beyond approaches that devolve only the responsibility for program administration.

The vision of Aboriginal Peoples is that they must have an opportunity to be involved in the way programs are designed, controlled, and evaluated, not just in the way they are delivered. This suggests an approach where governments concentrate on strategic planning and the development of standards, and direct services are provided by Aboriginal organizations.

It is clear that if governments want a true partnership with the Aboriginal Peoples, they must significantly revise and simplify their administrative requirements. Multiply the administration involved in Pathways by more departments and more governments, and it quickly becomes apparent that entering into partnerships with government is not a viable option for many Aboriginal communities right now. The onus is clearly on government to adapt its systems and policies so that a true partnership is possible.

There are many questions about how these changes would work in practice. For example, how can accountability to the taxpayers and parliament be achieved as funding and program design become further and further removed from direct government control? In areas bearing on the inherent rights of the Aboriginal Peoples, however, perhaps these questions of accountability to non-Aboriginal systems and governments are becoming irrelevant.

NOTES

1   The Pathways to Success strategy was launched in 1990 by Employment and Immigration Canada. In 1993, programs administered by Employment and Immigration Canada, including Pathways, became part of the new Department of Human Resources Development Canada.

2   In Manitoba, for example, similar issues are now confronting the Pathways to Success process. Manitoba's approach in negotiating distinct treaty/status Indian and Métis board structures has been supported with reference to the precedents set in Saskatchewan.

REFERENCES

Employment and Immigration Canada. 1990a. *Pathways to success: Aboriginal employment and training strategy, background document.* Ottawa: Employment and Immigration Canada.

————. 1990b. *Pathways to success: Aboriginal employment and training strategy, a policy and implementation paper.* Ottawa: Employment and Immigration Canada.

————. 1989. *Success in the works: A labour force development strategy for Canada.* Ottawa: Employment and Immigration Canada.

PART III

ISSUES AND DEBATES

CHAPTER 8

THE FINANCING OF ABORIGINAL SELF-GOVERNMENT[1]

ALLAN M. MASLOVE AND CAROLYN DITTBURNER
CARLETON UNIVERSITY

As negotiations toward self-government proceed, it is important to direct attention to possible financial arrangements and their ability to support self-government. This paper discusses practical considerations involved in setting up effective financial structures for the operation of Aboriginal self-government in Canada.

To this end, the paper is divided into three principal sections:

1. A review of the types of transfers that Aboriginal governments might receive from governments, primarily federal, but provincial as well;
2. A discussion of the importance and capacity of Aboriginal governments to generate revenues on their own; and
3. An examination of the administrative and political considerations involved in managing financial arrangements to support self-government.

While we acknowledge that there is tremendous diversity within the Aboriginal community and that this diversity may be expressed in different self-governing arrangements, we have chosen to concentrate this examination on the situation of land-based Aboriginal communities. Other self-government arrangements, such as public or non-land-based forms of government, are not explicitly discussed, though some of the issues we raise may apply.

TRANSFERS FROM OTHER GOVERNMENTS

Currently, the major source of financing for Aboriginal communities is cash transfers from the federal and provincial governments. There is no clear model that determines funding to all bands, as funding is adjusted at the donor's discretion. Chiefs and councils must negotiate annually on every item in the band's operating budget, and are ultimately accountable to the minister of Indian Affairs and Northern Development. Besides funds provided through cash transfers, a 1988 amendment to the Indian Act provides bands with the authority to impose municipal-style property taxes on reserve lands, though the majority of bands remain heavily dependent on federal government transfers.

For the most part, the sources of funding will remain the same under self-government arrangements, although the form of these transfers must change in important ways. The major dimensions along which changes are required to support self-government relate to the "formula" that determines funding. The formula determines the base funding (also referred to as "core funding") that will be provided to support the principal structures and services under self-government. It also determines the conditional grants that may be available to supplement base funding on a program-specific basis. The mix of government transfers employed under self-government arrangements (that is to say, the balance between base funding and conditional grants) affects the manner in which the governments will operate. Therefore, the formula must be sensitive to the circumstances of each community.

It is very important to consider the role that base funding might play in self-government financial arrangements. Regardless of the other funding sources that are developed, base funding from the federal government, whether provided through the Department of Indian Affairs and Northern Development or another federal agency, will be crucial to virtually all Aboriginal communities that enter self-government arrangements. An essential characteristic of self-government financing must be that the bulk of base funding is paid in unconditional grants. This will ensure that Aboriginal governments have the opportunity to exercise the discretion that self-government implies. We will return to this point later in the paper.

In considering the role that base funding will play in the financing of self-government, it is important to consider:

1. The rationale for providing base funds;
2. The potential for base funding to be subject to the principle of equalization; and
3. The extent to which these funds should be conditional.

The principle of entitlement, or Aboriginal right, as a basis for granting federal block transfers to Aboriginal governments, has dramatically different consequences for self-government than does the principle of the fiduciary, or trust, relationship. The distinction is between recognition and paternalism (Cassidy and Bish 1989). Paternalism is inconsistent with fiscal self-government, for it implies an ongoing caretaker role for the federal government rather than recognition of the ability of Aboriginal communities to govern themselves.

There is an inconsistency inherent in the choice of entitlement or recognition as a rationale for self-government financing arrangements. This inconsistency is rooted in the inverse relationship between entitlement and fiscal capacity, which suggests that despite political independence, a large measure of fiscal dependence must persist. Given the economic circumstances and prospects of many Aboriginal communities, fiscal "independence" cannot, in practical terms, be realized as anything more than a supplement to core funding transfers.

This problem is magnified by the failure of non-Aboriginal society to view these grants from the same perspective as Aboriginals as far as rights are concerned. The conclusion of Aboriginal self-government agreements, and even the recognition of Aboriginal rights in these agreements, does not change these differing perceptions. The consequence is that the federal government (and the respective provinces, to the extent they are involved) will come under pressure to treat self-government funding as "just another government program," subject to the same cutbacks and restraints. Therefore, it is important that the financial components of the agreements be written to insulate them as much as possible from this pressure.

Another major attribute affecting the relationship between fiscal arrangements and the effectiveness of self-government is that of equalization. The equalization principle starts with the argument that grant entitlement should be inversely related to the wealth or resources available to each community. This raises two principal issues for self-government financial arrangements. First, to whom should each community be equalized, and what should determine the point of reference to serve as a basis for equalization payments? Second, when a community becomes better off, its entitlement diminishes. How can the process be structured to ensure that equalization does not act as a disincentive for economic development initiatives undertaken by the community?

Regarding the first question, equalizing fiscal capacities among Aboriginal governments themselves would likely institutionalize poverty in Aboriginal communities. Alternatively, to use the provinces as a point of reference does not seem feasible, since there is enormous disparity in available revenue sources, and economic bases, between provinces and Aboriginal communities. This suggests that a simple adaptation of the federal-provincial equalization formula will not suffice. To give meaning to the term equalization, the context of a community's average income and wealth (and the government's fiscal capacity flowing from that), relative to some non-Aboriginal standard that does not involve comparison between Aboriginal and provincial governments, must be considered.[2]

It is also necessary to try to reconcile equalization with incentives for economic development within Aboriginal communities. Any formula for base funding implies that as economic development progresses, the amount of the transfer will decline, other factors being equal. A formula must be developed, therefore, to encourage recipient governments to move toward greater reliance on their own revenue-raising efforts, including economic development (Aniol 1990).

Hawkes and Maslove (1989) define the ratio of the change in fiscal transfer, and the change in fiscal capacity, as the "transfer reduction rate" (TRR). They contend that the TRR should be between zero and a small positive number less than one. This TRR allows the amount of transfers to be reduced as fiscal capacity increases, thereby preserving the equalization principle, but it does not reduce fiscal transfers so rapidly as to discourage economic development activity. It may be desirable to allow a community to achieve a certain threshold level of development before any reduction in transfers occurs. This would allow the community adequate time, and adequate incentive, to develop a viable infrastructure.

Section 19 of the Vuntut Gwich'in First Nation Self-Government Agreement (1992) provides an example of the way equalization has been incorporated into self-government agreements. This agreement states that the federal grant shall be reduced as Vuntut Gwich'in develops its own revenue capacity, but at a ratio of less than one to one (1:1). The Agreement does not specify what a desirable rate might be. A rate much beyond one-half to one (0.5:1), however, might create undesirably strong disincentive effects.

The issue of the conditionality of fiscal transfers is also critical to understanding the operation of self-government. An Aboriginal government that receives its total grant as an unconditional transfer, could maximize flexibility in the budgeting process, allowing it to freely pursue community priorities as they change over time (Maslove 1990). Such flexibility and discretion would enable Aboriginal governments to strengthen their accountability to constituents, rather than to the federal government, and to make decisions with a degree of independence.

There may sometimes be advantages to limited reliance on conditional funding, in addition to the unconditional base funding. Conditional grants provide some assurance that future Aboriginal administrations will provide services according to specified conditions, or at some minimum level. In the area of public health, for example, it may be in the best interests of both national and Aboriginal governments to adhere to certain national standards. The key point to stress, however, is that the fiscal transfer regime, if it includes conditional funding, must first incorporate sufficient unconditional grants to support a degree of autonomy that is consistent with the concept of self-government.

In addition to base funding, conditional grants from both the federal and provincial governments will undoubtedly play an important role in the financing of Aboriginal self-government. Intergovernmental, conditional, and matching grant arrangements have been prominent in the Canadian federal system; the federal government regularly enters into such arrangements with the provinces, and the provinces are involved in a wide range of matching grant systems with their municipal governments and school boards. Presumably, as Aboriginal self-government becomes more established, such arrangements will be available to them as well. An analysis of the impact of conditional grants on the effective operation of Aboriginal governments, and an examination of the instances where such arrangements would be attractive, are essential components of discussions about self-government financing.

Conditional, matching grants may be very attractive for the recipient Aboriginal government. If federal or provincial governments are interested in supporting programs in areas such as health care, education, or social welfare, it may provide an opportunity for an Aboriginal government to provide a desired service at substantially reduced costs. For example, fifty-fifty cost sharing arrangements are quite common, and in some areas the donor government pays more than half the costs (Maslove 1990).

Conditional arrangements, however, also tend to reduce the budgetary flexibility of the recipient government. Once it undertakes specific programs, the recipient government may find it difficult to terminate, or even modify, them in response to changing local conditions. Termination may be difficult because both client groups and providers defend established programs; modifications may be difficult because the donor government generally specifies conditions and standards that must be met for funding to continue (Maslove 1990).

In thinking of where and when conditional grants from the provincial or federal governments may be appropriate, the characteristics of the relevant public services must be considered. The level of conditionality should be related to the attributes of the corresponding service areas (Hawkes and Maslove 1989). Where there is a national or provincial interest at stake (as there is in the area of public health), conditional grants may be more appropriate; whereas a purely local interest, such as recreation or road maintenance, might be better financed within the framework of the unconditional base funding. An example of transfers and grants to a system of self-government currently in place may offer further insight into how such arrangements translate in reality.

The Sechelt model of Aboriginal self-government is based on federal legislation—the Sechelt Indian Band Self-Government Act (1986). Funds for this self-government arrangement are in the form of cash transfers, as determined by a fiscal formula adjusted in response to changes in costs and population. Additional conditional grants, however, can also be arranged between the band and the federal government. It is not clear whether this fiscal arrangement incorporates an explicit equalization factor.

The band can also raise revenue through local taxes because of section 14(e) of the Sechelt Indian Band Self-Government Act. The band has full taxing powers over band members and non-Indian residents and enterprises. These powers raise interesting questions about the potential for Aboriginal governments to generate revenue from within their own community to supplement transfers and grants from other governments.

SELF-FINANCING OF SELF-GOVERNMENT

At a recent conference on Indian governments and taxation, Ovide Mercredi (1991), the national chief of the Assembly of First Nations, recognized the importance of taxation as a means of governance:

> First Nations did not give up their concept of sharing, or in the vernacular of today, taxation jurisdictions. . . . We take the position accordingly, that at no time did our First Nations give up the right to govern ourselves, and at no time did we give up our jurisdiction in relation to taxation, a fundamental function of governing.

There is a strong rationale for Aboriginal governments to generate revenue from within their own communities, although the potential for revenue generation varies widely from community to community. In practical terms, self-generated revenues will often only be supplements to the transfers from federal and provincial governments. Yet, the principle at stake is important.

Self-financing may take a variety of forms, and the potential of each form must be considered on a community-by-community basis. We address three aspects of self-funding below:

1. The historical precedents for self-financing found in Aboriginal culture;

2. Why the principle of self-financing is important to Aboriginal self-government; and
3. The potential revenue sources upon which Aboriginal communities might draw.

Self-financing (or, to use a more politically charged term, self-taxation) is nothing other than the set of arrangements by which communities collectively provide for the needs of their members—or, as Chief Mercredi stated, "sharing."[3] Such arrangements have traditionally been important characteristics of Aboriginal societies. Self-taxation is really no more than the adaptation of these arrangements to the monetary society in which the Aboriginal Peoples now live.

Examples of ways in which members of Aboriginal communities have provided for each other through non-monetary means can be found in the anthropological literature. We cite only a few examples by way of illustration:

1. McMillan (1988), in his discussion of Assiniboine and Plains Cree hunting, discusses the communal hunt that involved the sharing of the game with other members of the community;
2. According to Driver (1969), even when a mature hunter went out alone and brought home game, he usually shared it with other families in the community if they were in need. Furthermore, whenever a visitor made a social call, he or she was always offered food. A good hunter could, therefore, expect plenty of visitors in times of need;
3. In the Inuit culture, sharing of food was essential for small groups of people living together harmoniously. By sharing in all hunters' successes, they could adjust for the vagaries of individual luck and reduce hostility arising from jealousy. When a man killed a seal at a winter sealing camp, it was taken to his igloo, where his wife butchered it, giving different portions to the wives of the other hunters, according to their relationships. The hunter kept little for himself but would share in the future successes of all his partners (McMillan 1988);
4. Chiefs and nobles of the northwest coast people controlled access to group-held territories and rights. Skillful management of the group's labor and resources allowed chiefs to accumulate wealth, which would be publicly distributed at feasts and potlatches. Commoners, who lacked inherited claims to titles or ceremonial privileges, shared in the group's greater prestige and provided the labor necessary to accumulate food and wealth (McMillan 1988); and
5. An important function of the Mik'maq district chiefs was the annual

reapportionment of hunting territories. These territories were reassigned as family sizes, and, therefore, the land needs of individual families, changed (Morrison and Wilson 1986).

The precedents established by these and other aspects of traditional Aboriginal culture point to the commitment of Aboriginal communities to provide for the needs of their members and neighbors. While current conditions prevent Aboriginal communities from being fully self-sufficient, the importance of encouraging and expecting some level of self-financing within these communities remains.

Self-financing is a key element in the development of effective systems of Aboriginal self-government. Its importance rests on three arguments:

1. Self-financing would gain for Aboriginal governments greater legitimacy in the eyes of non-Aboriginal people;
2. It would reinforce their legitimacy within their own communities; and
3. It would enhance the independence and autonomy enjoyed by the Aboriginal governments.

The establishment of self-financing mechanisms would grant Aboriginal governments greater legitimacy in the non-Aboriginal society by demonstrating a commitment to self-government and to Aboriginal Peoples assuming responsibility for themselves. Given the amount of intergovernmental interaction inherent in the establishment of self-government, goodwill between governments would facilitate an effective working relationship that was advantageous to all parties involved. Indeed, one might go further; in the absence of efforts to self-finance, could Aboriginal governments resist, over time, being pushed back into the role of administrative and service delivery agents of the federal government?

A certain degree of self-financing would also enhance the legitimacy of the government within its own community. Whereas the Boston Tea Party demonstrated that there could be no taxation without representation, self-financing within Aboriginal self-government adheres to the reverse proposition—there can be no effective representation without taxation.[4]

The collection of even modest taxes and fees would facilitate a greater political consciousness among community members. Supporting citizens take a greater interest in the decisions and trade-offs their governments make, and demonstrate greater appreciation of the cost of providing services (Bish 1987). Self-reliance promotes a culture of accountability to the community that is qualitatively different from the accountability that exists when all funds are provided from sources external to the community.

Finally, and perhaps most importantly, by enhancing its legitimacy in both non-Aboriginal and Aboriginal communities, by instilling a greater sense of political consciousness, and by fostering a greater appreciation for the costs involved in service provision, self-financing arrangements would enhance the independence of Aboriginal governments and instill a sense of ownership among the community members they represent. Without self-financing, Aboriginal governments would rely exclusively on other governments for financial resources. This would risk reverting to a colonial-style mentality and colonial-style treatment from funding governments.

Given the importance of self-financing, the mechanisms for setting up such arrangements under self-government need to be considered. In particular, what potential revenue sources can Aboriginal governments access, and to what extent can they supplement other sources of revenue?

The capacity for self-taxation to generate additional revenue has been realized in some communities in the United States, where bands have been given extensive tax powers. The result has been the generation of revenue from sales tax, tobacco tax, income tax, interest charges on the leasehold on Indian land, a bingo tax, and a tax on oil and gas (Aubry 1992).

In the Canadian context, Bish (1987) discusses the extent to which some bands have supplemented federal Indian Affairs funding with revenues from leaseholds, band enterprises, and user charges. As referred to earlier, the potential for self-taxation has been further realized in Canada because of section 14(e) of the Sechelt Indian Band Self-Government Act. This legislation provides the Sechelt government with full taxing powers over band members and non-Indian occupants (Taylor and Paget 1989).

There are a number of mechanisms Aboriginal governments could use to generate revenue from within their own communities. Potential sources of revenue, in increasing order of difficulty (decreasing order of feasibility), include:

1. USER FEES. User fees represent a potential source of revenue for many Aboriginal communities. Aboriginal governments might wish to charge those who use recreation services, water and sewer services, and garbage collection proportionate to the level of use. Revenue for road maintenance might also be generated through user fees, in a fashion comparable to the system used by Canada's national parks: permits purchased for a specified period display the government's authorization to use the road services within its jurisdiction;[5]

2. PROPERTY TAXES. Because of the 1988 taxation amendments to the

Indian Act, many reserves already use bylaws to impose property taxes on non-Aboriginal interests on reserve lands, particularly leaseholds. This could easily be extended, for example, to land that is leased to community members for housing. An annual lease fee, or user fee, could be assessed. There is an obvious, if rough, analogy to property taxation;

3. PAYROLL TAXES. Potential sources of revenue for some Aboriginal communities might include a payroll tax directed at enterprises operating on reserve lands. While a simple payroll tax could be administered fairly easily, its rate would have to be very low in order not to drive the tax base away. The number of communities for which a payroll tax would be an attractive option (that is, those with significant employment) would be small;

4. GAMING.[6] Considerable attention has, at least superficially, been directed to on-reserve gaming enterprises. Casinos, bingo halls, and the like are attractive because they offer the prospect of revenues and employment for residents of a reserve. The few reserves that have constructed such facilities have apparently found these prospects realized.[7] The potential for casinos and similar facilities to generate revenues for Aboriginal governments is probably limited, because gambling is likely to be profitable for only a small number of communities. There are two reasons for this. First, while the few reserves that have operated casinos have found them to be quite profitable, only a small number of enterprises are in operation. If they were to become widespread (whether operated by Aboriginal communities or by other governments), it is likely that they would dilute one another's profitability. Second, success is very much dependent upon proximity to population centers. Communities that are isolated won't likely find gaming a viable source of revenue from non-residents.[8] Partly in response to these realities, provincial governments and Aboriginal governments and organizations have recently begun to explore partnerships aimed at insuring Aboriginal involvement in major gaming enterprises being developed in a number of urban centers;[9] and

5. OTHER TAXATION POSSIBILITIES. In principle, excise (for example, on tobacco products) and sales taxes could be levied at rates equal to or less than provincial taxes without driving away the tax base. To be realistic alternatives, and to insure that compliance and administration costs did not become too onerous, these taxes might require the participation of all Aboriginal governments. This would require respective provincial governments to act as tax collectors. A final possibility, though perhaps

the least likely, would be a personal income tax. This would be a tax levied at a common rate, by all communities, and collected for them through the existing income tax system.

While various sources of revenue can be envisioned, the forms employed by Aboriginal governments must be tailored to the unique circumstances of each community. In assessing the applicability of a certain tax base, or revenue source, to a particular community, important factors to be considered include:

1. The mobility of the tax bases;
2. The technical capacities of the government; and
3. The extent to which a certain form of taxation might be used as an instrument for other policy goals.

As already suggested, the Aboriginal government must consider the possibility that those adversely affected by a particular tax might choose to leave the government's jurisdiction rather than pay taxes. This is particularly a problem in small communities. A key consideration in assessing feasibility and levels of various taxes would be the more general taxation environment in which a particular community exists. As a rule, if the same or similar taxes exist elsewhere (and if other considerations are comparable), a tax imposed by an Aboriginal government would not invoke a "flight" of taxpayers or tax-generating activities and businesses.

Generally, an Aboriginal government would want to consider forms of taxation and revenue where the administration is proportionate to the technical capacities of the government and its staff. More sophisticated taxes might prove difficult for some communities to administer. Administrative costs could easily exceed the revenue collected and defeat the purpose of a tax. Collection on behalf of Aboriginal governments by federal or provincial authorities, as suggested above, would be required for some taxes. Such arrangements are not easy to negotiate or to maintain.

Finally, in assessing the desirability of any particular form of taxation, an Aboriginal government might want to consider the extent to which it serves as a means for achieving other policy goals. Through taxation, a government can change the behavior of its constituents, perhaps by providing incentives for investment or perhaps by regulating land use. In these and other ways, an Aboriginal government might wish to consider the potential of a tax to serve as a powerful policy instrument, rather than simply as a means of raising revenue.

OPERATING FINANCIAL ARRANGEMENTS

We have argued that financial arrangements that support and are consistent with self-government are important prerequisites to success. Accordingly, how, and in what form, funding becomes available to Aboriginal governments has been the focus of our discussion. Yet, success also requires that new community-based governments effectively administer the resources for which they will become responsible. This final section of the paper will, therefore, briefly deal with important issues relating to the financial operations of Aboriginal governments.

Aboriginal self-government requires new models of governance for Aboriginal communities—at least new relative to the era of the Indian Act. These new models must address the structures and processes by which governments will relate to their peoples. Issues of the mechanics of financial administration, although sometimes mundane, are also important. We discuss each of these in turn.

New links between Aboriginal governments and their peoples must be forged to replace the dissolving links between current Aboriginal administrations and federal and provincial governments. This is not to imply that current tribal administrations are not representative or that they are not responsive to the needs of their communities. However, it is the case that federal control is part and parcel of current funding arrangements. This requires Aboriginal administrations to assume a particular relationship with the federal government and converts tribal administrations into agents of the federal government.[10]

Under current arrangements, Ottawa's approval is constantly required, policy development resides in Ottawa, Aboriginal administrations must negotiate initiatives with Ottawa, rigid reporting requirements are maintained, and funds are largely non-fungible.[11] Fortunately, under the recent Alternative Funding Arrangements initiative, the last two restrictions have been relaxed.

The focus of financial accountability under self-government will shift dramatically to the community, and away from the minister of Indian Affairs. This shift is clearly desirable and to be encouraged. Indeed, it is a reason for seeking self-government in the first place. However, the impact of the change should not be downplayed. Aboriginal governments will be much more "on the firing line" than is the case now.

One area of financial management that will be dramatically affected is budgeting. For a politically autonomous government, the budget serves several purposes. It is, first and foremost, a means of control. Through the budget, central managers control operating managers, and the latter control their operations. This is the traditional and most narrow role of the budget.

Tribal budgets serve the control function, even for administrations operating under the Indian Act, but there will be dramatic changes under self-government. The budget is a plan. It specifies:

1. What the government intends to do and not do;
2. In what order, and how fast, it intends to carry out its planned activities; and
3. How it intends to finance its planned activities.

As such, the budget is an important, probably the most important, statement of the government's action plans and political priorities.

Budgeting is central to governing. This statement holds true, with particular force, for small governments, whose capacities for non-budgetary actions (for example, regulation) tend to be limited. Therefore, budgeting should meet the same criteria of democracy, justice, and fairness that apply to government itself. The budget must reflect community values, and it must respond to changes in those values.

The process by which the budget is determined takes on special significance. Second only to the selection of the government itself, the annual budget cycle can become the primary vehicle for communication between the government and the community. To meet this ideal, however, the process must be non-arbitrary and systematic, and it must be clear that various interests in the community have been heard.

In practical terms, a series of structure and process questions must be addressed. First, a system must be established to enable the decision-makers to determine government-wide trade-offs. Because of the nature of their financial relationship with the federal government, current tribal administrations often do not confront these decisions. Each program, and its accompanying funding, is often established largely in isolation from other program and funding decisions. Combine this with the restricted fungibility of funds (or complete non-fungibility) and the result can often be characterized as a series of parallel, or "earmarked," budgets, each relating to a particular service area, such as roads, housing, or education.[12]

Under self-government, Aboriginal governments will possess greater powers to manage financial resources. The parallel budgets will replace consolidated budgets, and governments will decide how much to spend on each function, with the knowledge that more money for education, for example, will mean less money for roads. They will also have to decide the emphasis to give to housing relative to health care. To support self-government, a budget system must be in place to effectively facilitate these decisions.

Among the issues to be decided are:

1. The roles of the administrative and political officials, however selected, in the Aboriginal government;
2. The structure of the political body (for example, the tribal council);
3. The forum(s) in which decisions are to be made; and
4. The role and form of community participation.

While the legislative council of the Aboriginal government is likely to be the formal and ultimate authority for budget approval, the process prior to that approval has important consequences. Each community must decide how council members will participate in this process. For example, a budget committee may recommend a budget to full council, or the council may act as its own budget committee. Each must also decide how administrative officials will serve the budget committee—as advisors, advocates, or voting members. And each must decide if representatives of the community at large will be represented on the committee, and whether the committee (or council) will hold public meetings to explain the budget decisions and solicit reactions.

There in no single "correct" model. Each community must decide for itself what procedures are consistent with its traditions, and what style it wishes its new government to adopt. These decisions must be considered as part of the financial management system, along with decisions about taxation and other sources of funding. Though changes will likely evolve as experience accumulates, it is central to the initial success of self-government that these structures and processes be in place from the beginning.

Finally, a few words on the mechanics of financial administration. Human skills and knowledge are obviously required to operate sophisticated systems of financial administration and budgeting. Communities entering self-government will likely have already developed such skills, through previous tribal administration offices, dealings with the federal and provincial governments, and through the self-government negotiation process itself. It may be the case, in light of the expanded responsibilities, that the community will want to train additional members, to ensure that new operating systems and procedures are clearly understood. Such investments in human capital should be undertaken before assuming new responsibilities.

Investments in physical capital may also be required, especially in computer systems. A minimum of institutional capital should also be in place—legal authorities for taxation, contracting, and the like.

The need for investments in various forms of capital should be carefully considered in advance. The costs should be incorporated into the estimates for set-up costs in preparation for self-government.

CONCLUSION

Appropriate fiscal arrangements are a crucial element in the success of Aboriginal self-government. Federal transfers will continue to play a central role under self-government; however, in several important respects, the form of these transfers will change.

Inflexible conditional transfers under the Indian Act will have to be converted to unconditional funding that will maximize the fiscal flexibility of emerging Aboriginal governments. With this shift, the focus of accountability will move from the federal government to Aboriginal communities. Unconditional transfers will also have to incorporate some form of "equalization," to ensure that poorer communities receive more federal support. While the equalization principle is borrowed from federal-provincial arrangements, these agreements are not likely to provide much practical guidance to Aboriginal governments. In addition to unconditional base funding, some limited role is still likely to emerge for conditional grant programs, to share costs of particular services.

The success of self-government also depends on the readiness of Aboriginal communities to support their own governments financially. While recognizing that the poverty of many communities will severely limit the scope of self-financing, the principle is important. Self-financing will enhance the independence and autonomy of the Aboriginal governments, reinforce the accountability of governments within their own communities, and enhance their legitimacy in the eyes of non-Aboriginals.

Self-government financing systems will require new decision-making and budget systems in many communities. It is important that these institutional elements be in place from the outset to provide for both the substance and perception of fair and accountable government.

NOTES

1   We are grateful to Katherine Graham and Leigh Anderson for the helpful comments they provided on an earlier draft.

2   Local government might also be considered as a reference point for equalization payments. While not equalization grants in the federal–provincial
sense, provincial–municipal grant schemes that treat northern municipalities
differently from their southern counterparts, or that allow for differences in
population size or density, could be seen as efforts at equalization. These
approaches might be adapted to the financing arrangements for Aboriginal
self-government.

3   A continuum of governance arrangements might be envisioned, with informal, family-based, unspoken rules of behavior on one end, and formal,
institutionalized, legalized forms of governance on the other. A parallel
continuum of financial arrangements, ranging from less formal to more
formal arrangements, might also be envisaged. As governance becomes more
formalized through the establishment of Aboriginal self-government, forms
of financing must also change in order to adapt. In this way, self-financing,
or self-taxation, may be seen as a more formal, institutionalized expression
of the ways in which Aboriginal communities have traditionally provided for
themselves.

4   We acknowledge Hugh Mackenzie, executive director of the Ontario Fair
Tax Commission, as the source of the reverse Boston Tea Party analogy.

5   As an alternative way of employing user fees for road services, the Mohawks
of Kahnawake have suggested a system of toll booths to charge non-resident
vehicles traveling on roads connected to the Mercier bridge (Aubry 1992).

6   It is beyond the scope of this discussion to address gaming as a strategy for
economic development. It is worth pointing out that there is a close link
between economic development and the potential of an Aboriginal community to raise its own revenues. This analysis, however, is limited to examining
the revenue potential of gaming.

7   The Roseau River First Nations in southern Manitoba, for example, have
watched thirteen Indian casinos in neighboring Minnesota turn gambling into
a lucrative economic development activity. Roseau River and other Aboriginal communities are increasingly viewing expanded gaming facilities, not
only as a means of exercising their sovereignty, but as a means of generating
much needed employment and revenue within their community (Platiel
1992).

8   Approximately one-third of bands are located within fifty kilometers of the
nearest DIAND regional center, and are classified as having good access to
major urban markets (Nicholson and Macmillan 1986).

9   See Richard Mackie, Toronto *Globe and Mail*, "Provinces make moves
towards Native Casinos," July 4, 1994 edition, pp. A1 and A2.

10 It should also be pointed out that federal government control arises primarily
from its "exposure" in the context of ministerial responsibility.

11 Fungibility of funds refers to the ability of an organization to use funds from
one source, or intended for one purpose, to replace funds from another source,
or for another purpose. Non-fungibility means that if an organization saved

money (or secured additional funding) intended for a particular purpose, the "extra" money could not be reallocated for another purpose.

12 "Earmarked" budgets may be derived from two different sources. They may be rooted in the funding relationships with the federal government that emphasize project- or program-specific grants; this situation would disappear under self-government financial arrangements. In addition, these parallel budgets may be the byproduct of special purpose bodies established by Aboriginal governments themselves. Self-government financing will not necessarily remove the pressure for special purpose bodies to retain earmarked budgets. The more autonomous the special purpose bodies, the less comprehensive Aboriginal government budgeting may be.

REFERENCES

Aniol, Richard. 1990. Fiscal arrangements: Creating unique financial transfers for Indian governments. Paper presented at the National Indian Government Conference. Toronto: unpublished.

Aubry, Jack. 1992. Give natives tax powers, report urges. Ottawa: *Ottawa Citizen,* December 26, p. A1.

Bish, Robert L. 1987. *Financing Indian self-government: Practice and principles.* Victoria: University of Victoria, School of Public Administration.

Cassidy, Frank, and Robert L. Bish. 1989. *Indian government: Its meaning in practice.* Lantzville, BC, and Halifax: Oolichan Books and The Institute for Research on Public Policy.

Driver, Harold E. 1969. *Indians of North America,* 2d ed., rev. Chicago: University of Chicago Press.

Hawkes, David C., and Allan Maslove. 1989. Fiscal arrangements for Aboriginal self-government. In *Aboriginal Peoples and government responsibility: Exploring federal and provincial roles,* ed. David C. Hawkes. Ottawa: Carleton University Press.

Maslove, Allan M. 1990. Financing Indian government. Paper presented at the National Indian Government Conference, Osgoode Hall Law School. Toronto: unpublished.

McMillan, Alan, D. 1988. *Native peoples and cultures of Canada: An anthropological overview.* Vancouver: Douglas & McIntyre.

Mercredi, Ovide. 1991. Paper presented at the Indian government and taxation conference. Whistler, BC: unpublished.

Morrison, R. Bruce, and C. Roderick Wilson. 1986. *Native peoples: The Canadian experience.* Toronto: McClelland and Stewart.

Nicholson, J. Phillip, and Paul Macmillan. 1986. *An overview of economic circumstances of registered Indians in Canada.* Ottawa: Indian and Northern Affairs Canada.

Platiel, Rudy. 1992. Natives gamble on self-government right. Toronto: *Globe and Mail,* November 13, p. A6.

Sechelt Indian Band and Government of Canada. 1986. *Sechelt Indian Band self-government act.* Ottawa: Sechelt Indian Band and Government of Canada.

Taylor, John P., and Gary Paget. 1989. Federal/provincial responsibility for the Sechelt. In *Aboriginal Peoples and government responsibility: Exploring federal and provincial roles,* ed. David C. Hawkes. Ottawa: Carleton University Press.

Vuntut Gwich'in First Nation, Government of Canada, and Government of the Yukon. 1992. *Self-government agreement.* Ottawa: Vuntut Gwich'in First Nation, Government of Canada, and Government of the Yukon.

CHAPTER 9

GEOGRAPHIES OF
ABORIGINAL SELF-GOVERNMENT

EVELYN J. PETERS, QUEEN'S UNIVERSITY

While the available material on Aboriginal self-government has expanded remarkably since the early 1980s, much of the research has focused on Aboriginal rights, and on outlining possible structures and institutional arrangements for self-government, primarily for land-based models. It is time to move beyond these issues to consider some of the practical questions involved in implementing self-government. Some of these questions have to do with the geographies of self-government.

The term *geography of self-government* is used here to refer to the spatial configuration of the jurisdiction and responsibility that Aboriginal governing bodies exercise over their citizens. Self-government arrangements have to be implemented "on the ground," in particular locales and over particular territories. Existing work in politics, public administration, and law has not given due emphasis to the spatial aspects of self-government. There has been some work on issues of scale, boundaries, and public administration (Franks 1987; Wolfe 1989; Bish 1990), and on the possibility of self-government off a land base (Dunn 1986; Weinstein 1986; Groves 1991). However, space, place, and territory have a number of important implications for the lives, lands, and cultures of the Aboriginal Peoples that have not been carefully considered.

This chapter begins with a brief overview of the treatment of questions of geography in the existing literature on Aboriginal self-government. It then addresses some of the implications of geography. I put forth the argument that spatial arrangements can affect public perceptions of the Aboriginal Peoples, the maintenance of Aboriginal cultures, and the administrative efficiency of Aboriginal governments. The intent is not to prescribe concrete solutions. Instead, the object of the analysis is to present an important perspective on Aboriginal self-government that has often been overlooked.

SPATIAL ARRANGEMENTS AND SELF-GOVERNMENT:
SOME EXAMPLES

The importance of examining the geographies of self-government derives from the increasing spatial complexity both of models of self-government, and of existing agreements and negotiations.

Until recently, most of the literature on Aboriginal self-government has focused on land-based populations (Groves 1991). Weinstein (1986) claims that national Aboriginal organizations came to a tacit understanding to downplay issues relating to self-government off a land base in order to concentrate on other priorities. For their part, researchers exploring the possibilities of Aboriginal self-government have most often pointed out the difficulties of implementation off a land base, and then concentrated their analysis on land-based arrangements.

Some writers have argued that Aboriginal territories represent a prerequisite for self-government. Knight (1988, p. 126), for example, has written that, without control over territory, Indigenous Peoples:

> . . . exist essentially as dissenting voices within states. As such, indigenous peoples face the full range of means available to states for 'dealing' with them, from liberal encouragement to tyrannical threats of violence.

While exclusive Aboriginal territories may provide opportunities for the greatest level and scope of jurisdiction, there are other possibilities. Cassidy (1991, p. 1) makes a useful distinction between self-government and self-determination.

Self-determination is the right and the ability of a people or a group of peoples to choose their own destiny without external compulsion. It is the right to be sovereign, to be a supreme authority within a particular geographic territory. *Self-government* is a term that is often associated and sometimes used interchangeably with the terms *self-determination* and *sovereignty*. Such a practice can be misleading, for a group of people can exercise self-government—that is, they can make quite significant choices concerning their own political, cultural, economic, and social affairs—without actually having sovereignty or experiencing self-determination.

Chamberlin (1988, p. 15) calls the association between "distinctive authority" and territorial designations a "stubborn delusion, part of the mistaken notion that sovereignty is absolute and always territorially defined."

A number of researchers have put forward models of self-government in urban areas (Weinstein 1986; Tizya 1992). Dunn (1986), for example, argues that, in urban areas, Aboriginal people could be treated as a "community of interest" whose "territory" would be cultural rather than geographical. Models for self-government over traditional territories and treaty areas have also been proposed (Groves 1991; Tizya 1992).

The strategy of associating categories of land with different rights and jurisdictions[1] has produced a considerable variety of spatial bases for self-government, some of them quite complex.[2] For example, the geography of self-government for each of the fourteen Yukon First Nations, includes two categories of the settlement areas, as well as the Nations' traditional territory.[3] There are provisions for lands that have historically been shared among nations, as well as for activities and claims that cross provincial boundaries. In addition, each First Nation has some jurisdiction over its citizens, wherever they reside in the Yukon.

Innovations also continue to emerge in ongoing negotiations for self-government. The Nishnawbe-Aski Nations in northern Ontario, for example, have proposed a threefold system of land classification modeled on the Cree sections of the James Bay Agreement (Nothing and Wolfe 1993). Because the Aboriginal Peoples are the overwhelming majority in the area, Nishnawbe-Aski Nation negotiators are also proposing that a northern Ontario "public" government be established under provincial legislation. This would provide a vehicle for accessing off-reserve authority over land use.

Both models of self-government, and existing arrangements, display an increasingly complex geography. The variations have resulted from the particular interests of the Aboriginal, provincial, territorial, and federal governments in the negotiations.[4] However, it may be time to look at some of the implications of the spatial configurations of self-government, and to move beyond circumstantial and political elements in determining what these configurations should be. More general principles can be developed to contribute to the spatial foundations of self-government arrangements.

SPATIAL ARRANGEMENTS AND SELF-GOVERNMENT: SOME PRINCIPLES

This section turns to some general principles. It identifies the relationship between spatial arrangements and the representation of Aboriginal cultures to the general public, the maintenance of these cultures and traditions, and administrative efficiency.

1. SPATIAL ARRANGEMENTS CHALLENGE OR REPRODUCE IMAGES OF A GROUP

Ranging from taken-for-granted public perceptions about where certain groups belong in space, to actual legislation confining groups to particular areas, the social definition of minority groups frequently incorporates a spatial component. Chamberlin (1988, p. 14) explains:

> Naming is one way of imposing a definition upon other people. Another way is by territorial designations. . . . Putting people in their place is much more than a figure of speech. It is the basis of all codes of conduct; and it is the basis of colonial settlement.

The socio-spatial dimensions of society continually shift as boundaries are drawn to put real or symbolic distance between those who "belong" and those who, because of some perceived cultural difference, are believed to be out of place.[5] Spatial arrangements, then, can reflect who are "outsiders" and "insiders" in society (Sibbley 1992).

Spatial arrangements not only reflect public perceptions about the nature and attributes of a group of people, they can also shape these perceptions. Anderson's (1991, p. 29) work on Vancouver's Chinatown, for example, argued that: "state practices institutionalized the concept of a Chinese race, but it was in space that the concept became materially cemented and naturalized in everyday life." The idea of Chinatown itself contributed to the definition of what it meant to be Chinese, and separate and different, in Vancouver.

In Canada, there is a long history of putting Aboriginal people "in their place." Early federal legislation created a separate legal and political status for "Indians,"[6] but the reserve system provided a spatial map of where "Indians" belonged in Canadian society. Late nineteenth- and early twentieth-century thought assigned "Indians" to reserves with the objective of imposing Christianity, "civilization," and agriculture upon them. Participation in urban and industrial life was assumed to require complete assimilation into Euro-Canadian society. In time, the isolation of many reserves became an integral component of the relationship between "Indian" and non-Indian society,[7] and unassimilated "Indians" were perceived to belong in places separate from modern urban society (Peters, in progress). The association of "Indians" with reserves was strengthened by the federal government's definition of its responsibility as only involving Indians on reserves.

The spatial component of government policies, therefore, reinforced public perceptions of what it meant to be "Indian." "Indians" in their place meant Indians on the reserve, turning the tension between "Indianness" and European "civilization," into a tension between "Indianness" and city life. These images are often extended to all Aboriginal people, as reflected in the Native Council of Canada's statement in the constitutional debates (1992, p. 10): "There is a strong, sometimes racist perception that being Aboriginal and being urban are mutually exclusive." The colonial legacy of attempting to place Aboriginal people away from "civilized" society may also be at the root of the disjuncture between general public support for land claims and self-government, and local protests about their implementation (McNab 1992, p. 45). Aboriginal people are not supposed to be where they interfere with the economic interests of non-Aboriginal people.

Spatial arrangements of self-government can begin to challenge the colonial legacy of definitions about where Aboriginal Peoples belong, as peoples who maintain their cultures and values, and as peoples who have enforceable rights. Where Aboriginal Peoples have rights to be self-governing sends a strong message about the appropriate place of Aboriginal Peoples and Aboriginal cultures in Canadian society. It is in this context that demands for self-governing institutions in urban areas, and for mobility of rights, take on particular significance. These initiatives contradict the message that Aboriginal cultures, communities, and values are incompatible with, or inappropriate in, the urban, industrial milieu. They are statements that "Aboriginality" has a place everywhere that Aboriginal people live in this country.

This is a general argument. It pays little attention to the concrete details of varying jurisdiction and structures appropriate in different areas for different cultural groups, or to the concrete problems involved in implementation. At the same time, the point is not trivial. When Aboriginal Peoples negotiate the spatial organization of self-government arrangements, they are involved in the complex activity of communicating, by symbol, the culture of which they are a part. It is important to step back and to ask: what does this say about the appropriate place for Aboriginal Peoples, cultures, and communities in Canadian society?

2. Spatial Arrangements Support or Erode Culture

Spatial arrangements play an important part in the maintenance of culture and group identities. Spatial practices codify particular value systems. They reflect what is central and what is peripheral to a group or society, what is private and what can be shared, and what or who belongs where (Sibbley 1992). Places can anchor identity, and territory can become "a focus and symbol of group membership" (Smith 1986, p. 482). Finally, spatial arrangements can shape social relationships. They can mold people into communities with common interests because "the territory becomes the object to which other attributes are assigned" (Sack 1983, p. 59). Public goods and services, for example, can be assigned by territory, creating a shared interest among residents. Obviously, spatial arrangements can also divide existing communities, and create inequalities and conflicts.

There are significant differences between European and Aboriginal approaches to the relationship between self-determination and land (Erasmus 1989; Groves 1991; Nothing and Wolfe 1993). Land and place also have a different role in Aboriginal cultures and identity than they have in European societies (Coolican 1985; Little Bear 1987). These different perspectives led Bowles (1992, p. 133) to argue that it is "dangerous and potentially destructive for First Nation Peoples to negotiate with our society" until Anglo-Europeans confront and understand the values and assumptions underlying their own relationship with land.

Shkilnyk's (1985) study demonstrates the potential destructiveness of imposed and foreign geographies.[8] She argues that, in the context of the destruction of the economic base of the Grassy Narrows' community, the relocation of the band to a new reserve was crucial. Shkilnyk (1985, p. 53) notes:

> The exodus from the old reserve was a turning point. . . . Men and women gave up traditional roles and occupations when they ceased to trap as a family, and the special relationship of the people to the land, which had cushioned all previous crises, was severely undermined by the imposed economic, political, and *spatial order* of the new reserve. All the people date the beginning of their time of troubles from this event. (Emphasis added)

Relocation and the spatial configuration of the new reserve were not the only contributing elements, but Shkilnyk argues they were a significant added stress. The result for many members of the community was a loss of a sense of identity, or, as Shkilnyk (1985, p. 17) puts it: "depression, hopelessness, a loss of moorings and erosion of the symbols of reference essential to life's continuity."

It is not difficult to find examples of how the colonial regime, applied over space, distorts the social relationships of Aboriginal Peoples and cultures. Perhaps most familiar is the artificially imposed distinction between reserve and urban First Nations Peoples. Its serious implications for funding has driven a wedge between these populations, distorting the social realities of people.

A less well-known example has to do with the Mocreebec of Quebec and Ontario. The Mocreebec community consists of approximately a thousand people living on Moose Factory Island. They are descendants of Quebec Cree who traditionally used both sides of James Bay for subsistence. While the majority are beneficiaries of the James Bay Agreement, their current residence in Ontario means that they do not receive the community-based benefits Quebec Cree bands receive. Because they are not "Ontario Indians," they do not receive benefits or recognition under Treaty 9. The Mocreebec argue that their historic patterns of settlement should be recognized and accommodated. Neither the federal government nor the provincial governments of Ontario and Quebec have been prepared to accommodate the social reality of the Mocreebec—a reality that challenges provincial boundaries (McQueen 1991).[9]

The potential of spatial arrangements to have an impact on culture and identity suggests that the geographies of self-government agreements must be taken seriously. Revitalizing their cultures is an important priority in Aboriginal Peoples' demands for self-government. Aboriginal geographies are an important part of these cultures. Spatial practices of governance codify particular value systems, and it is important for Aboriginal Peoples to insist that these value systems be their own. The "right to define the content of one's own culture" and the right of First Nations to shape their cultures over time (Standing Committee 1990) should include the right to negotiate spatial arrangements of self-government that reflect and support Aboriginal cultures.

3. SPATIAL ARRANGEMENTS AFFECT GOVERNMENTS' ABILITIES TO
   FUNCTION EFFECTIVELY

The spatial configurations of self-government will both represent Aboriginal culture and house it: they are symbolic and functional at the same time. Appropriate spatial organization is an essential, if neglected (Bours 1989), prerequisite for the smooth functioning of governments.

Various spatial elements are involved in the administrative efficiency of governments. To maximize technical efficiency in the administration of services, for example, boundaries need to take account of economies of scale and distribution. Ideally, jurisdictional boundaries match processes and activities to minimize the extent of externalities[10] and spill-overs. Fragmented and complicated administrative zones lend themselves to disparity between people living in different areas, and can lead to overlapping provision of services, as well as confused lines of accountability.

The literature on Aboriginal self-government has recognized issues of economies of scale and distribution (Franks 1987; Wolfe 1989; Bish 1990), and, therefore, these issues will not be explored here. The problem of externalities has, however, received less attention. In the Yukon, for example, most First Nations communities are next to, or within, existing municipal boundaries. First Nation governments will operate autonomously from the municipal system. Yet no structures for dealing with externalities were mandated in either the Umbrella Final Agreement or the Draft Self-Government Agreement.

There is considerable concern in the non-Aboriginal community about the social, economic, and environmental externalities associated with Aboriginal self-government (McNab 1992). Penner (1983, p. 65) makes the point that:

> Governments adjacent to First Nations jurisdictions may be concerned that Indian developments will be incompatible with their own needs, for instance, in regard to zoning. It must be remembered, however, that Indian jurisdictions may have the same concerns about their neighbours.

These issues may be some of the most challenging and difficult in implementing self-government. The potential for cooperation, as well as for conflict, makes research on appropriate mechanisms to address externalities crucial.

The capacity of administrative structures to deal with the spatial complexity of governing arrangements has received even less attention in the literature. Since the mid-1980s, a number of researchers have put forward models of self-government for urban Aboriginal Peoples (Dunn 1986; Reeves 1986; Weinstein 1986). Citizenship models have also been advanced. They involve First Nations' jurisdiction over citizens outside their territory (Bish 1986). Finally, there have been proposals to establish governance over traditional or treaty territories (Groves 1991; Tizya 1992, p. 9). In these models, the nation whose traditional or treaty territory it was, could have jurisdiction over, and provide services to, all Aboriginal residents in the area. If these residents belonged to another First Nation, reimbursement for services could be obtained from that resident's nation of origin.

Because all self-government arrangements have a spatial component, it is important, at some point, to map out their configurations in combination. In other words, it is necessary at some time to switch the focus from separate

TABLE 1: COMPOSITION OF THE ABORIGINAL POPULATION, REGINA, SASKATCHEWAN, 1982	
Status Indians* (estimated population—7157)	
Reserve origin	27 reserves in Saskatchewan, plus others in other provinces
Treaty areas of origin	Treaties 1, 2, 3, 4, 5, 6, 7, and others
First Nations of origin	Assiniboine, Blackfoot, Cree, Dakota, Ojibwa, and others
Provincial origin	British Columbia, Alberta, Saskatchewan, Manitoba, Ontario, Nova Scotia
Country of origin	Canada and the United States
Métis and Non-Status Indians (estimated population—4507)	
Communities of origin	Not identifiable from survey
First Nations of origin	Not identifiable from survey
Provincial origin	British Columbia, Alberta, Saskatchewan, Manitoba, Ontario
Countries of origin	Canada and the United States
*This was the terminology used in the survey	
Source: E. J. Peters, from The Institute of Urban Studies Data Base 1982	

models to a perspective that examines what happens in particular places in terms of combinations, overlap, or areas unassigned to Aboriginal government jurisdictions. Implementing some of these alternatives may create combinations that are extremely complex for both Aboriginal and non-Aboriginal governments.

The Aboriginal population in a large metropolitan center can be quite varied in terms of its origins. Table 1 provides information about the origins of Aboriginal people in Regina, Saskatchewan, in 1982.[11] The Regina situation is almost certainly not more complex than that of most other metropolitan areas. If self-government arrangements are negotiated on a band-by-band basis, each with jurisdiction over citizens off the reserve, there could be more than twenty-seven different regimes governing First Nations citizens and services for citizens in this city. This still leaves out a large number of Aboriginal people who are not members of First Nations. The establishment of urban self-governing institutions could provide opportunities for these people, but it would also add to the complexity of governing.

Self-government arrangements for urban Aboriginal people based on traditional or treaty areas could simplify the picture. Regina is in the Treaty 4 area and in the Plains Cree traditional territory (Mandelbaum 1979). Services and government could be the responsibility of the Cree Nation or a Treaty 4 group. The implications, though, are that the regional governing body may be seeking reimbursement for services from at least five other nations, or at least seven other treaty groups. Provincial boundaries provide an additional territorial overlay. These levels of potential complexity have serious implications for the efficiency and accountability of Aboriginal governments.[12]

The variety of models of self-government, as they are applied in space, also leads to questions of equity and access. Some self-government arrangements, for example, may have reserve boundaries as their territorial base. Reserve-based governments may extend their responsibilities to citizens within provincial boundaries. Some arrangements could be based on treaty territories, others on traditional territories.[13] Aboriginal groups without a land base may create self-governing institutions in some places but not in others. Some places could fall completely outside the jurisdiction of any Aboriginal government. The result could be that Aboriginal people have extremely uneven access to institutions of self-government depending on where they live.

The Native Council of Canada (1992, p. 17) has argued that:

> In some areas, such as culture, education and child welfare, Aboriginal peoples should have rights to services controlled by and accountable to themselves wherever they live, even outside of traditional territories. Without such basic protection, the majority of Aboriginal peoples face yet further generations of enforced assimilation.

If this is true, then the potential lack of equity in access to self-governing institutions, as implemented in space, is of serious concern.

The potential for inefficiency and inequity to emerge from the combination of a variety of spatial bases for self-government is a strong argument for coordination and cooperation among Aboriginal Peoples in designing the spatial bases of self-government. Clearly, there is a tension between administrative rationality and the importance of having spatial arrangements that reflect varied and unique cultures. Moreover, Bennett (1989,

p. 312) points out that the dominance of administrative rationality may "undermine community identity and the requirements of representation, accountability and participation." At the same time, ignoring the spatial bases for administrative rationality may interfere with the smooth functioning of Aboriginal governments. At this point, there is a pressing need to begin to recognize and find ways of accommodating these issues.

CONCLUSION

I have argued that the geography of self-government has implications for the representation, preservation, and construction of Aboriginal cultures, and for the efficacy of governing arrangements. I have not explored implications for particular arrangements or types of agreement. This is partly because of the limited scope of this paper. It is also because there is not a large body of relevant research on which to draw. Geographers have paid virtually no attention to issues of Aboriginal self-government. Even political geographers have focused primarily on states, and not on nations within states. Researchers in politics, law, and public administration have had very little to say about geographic questions. In this context, then, I appeal for more research on spatial issues associated with the implementation of Aboriginal self-government.

At the same time, I recognize that my concern with the geography of self-government derives from a non-Aboriginal structure of knowledge, in which individual disciplines have responsibility for different perspectives. Moreover, my view of the implications of geography are rooted in western concepts of place and space. It may be that the issues I have raised have a far different significance when viewed from an Aboriginal perspective. The starting point for research, then, must be Aboriginal perspectives on these issues.

NOTES

1 This idea may have first emerged during negotiations with the Cree over the James Bay Agreement (MacGregor 1989).
2 Readers interested in exploring the geography of existing agreements should consult the following references: for the Quebec James Bay Cree, see Peters (1989; forthcoming) and Moss (1985); for the Quebec James Bay Inuit, see LaRusic (1985) and Rostaing (1984); for the Sechelt Agreement, see Cassidy and Bish (1989), Etkin (1988), and Taylor and Paget (1989); and for Nunavut, see Canadian Arctic Resources Committee (1993) and Duffy (1988).
3 This geography derives from both the land claims settlement and the self-

government agreements that the fourteen Yukon First Nations negotiated concurrently. In the Umbrella Final Agreement that represents the land claims agreement, the section on self-government was developed as a statement of principle and as an enabling provision subject to negotiations with each Yukon First Nation. Thus, each First Nation negotiates the details of its own land claim and self-government agreement. For more information, see Courchene (1993), Graham (1992), and Joe (1991).

4   For example, Quebec's intention in negotiating the James Bay Agreement was to affirm its presence and jurisdiction over the territory, and to open up the area for economic development (Ciacca 1976). A major objective of the Cree was to secure their way of life, based on harvesting activities. Unable, in the face of Quebec's objectives, to gain jurisdiction over the whole territory, Cree negotiators settled for high levels of jurisdiction over relatively small areas, with a detailed set of principles governing the impact of economic development on the hunting, fishing, and trapping economy (Feit 1980; 1988). Taylor and Paget (1989, p. 298) point out that the Sechelt agreement "was developed for a highly urbanized, strategically located, relatively prosperous band, holding lands with immense development potential." The band's main objective coincided with that of the B.C. government—to integrate Aboriginal self-government within the provincial system of local government.

5   This is not a simplistic argument that social structure can be read from the landscape. Landscapes and their histories are complex iterations of socioeconomic and political processes (Duncan and Duncan 1988).

6   I place "Indians" in quotation marks to reflect the imposition of this term on First Nations Peoples.

7   Note, for example, the title of Heather Robertson's (1970) book *Reservations are for Indians.*

8   Geographic configurations are not deterministic. Aboriginal cultures have been extraordinarily resilient in the face of the reshaping of Aboriginal spaces and places (Kayahna Area Tribal Council 1985). However, Brody (1981) warns that, while Indian cultures have proved flexible enough to avoid or accommodate encroachments, there are limits beyond which these strategies cannot be extended.

9   There are many other examples of ways colonial geographies distort Aboriginal social realities (Groves 1991; Clatworthy and Smith 1992). A notable recent example includes the Dene in Saskatchewan, Manitoba, and the Northwest Territories (adherents of Treaties 5, 8, and 10), who mounted a court challenge in 1991 against the proposed Nunavut agreement, because their claims to the Northwest Territories had not been fully determined and settled. A further example is reflected in the settlement made to the Tetlin Gwitchin, who are based in Fort McPherson, NWT. The settlement included some land in the Yukon (McQueen 1993). The effects of colonial geographies are not trivial. Note, for example, the federal government's relocation of

Inuit families from northern Quebec to Grise Fiord and Resolute Bay in the Northwest Territories in 1953.

10 In this context, externalities refer to the negative or positive effects of activities within one area on other areas.

11 Table 1 relies on data from a 1982 survey in Regina by the Institute of Urban Studies, Winnipeg (Clatworthy and Hull 1983). Surveyors contacted approximately ten percent of the total urban population through random survey techniques in order to interview people of Aboriginal origins. At present, the level of detail in the resulting data base is not available from other data sources. The Aboriginal Peoples Survey may provide similar information for other metropolitan areas when it becomes available.

12 Aboriginal people are also citizens of provincial and federal governments, and may be citizens of municipal governments. Depending on the nature of specific self-government agreements, these three levels of government will also be delivering services to, and making laws for, Aboriginal people. Clearly the complexity of Aboriginal self-government arrangements affects the functioning of these other levels of government as well. I am limiting the focus of this paper, however, to implications for Aboriginal governments.

13 While Aboriginal title is the basis of treaty negotiations, some treaties were signed by more than one nation, and most nations signed more than one treaty. It is not straightforward to map traditional territories onto treaty territories.

REFERENCES

Anderson, K. J. 1991. *Vancouver's Chinatown: Racial discourse in Canada 1875–1980.* Kingston: McGill-Queen's University Press.

Bennett, R. 1989. *Territory and administration in Europe.* New York: Printer Publishers.

Bish, R. L. 1990. Community models of Indian government. In *Keeping the circle strong.* Toronto: Osgoode Hall Law School.

———. 1986. *A practical guide to issues in Gitksan-Wet'suwet'en self-government.* Victoria: School of Public Administration, University of Victoria.

Bours, A. 1989. Management by territory and the study of administrative geography. Pp. 72–92 in *Territory and administration in Europe,* ed. R. Bennett. New York: Printer Publishers.

Bowles, P. A. 1992. Cultural renewal: First Nations and the challenge to state superiority. Pp. 132–50 in *Co-existence? Studies in Ontario–First Nations relations,* ed. B. W. Hodgins, S. Heard, and J. S. Milloy. Peterborough, ON: Trent University.

Brody, H. 1981. *Maps and dreams: Indians and the British Columbia frontier.* Vancouver: Douglas & McIntyre.

Canadian Arctic Resources Committee. 1993. *Northern Perspectives* 21:1.

Cassidy, F. 1991. Self-determination, sovereignty, and self-government. Pp. 1–17 in

Aboriginal self-determination, ed. F. Cassidy. Halifax: Institute for Research on Public Policy.

Cassidy, F., and Robert L. Bish. 1989. *Indian government: Its meaning in practice.* Lantzville, BC, and Halifax: Oolichan Books and the Institute for Research on Public Policy.

Chamberlin, J. E. 1988. Aboriginal rights and the Meech Lake accord. Pp. 11–20 in *Competing constitutional visions: The Meech Lake accord,* ed. K. E. Swinton and C. J. Rogerson. Toronto: Carswell.

Ciacca, J. 1976. Opening remarks to the Standing Parliamentary Committee of the National Assembly of Quebec convened to examine the Agreement with the James Bay Crees and the Inuit of Quebec prior to its signature. Pp. xi–xxiv in *The James Bay and Northern Quebec Agreement.* Montreal: Editeur officiel du Québec.

Clatworthy, S. J., and J. Hull. 1983. *Native economic conditions: Regina and Saskatoon.* Winnipeg: University of Winnipeg, Institute of Urban Studies.

Clatworthy, S. J., and A. H. Smith. 1992. *Population implications of the 1985 amendments to the Indian Act.* Ottawa: Assembly of First Nations.

Coolican, M. 1985. *Living treaties: Lasting agreements.* Ottawa: Department of Indian Affairs and Northern Development.

Courchene, T. J. 1993. *Aboriginal self-government in Canada.* Australia: Occasional Lecture Series, Australian Senate.

Courchene, T. J., and L. M. Powell. 1992. *A First Nations province.* Kingston: Queen's University, Institute of Intergovernmental Relations.

Duffy, R. Q. 1988. *The road to Nunavut.* Montreal: McGill-Queen's University Press.

Duncan, J., and N. Duncan. 1988. Rereading the landscape. *Environment and Planning: Society and Space* 6:117–26.

Dunn, M. 1986. *Access to survival: A perspective on Aboriginal self-government for the constituency of the Native Council of Canada.* Kingston: Queen's University, Institute of Intergovernmental Relations.

Erasmus, G. 1989. Twenty years of disappointed hopes. Pp. 1–42 in *Drumbeat: Anger and renewal in Indian country,* ed. B. Richardson. Toronto: Summerhill Press.

Etkin, C. E. 1988. The Sechelt Indian Band: An analysis of a new form of Native self-government. *Canadian Journal of Native Studies* 8(1):73–105.

Falconer, P. 1985. Urban Indian needs: Federal policy responsibility and options in the context of the talks on Aboriginal self-government. Winnipeg: unpublished.

Feit, H. A. 1988. The power and the responsibility: implementation of the wildlife and hunting provisions of the James Bay and Northern Quebec Agreement. Pp. 74–88 in *James Bay and Northern Quebec: Ten Years After,* ed. S. Vincent and G. Bowers. Montreal: Recherches Amerindiennes au Québec.

———. 1980. Protecting indigenous hunters' ways of life: The social and environmental protection regime in the James Bay and Northern Quebec

Aboriginal Rights Agreement. Paper presented at the Conference on Social Impacts of Natural Resource Development on Indigenous Peoples. New York: Cornell University, unpublished.

Franks, C. E. S. 1987. *Public administration questions relating to Aboriginal self-government*. Kingston: Queen's University, Institute of Intergovernmental Relations.

Graham, R. 1992. Implementation of Indian self-government under the Yukon Indian land claim. Kingston: Queen's University, School of Public Administration, unpublished.

Groves, R. 1991. Territoriality and Aboriginal self-determination: Options for legal pluralism in Canada. Pp. 223–45 in *Proceedings of the VIth international symposium on folk law and legal pluralism*. Ottawa: Commission on Folk Law and Legal Pluralism.

Hawthorn, J. B. 1966. *A Survey of the contemporary Indians of Canada: A report on economic, political, educational needs and policies*. Ottawa: Indian Affairs Branch.

Joe, D. 1991. Sharing power: How can First Nations government work? Pp. 63–70 in *Aboriginal self-determination*, ed. F. Cassidy. Halifax: Institute for Research on Public Policy.

Kayahna Area Tribal Council. 1985. *The Kayahna region land utilization and occupancy study*. Toronto: University of Toronto Press.

Knight, D. B. 1988. Self-determination for indigenous peoples: The context for change. Pp. 117–34 in *Nationalism, self-determination and political geography*, ed. R. J. Johnston, D. B. Knight and E. Kofman. London: Croom Helm.

LaRusic, I. 1985. *Sketches of communities in northern Quebec*. Montreal: Recherches Amerindiennes au Québec.

Little Bear, L. 1987. Self-Government and the Canadian political system. Pp. 59–62 in *Issues in entrenching self-government*, ed. D. C. Hawkes and E. J. Peters. Kingston: Queen's University, Institute of Intergovernmental Relations.

MacGregor, R. 1989. *Chief: The fearless vision of Billy Diamond*. Markham, ON: Viking.

Mandelbaum, D. G. 1979. *The Plains Cree: An ethnographic, historical and comparative study*. Regina: University of Regina, Canadian Plains Research Centre.

McNab, D. T. 1992. Making a circle of time: The treaty-making process and Aboriginal land rights in Ontario. Pp. 27–49 in *Co-Existence? Studies in Ontario-First Nations relations*, ed. B. W. Hodgins, S. Heard, and J. S. Milloy. Peterborough, ON: Trent University.

McQueen, A. 1993. Personal communication.

———. 1991. We have always been here: Negotiating an Aboriginal community identity at Moose Factory Island, Ontario. Pp. 14–25 in *Indigenous peoples and the state*, ed. E. J. Peters. Kingston: McGill-Queen's University Press.

Moss, W. 1985. The implementation of the James Bay and Northern Quebec agreement. Pp. 684–94 in *Aboriginal Peoples and the law: Indian, Metis and Inuit rights in Canada,* ed. B. W. Morse. Ottawa: Carleton University Press.

Native Council of Canada. 1992. *Decision 1992: Background and discussion points for the First Peoples forums.* Ottawa: Native Council of Canada.

Nothing, B., and J. Wolfe. 1993. Reintegrating people, land and government: The Nishnawbe-Aski nations in Northern Ontario. Pp. 121–31 in *Indigenous land rights in Commonwealth countries: Dispossession, negotiation and community action,* ed. G. Cant, J. Overton and E. Pawson. Christchurch, N.Z.: University of Canterbury Printery.

Penner, K. 1983. *Indian self-government.* Ottawa: Supply and Services.

Peters, E. J. In progress. Placing "Indians": Implications of reserve policy for public perceptions of Aboriginal people.

———. Forthcoming. Whose north? The James Bay and Northern Quebec Agreement and its implications. In *Geographic perspectives on the provincial norths,* ed. M. Johnston. Copp Clark Pitman Ltd.

———. 1992. Protecting the land under modern land claims agreements: The effectiveness of the environmental regime negotiated by the James Bay Cree in the James Bay and Northern Quebec Agreement. *Applied Geography* 12:133–45.

———. 1989. Federal and provincial responsibilities for the Cree, Naskapi and Inuit under the James Bay and Northern Quebec, and the northeastern Quebec agreements. Pp. 173–242 in *Aboriginal Peoples and government responsibility: Exploring federal and provincial roles,* ed. David C. Hawkes. Ottawa: Carleton University Press.

Reeves, W. 1986. Native societies: The professions as a model of self-determination for urban Indians. Pp. 342–58 in *Arduous journey: Canadian Indians and decolonization,* ed. J. R. Ponting. Toronto: McClelland and Stewart.

Robertson, H. 1970. *Reservations are for Indians.* Toronto: James Lewis & Samuel.

Rostaing, J. P. 1984. Native regional autonomy: The initial experience of the Kativik regional government. *Inuit Studies* 8(2):3–39.

Sack, R. D. 1983. Human territoriality: a theory. *Annals of the Association of American Geographers* 73:55–74.

Shkilnyk, A. M. 1985. *A poison stronger than love: The destruction of an Ojibwa community.* New Haven, CT: Yale University Press.

Sibbley, D. 1992. Outsiders in society and space. Pp. 107–22 in *Inventing places: Studies in cultural geography,* ed. K. Anderson and F. Gale. Melbourne, Aust.: Longman Cheshire.

Smith, G. E. 1986. Territoriality. Pp. 312–14 in *The dictionary of human geography,* ed. R. J. Johnston, D. Gregory, and D. M. Smith. Oxford: Basil Blackwell.

Standing Committee on Aboriginal Affairs. 1990. *Unfinished business: An agenda for all Canadians in the 1990s.* Ottawa: House of Commons Standing Committee on Aboriginal Affairs.

Taylor, J. P., and G. Paget. 1989. Federal/provincial responsibility and the Sechelt. Pp. 297–348 in *Aboriginal peoples and government responsibility: Exploring federal and provincial roles,* ed. David C. Hawkes. Ottawa: Carleton University Press.

Tizya, R. 1992. Comments on urban Aboriginals and self-government. Pp. 45–52 in *Aboriginal governments and power sharing in Canada,* ed. D. Brown. Kingston, ON: Queen's University, Institute of Intergovernmental Relations.

Weinstein, J. 1986. *Aboriginal self-determination off a land base.* Kingston, ON: Queen's University, Institute of Intergovernmental Relations.

Wolfe, J. 1989. Approaches to planning in Native Canadian communities: A review and commentary on settlement problems and the effectiveness of planning practice. *Plan Canada* 29:2.

CHAPTER 10

ABORIGINAL WOMEN AND SELF-GOVERNMENT[1]

MARGARET A. JACKSON, SIMON FRASER UNIVERSITY

It has been argued that the application of Canadian law is becoming more sensitized to questions of gender equality (Brockman and Chunn 1993). However, the fear has been expressed that the increased emphasis on customary law that is expected to accompany movement toward Aboriginal self-government may not capture this trend. It is a "Catch 22" situation. The arguments of certain Aboriginal women's groups (for example, the Native Women's Association of Canada—NWAC) are resisted by other Aboriginal women's groups and other traditional First Nations groups (for example, the Assembly of First Nations—AFN), in part because it is felt that public examination of the issue might jeopardize hard-won steps toward self-government (Fleras and Elliott 1992). Meanwhile, some have suggested that a return to customary law should not provoke any such concerns, since one of the goals of self-government is to create local community governance structures based on traditional Aboriginal values.

In this chapter, an overview of self-determination/self-government issues will be presented from the perspective of Aboriginal women. It is their voices that carve out the various positions taken, and it is their voices that policy makers and legislators must weigh. My purpose is to provide a summation and analysis of their perspectives. After establishing the historical context, I present a selection of the positions held by Aboriginal women and an analysis of possible future policy directions.

A review of recent Canadian legal history provides the context for the discussion. It is not my intention to provide a legal analysis of the issues, since this has already been completed by Aboriginal women lawyers (Turpel 1989; Monture-OKanee 1992; Nahanee 1992). Rather, I wish to describe the socio-legal policy context—the values in conflict, the stakeholders, and the decisions that have been made earlier that can bring us to an understanding of present positions.

THE POLICY ENVIRONMENT: FOUR HISTORICAL JUNCTURES

Four important junctures in recent history have influenced the current policy environment pertaining to Aboriginal women and self-government/self-determination.[2] These are:

1. The repeal of section 12(1)(b) of the Indian Act in 1985;
2. The increasing cultural sensitivity shown by some judiciary in the early 1980s;
3. Entrenchment of the Charter of Rights and Freedoms in the Canadian Constitution in 1982; and
4. More recent constitutional talks that involved consideration of self-government for the Aboriginal Peoples.

Together, these developments have provided the triggering stimulus for Aboriginal women's interests and perspectives.

1. REPEAL OF SECTION 12(1)(b): BEGINNING OF THE PATH?

The repeal of section 12(1)(b) of the Indian Act in 1985 was, perhaps, the first signal given to Aboriginal women in Canada that they could achieve some measure of self-determination.

The legacy of the 1876 Indian Act cannot be overemphasized here. The intent of the original act (and subsequent versions) was to regulate the use of reserve land and persons eligible to use reserve land (Moss 1990). One consequence of the government's decision to "enfranchise" Aboriginal people under the act was to have them lose their Aboriginal status. There was the clear government intent to absorb all Indians into Canadian society, such that there would be no need to even have an Indian department (Moss 1990).

The impact of government policy on Aboriginal women was particularly discriminatory because section 12(1)(b) took away their Indian status when they married non-Indian men. Penalties included deprivation of rights, such as employment and accommodation rights, ostracism, and exclusion from involvement in tribal life (Fleras and Elliott 1992).

In the 1970s, one Aboriginal woman, Jeanette Lavell, lost her challenge of the Indian Act in the Supreme Court of Canada. According to NWAC (1992, p. 13), the then-existing Bill of Rights was "simply another statute which could not override another statute." In 1981, however, Sandra Lovelace, another Aboriginal woman, succeeded in having the United Nations Committee on Human Rights declare the Indian Act provision discriminatory. The Lovelace decision was considered a landmark case because there was a recognition of "a right for minority groups and their members to define themselves" (Moss 1990, p. 294). In 1985, after the Charter of Rights and Freedoms was entrenched in the Constitution, Mary Two-Axe Early, the founder of a group called Indian Rights for Indian Women, won a case similar to Lavell's in the Supreme Court. These events paved the way for Parliament to adopt Bill C-31, which returned Indian status to thousands of Aboriginal women.[3]

As a result of Bill C-31, 70,000 men, women, girls, boys, and old and young people were added to the federal Indian registry and band lists (NWAC 1992). According to NWAC (1992), the status Indian population grew from 360,000 to 487,000 in a little over four and a half years.[4]

2. CULTURAL SENSITIVITY IN THE COURTROOM: UNEQUAL JUSTICE?

Ironically, the second force contributing to the modern Aboriginal women's movement has been the increasing sensitivity shown by the Canadian judiciary. This was especially evident in the Northwest Territories during the 1980s, where customary law was considered in the sentencing of some Aboriginal offenders. Here the policy focus shifts to the justice system. For Aboriginal women, concerns have arisen because Aboriginal offenders (for the most part male) have been treated unequally by the Canadian justice system in the name of fair justice, but the result has often been injustice for Aboriginal women.[5] One high-profile case illustrates the concerns.

A one-week sentence was handed down by a judge for three Inuit men accused of raping a thirteen-year-old girl. The trial judge reasoned that cultural factors should be taken into consideration. He noted that Inuit people do not regard having sex with a girl under fourteen as a crime. He stated (quoted in Jackson 1985, p. 6):

> A culturation process does not include the term statutory rape, jailbait, and other terms suggesting prohibition. Rather the morality or values of the people here is that when a girl begins to menstruate, she is considered ready to engage in sexual relations. That is the way life was and continues to be in the smaller communities.

In passing sentence, the trial judge described the three accused as a credit to the community and to their country. He also noted they used no violence and pleaded guilty, thus relieving the victim from the ordeal of three separate trials.

Although the trial judge attempted to incorporate Aboriginal standards for acceptable behavior into his decision, his efforts to be sensitive to the local culture were rejected on appeal. The Court of Appeal asserted that courts are responsible for maintaining the law established by the Parliament of Canada and not for upholding community standards of behavior. The sentence was lengthened to four months. The appeal court decision implied that Aboriginal custom did not carry the same weight as Canadian law and, by extension, that Aboriginal Peoples were not equal to non-Aboriginal peoples.[6]

Aboriginal women are concerned about these types of decisions. They fear that the attendance to cultural context does not necessarily serve the interests of Aboriginal women and children. In this regard, family violence and sexual abuse are frequently cited. Aboriginal women argue that these kinds of crimes have no place in customary or in traditional law (Jackson 1985).

Another layer of difficulty for the current policy debate is that there has been no holistic approach, either legally or politically, to the role of customary law in Canada. Some argue that little or no customary law has been received into Canadian law (Haveman 1983), while others have suggested that it has been deformed when introduced into the non-Aboriginal court system.

Richstone (1983) has pointed out that once a non-Aboriginal standard is adopted to determine the validity of Aboriginal customary law, the essence of the customary law may be lost. A judge, for example, may employ classifications of thought that are alien to the original structure of the Aboriginal *lex loci*. Richstone cites the example of Judge Sissons' decision in the Northwest Territories. Judge Sissons implied that Inuit custom was acceptable under the common law, only because it complied with the requirements of English law.[7] The danger arises when an unconscientious ethnocentrism deforms a customary law, a precedent is established based on this distortion, and future cases follow from it (Richstone 1983).

Many Aboriginal people have expressed the concern that customary law can (and has) become distorted in the white man's courts. Therefore, they feel it must be applied in its traditional form and setting. They view this as one of the important goals of self-government.

3. CHARTER OF RIGHTS AND FREEDOMS: NEEDED SAFEGUARD FOR
   SELF-GOVERNMENT?

The third historical legal factor important for the current discussion was the entrenchment of the Charter of Rights and Freedoms in the Constitution Act

(1982). Groups such as NWAC have argued that any collective self-governing arrangement must have the equality provisions of the Canadian Charter (or a similarly focused document) structured into the agreement in order to protect Aboriginal women's individual rights (Platiel 1992). It is reasoned that customary law has traditionally held collective interests above individual interests in structuring social, political, and economical programs for Aboriginal communities. In the translation of such collective social values into operational mandates, the concern is that the interests of individual Aboriginal women could be overshadowed. This has happened in the past, and, some fear that, without a Charter safeguard, it could continue in the future.

The Charter, and other key provisions of the Constitution, have important implications for both individual rights and for self-government. With respect to individual rights, several sections, including 7, 15, 28, and 35, have been the subject of recent controversy.

Section 7 reads:

> Everyone has the right to life, liberty, and the security of the person and the right not to be deprived thereof except in accordance with the principles of fundamental justice.

It has already been argued that attendance to customary law does not necessarily constitute a negation of section 7 of the Charter. Mr. Justice de Weerdt, in the Saila case, for example, maintained that the principles of fundamental justice were not affected by the imposition of a customary form of punishment.[8] Therefore, the courts could give legal expression to community values through their sentencing decisions.

The courts' discretionary powers in sentencing, however, appear to have limits. The traditional method of discipline—ostracism by the community—is a well-recognized means of dealing with offenders who do not uphold customary traditions. However section 15(1) would appear to constrain the court's discretion. Section 15(1) states:

> Every individual is equal before and under the law and has the right to the equal protection and equal benefit of the law without discrimination and, in particular, without discrimination based on race, national or ethnic origin, colour, religion, sex, age or mental or physical disability.

Judges who consider Aboriginal customs in their sentencing are not meting out the same justice as that given to "white men" who do not possess

Aboriginal customs, even though the underlying rationale may be well intended.

The next relevant section is section 28. It states:

> Notwithstanding anything in this Charter, the rights and freedoms referred to in it are guaranteed equally to male and female persons.

Finally, section 35(4) states:

> Notwithstanding any other provision of this act, the Aboriginal treaty rights referred to in subsection (1) are guaranteed to male and female persons.

Thus, the Charter and the Constitution, and especially the above-noted sections, are at the basis of self-government discussions for many Aboriginal women.

There are other implications of the Charter for self-government. While NWAC (1992) supports the inherent right to self-government, it argues that it is an existing right within the context of section 35 of the Constitution Act. If self-government is an inherent right, NWAC reasons that the Aboriginal governments subsequently formed must not simply be the currently existing patriarchal forms of governance that were created by a "foreign government," that is, those created under the Indian Act. If it is not agreed that self-government is an inherent right (and thus falls outside of section 35), then it is argued that section 2 of the Charter and sections 7 to 15 do apply to all Aboriginal persons.

NWAC has expressed the fear that some Aboriginal groups, could, if given the opportunity, suspend the sections of the Charter that protect the individual rights described above. This could come about if Aboriginal governments have the opportunity to employ the notwithstanding clause of the Constitution Act.[9] Groups such as the AFN have long resisted the application of the Charter.[10] They hold that individual rights cannot override collective rights and that "the Canadian Charter is in conflict with our philosophy and culture" (quoted in NWAC 1992, p. 9).

4. The Constitutional Talks and Self-Government: Transcending to a Rights Perspective?

The fourth factor influencing Aboriginal women's perspectives on self-government is the recent constitutional talks. The efforts of Elijah Harper, former Aboriginal member of the Manitoba Legislature, forced attention in the Constitutional talks on the Aboriginal reality in Canada. This was in dramatic juxtaposition to the Quebec francophone concerns. Harper's actions were the culmination of a desire for cultural autonomy that had been growing since at least the 1980s.

In 1984, Marie Smallface Marule, in her article "Traditional Indian Government: Of the People, By the People, For the People," reported that a delegation from the Union of British Columbia Indian Chiefs had traveled to the United Nations to present their case to the under-secretary general of Political Affairs, Decolonization, and Trusteeships. They questioned why the colonial situations in Africa and Asia were being examined, but not those of the Aboriginal Peoples in the Western Hemisphere. It was, interestingly enough, shortly after this issue came to the attention of the UN, that the Canadian government appeared willing to negotiate changes to the Canadian Charter of Rights and Freedoms that added protection for Aboriginal rights and freedoms.

In 1990, Mr. Harper blocked approval of the Meech Lake Constitutional Accord because of his concern that Aboriginal issues were not being addressed in the constitutional process. As described by Mary Ellen Turpel (1989), the distinct society clause triggered a strong reaction from Aboriginal Peoples. She quotes from the prepared statement of the AFN:

> It perpetuates the idea of a duality in Canada and strengthens the myth that the French and English peoples are the foundation of Canada. It neglects the original inhabitants and distorts history. It is as if the peoples of the First Nations never existed. It suggests that historically and presently as well the French peoples in Quebec form the only distinct society in Canada. The amendment fails to give explicit constitutional recognition to the existence of First Nations as distinct societies that also form a fundamental characteristic of Canada. We were told for five years that governments are reluctant to entrench undefined self-government of Aboriginal peoples in the Constitution. Yet, here is an equally vague idea of a "distinct society" unanimously agreed to and allowed to be left to the courts for interpretation.

Later, in the "Canada Round" of constitutional talks, NWAC was not allowed to have a place at the federal government's constitutional talks along with other Aboriginal groups. NWAC appeared before the Federal Court of Canada on March 16, 1992, to argue that Aboriginal women were being denied the right to free speech as guaranteed under the Charter. The decision of the court was in their favor—a landmark ruling that further marked the legitimacy of the individual rights claims. In the decision, Mr. Justice Walsh stated that "NWAC is a bona fide, established and recognized national voice of and for Aboriginal women" (quoted in Nahanee 1992, p. 22). In essence, the court determined that the rights of the Aboriginal women (as represented by NWAC) had been violated by the Canadian government.

The more recent interventions by Aboriginal women in the self-government process have been described by one law professor at the University of Calgary (quoted in Mahoney 1993) as a "women's version of Elijah Harper." Just as Mr. Harper was concerned that Aboriginal rights to self-government were not being attended to in the constitutional talks, Aboriginal women are arguing that their individual rights are not being attended to in the self-government discussions.

ABORIGINAL WOMEN SPEAK

It has been fascinating to observe how strong the voice of Aboriginal women has become in the debates about self-government. Teressa Nahanee, among others, would surely argue that this was not an overnight discovery of tongue, since she herself has been speaking out since at least 1976. It is only recently, however, that public awareness has been raised and tentative listening has begun.

There is not a single Aboriginal women's voice. Rather, divergent opinions are being offered. In this section of the chapter, therefore, a representation of these voices are presented. For Aboriginal women, the key issues of concern have been the Indian Act, representation in constitutional talks, and the protection of individual rights.

The repeal of section 12(1)(b) of the Indian Act was received with qualified optimism by many Aboriginal women, but the issue of sexual discrimination was not completely addressed by the repeal of that one section. The continued existence of the act is a matter of considerable concern, and most Aboriginal organizations view reform efforts to date as piecemeal (Moss 1990).

According to Moss (1990, p. 287), it has generally been maintained by women's groups that current inequalities are a "federally created problem" and that the elimination of sex discrimination from the Indian Act is the government's responsibility. But there is no real evidence that the government is willing to reopen the act to grapple with residual sexual discrimination or with other difficult policy issues relating to Aboriginal status entitlement (Moss 1990).

The act has become a symbol of the struggle between Aboriginal collective rights, and individual human rights. Moss (1990) argues that, at least to some extent, the debate illustrates the difficulty of applying externally developed human rights' norms to cultures that resist them on grounds of conflict with traditional mores. To a greater degree, however, the problem may lie in the threat posed by imposing externally developed norms, even if they are consistent with current cultural norms.

One key to achieving balance between collective and individual rights would seem to lie in consultations with Aboriginal groups (Moss 1990). However, this raises an important question: Who should be consulted? The representation issue has emerged as a focal point for the current debates.

Not all Aboriginal women's groups have felt adequately represented at the constitutional talks on self-government, although there has certainly been a range of opinion in this regard. Wendy Grant, a vice-chief of a Musqueam reserve in British Columbia, for example, has stated (First Nations Summit 1992) that the Assembly of First Nations does have appropriate representation of women:

> If you look at the AFN right now, our percentage of elected women chiefs is close to the percentage of elected women in the House of Commons.[11]

She is concerned that the NWAC insistence on entrenchment of the Charter in any self-governing process would "jeopardize key elements of traditional Native government, law and society" (quoted in Scott 1992).

Jennie Jack of the AFN supports Grant's collective rights perspective:

> To say that male chiefs do not represent their constituency is to be disrespectful of all men and women within their communities who elect their leadership. (Quoted in Scott 1992)

She continues by stating that a more "collective" role is the appropriate one for Aboriginal women:

> Aboriginal women have always looked out for the greater good of all people—men, women, children, and elders—rather than worry about putting the women's issue first. It's basic survival, it has nothing to do (with) gender.

Bernice Hammersmith (1992, p. 56), in her article on Aboriginal women and self-government, takes a similar position. She believes Aboriginal women should not attempt to make their own voices heard in the public fora, but they should stay:

... back in their own nations, no matter how evil they think the situation
is. It is only by dealing with real concerns at the local level that we will
get back to the original values of our nations.

These Aboriginal women appear unwilling to focus upon gender
equality as an issue apart from self-government. The collective interest "of
all people" is seen to be the appropriate emphasis. Therefore, the individual
rights of Aboriginal women are not singled out for attention.

With respect to the individual or collective rights debate, there has also
been a variety of opinions. For example, the Ontario Native Women's
Association, representing about ten thousand women was among several
Aboriginal women's groups who felt that representation at the constitutional talks was not an issue. They took the position (quoted in Fine 1992)
that enough protection had already been incorporated into the wording of
the Charlottetown Accord, therefore, an entrenched Charter was not a
necessary condition for approval.

Rosemary Kuptana (quoted in Canadian Press 1992), head of the Inuit
Tapirisat of Canada, adopted a similar stance. She was quoted as saying:
"We are satisfied that the equality rights of Aboriginal women are not
prejudiced by the Charlottetown Accord."

Sheila Genaille (1992), president of the Métis National Council of
Women, strongly endorsed the Charlottetown Accord as well: "From a
Métis perspective, the constitutional agreement in Charlottetown provides
protection for Aboriginal women in future self-government agreements."
She further stated that the notwithstanding clause of the Charter did not
allow any government (Aboriginal or otherwise) to "shield themselves from
the gender equality rights (section 28) of the Charter."

These diverse and influential Aboriginal women appeared to have no
difficulty with an accord that did not absolutely entrench Charter rights in
self-governing arrangements, that is, they were not concerned about the
possibility that an Aboriginal government would use the notwithstanding
clause of the Charter to "opt out." Therefore, what are the other Aboriginal
women's groups, such as NWAC, concerned about? Why are they adamant
about having a Charter safeguard? On the surface, it may appear ironic that
the NWAC position demands the inclusion of certain elements of white
man's law—the Charter—in the self-government exercise. There are important underlying issues that need to be explored in order to arrive at an
understanding of the basis for these different positions.

An understanding of the different positions that Aboriginal women
have adopted in relation to self-government requires an analysis of the
objectives that Aboriginal women are seeking to attain. In addition to being

able to define themselves as Aboriginal, many Aboriginal women are also expressing a need to define themselves as women. The issue is one of self-determination. In this regard, Monture-OKanee (1991, p. 16) quotes Osennontion:

> The establishment, exercise and enforcement of government, is only one aspect of 'self-determination'. In our own language, we have a word that, of course, even better describes what we have been instructed to do. TEWATATHA: which best translates into "we carry ourselves"—a rather simple concept, some might say, but I think it says it all.

Monture-OKanee (1992) has difficulty with what she perceives to be the construction of woman as "other" in the line of questioning of Aboriginal feminist. She states that "when one gender is constructed as 'other', then the goal of equality will continue to be elusive" (p. 9).

Monture-OKanee (1992) describes a story told by Marie Wilson of the Gitskan Wet'suwet'en Tribal Council. Wilson likens the relationship between women and men to the eagle. An eagle soars to unbelievable heights and has tremendous power on two equal wings, one female and one male, that carries the body of life between them. In the same way, women and men are said to be balanced parts of the whole, yet they are very different from each other. They are not "equal," if equality is defined as being the same. Rather, equality in this case is the contribution of both wings to the flight.

Monture-OKanee (1992) examines the feminist mind and the perspective of Aboriginal women. While she finds a certain shared reality between the two approaches in thinking, she also finds differences. She makes reference to a Cree colleague, Winona Stephenson:

> I want to understand why feminists continue to believe in the universality of male dominance, the universality of sisterhood, and why they strive so hard to convert Aboriginal women. I want feminists to know why many Aboriginal women do not identify as feminist. I perceive two parallel but distinct movements, but there ought to be a place where we can meet to share, learn, and offer honest support without trying to convert each other. (p. 27)

This points out an important additional layer in the debate. The emphasis Aboriginal feminists place on the gender equality component of self-government contrasts with the emphasis of Aboriginal women who do not approach self-government from a feminist perspective. Those, such as

Monture-OKanee, who argue that racial and cultural inequality are as important as gender inequality, undoubtedly have a different perspective than feminists, such as Nahanee, who argue that the main concern for Aboriginal women relates to the gender issue and the protection of individual rights.

Monture-OKanee (1992, p. 28) has challenged the feminist point of view:

> Feminist thought can inform attempts to understand Aboriginal women's reality. But, feminism must be seen as only one tool which may or may not accurately inform our developing understanding.

Similarly, Lillian Head (quoted in Clark 1992, p. 48) has commented:

> Women are often the most oppressed in any marginalized group. Moreover, relationships that women seem to have with the land, Mother Earth, are very special. As Indigenous women we can't belittle the feminist movement because they too are going through struggles. Different women's groups are going through different experiences in terms of being oppressed by patriarchal societies.

In contrast, feminist arguments have been advanced by NWAC member Teressa Nahanee (1992) and others. In her paper, "Dancing with a Gorilla," Nahanee takes a feminist-legal theory approach. While her starting point is one that Monture-OKanee and Head would agree with—that Aboriginal women need to be included in the consultation process—Nahanee focuses on justice issues, and, in particular, on the reality of sexual and physical abuse of Aboriginal women. She notes that "customary" sanctioning of sexual offenders has been ineffective in curbing sexual violence, and that customary cultural values—such as kindness, reconciliation, and family cohesiveness—may actually prevent Aboriginal women from officially reporting violence in the home. She traces much of the difficulty to the fact that males have almost total control in Aboriginal communities through band councils that, ironically, were first established under the Indian Act.[12]

Nahanee expresses concerns about the types of cases in the Northwest Territories, cited earlier, and those occurring more recently in British Columbia. She feels these cases indicate why "culturally sensitive" judicial decision-making is detrimental to Aboriginal women. Interestingly, her "feminist" resolution appears quite similar to Monture-OKanee's. She states (p. 9): "There needs to be a return to traditional ways, healing circles, and a sharing of power between the men and the women."

According to Nahanee, Aboriginal women want to revive traditions that recognize equally valued roles for both men and women. She fears, however, that men are not willing to share power in many situations. For instance, she notes that women are told that they cannot participate in sweat lodges and other ceremonies when they are menstruating because men are afraid of "women" power.

Nahanee traces the history of Indian sexual inequality from the Lavell case. For Nahanee, the challenge Lavell made to the Indian Act in 1970 was a challenge to the patriarchal state. The court decision in Lavell clearly underpins the social values of equality that Nahanee feels should remain foremost in the movement toward self-government. The threats to equality, she believes, are very real. She notes that in the 1980s, the AFN and the Native Council of Canada both agreed that sexual discrimination should end; however, they felt that interim measures could be taken while further studies were pursued. The Native Women's Association of Canada, on the other hand, insisted amendments to the Indian Act that would end discrimination should be brought forward immediately.

Other Aboriginal women and women's groups support the Nahanee/NWAC position. Winnie Giesbrecht (Geisbrecht 1992), for example, president of the Indigenous Women's Collective of Manitoba, opposes self-government arrangements that do not have a guarantee of gender equality rights. She fears that Native politicians are no different from other politicians: "A politician is a politician. A politician is there for one reason—for themselves."

Freda Cooper (Cooper 1992), a fifty-nine-year-old Salish woman from Vancouver Island, takes the argument a step further. She questions the wisdom of returning to certain customary traditions. Pointing to a February 1992 B.C. Supreme Court decision, Cooper describes how a thirty-five-year-old Salish man was awarded $42,000 in damages for pain, suffering, and mental distress he suffered during his forcible initiation into the Coast Salish tradition of spirit dancing. She is also concerned about the protection of the Christian minority on reserves if there is a return to traditional spirituality.

It is clear that while Monture-OKanee is sensitive and appreciative of the feminist concerns about equality rights, she feels that this is only part of a larger rights issue. Her vision is for self-government based on Aboriginal values, not just values unique to Aboriginal women. She foresees a process by which both men and women undergo a healing process together in order to return to more traditional spirituality and self-determination. While Nahanee also sees the need for traditional healing, her emphasis is different. She does not want a return to customary law, if that means a return to the subservient role that Aboriginal women have been experiencing in Canada since the white society's patriarchal institutions distorted Aboriginal culture. She sees women in Canadian society engaging more fully in a participatory democratic system, and she sees a system that brings with it the safeguards of a Western legal system, including provisions of the Charter and the Criminal Code. She does not want this to be lost in the process of implementing self-government.

Like Monture-OKanee, Nahanee approaches the question of equality of rights from a human rights perspective. She argues that the Canadian government is racist in the way it deals with Aboriginals and that this constitutes a violation of the Universal Declaration of Human Rights. The difference between the two positions appears in how gender issues are collapsed into, or separated from, racial and cultural inequalities. The point has been made that the feminists appear to "lift away" the power issues from the larger question of Aboriginal self-determination.

Yet another perspective on the rights question is provided by Mary Ellen Turpel (1989). She has suggested that a lot of the confusion about "Aboriginal rights" may emerge because of ambiguous definitions. The very expression "Aboriginal rights" cannot easily be translated into anything meaningful for many Aboriginal people. These are expressions that have been "thought up and imposed on those peoples by the same culture that brought us the 'rights category'" (p. 37). But, according to Turpel, these are incompatible with Aboriginal approaches to an everyday world based on land, family, social life, and spirituality.[13]

CONCLUSION

This analysis highlights a dilemma. There is, for many Aboriginal people, the hope that a fading cultural identity can be recovered and that a strong desire for self-government and autonomy can be achieved. At the same time, for many Aboriginal women, there is an interest in preserving and extending gender equality. Thus, a central issue for Aboriginal women concerns what a return to traditional customs would involve. Would it involve a return to the historical subservience of Aboriginal women to Aboriginal men, or would it involve the equality of power between Aboriginal men and women that existed earlier but was distorted by the imposition of European patriarchal law and practices?[14]

On the basis of the current review, it is apparent that there is a need to articulate which Aboriginal social values are to be given priority in the development of self-governing structures. Once these values have been articulated, their implications for self-governing policies, structures, and procedures can be more carefully examined.

Policy-making is concerned with competing values and the achievement of social purposes. Social policies seek to effect compromises between social values that are in tension (for example, individual rights versus collective rights). In the widest sense, social policy seeks to address the balance between fairness to the individual and the well-being of society as a whole (Ekstedt 1991). In the self-government debates, we may ask: where is the balance to be struck? The Aboriginal Peoples must decide. It is important to get agreement on these underlying assumptions before proceeding to debate the form that specific self-governing structures should take. This is not a question of supporting or not supporting self-government. It is about getting the directions to self-government right, and about the need to have a map before starting the journey.

In some respects, Nahanee's stance, and the stance of Aboriginal women feminists, is less risky than the type of position adopted by Monture-OKanee. The latter position asserts that the unique Aboriginal way of being will, if allowed to develop, assure the protection of Aboriginal women. The former position is more skeptical. It asserts the necessity of a return to the unique Aboriginal way of being for healing, but the return requires an escort—the Charter. In this way, the journey can be observed by international bodies, such as the United Nations, as it twists and turns toward successful completion.

While difficult to judge, it may be that the harm done to customary Aboriginal ways of being is already too great for a return to spiritual balance without the imposition of structure and process. As Nahanee says, there are many Aboriginal people who are no longer in touch with their Aboriginal roots. What of the overwhelming proportion of Aboriginals who have become urbanized? What meaning does a healing circle have to someone born in a city where concrete, and concrete poverty, provide the surround?

It does appear to the present author that in both Nahanee's and Monture-OKanee's assessments, the debate needs to transcend self-government pragmatics to focus upon wider human rights issues if Aboriginal women are to have a stronger base from which to address their concerns.[15] An emphasis on social values, such as equality and freedom of speech, may be the better road to travel for at least two reasons:

1. It allows a wider support network to be accessed through international linkages, such as the UN Human Rights Sub-Committee on Indigenous Populations, and international and national women's groups, both feminist and otherwise; and
2. There is more certainty about how values such as equality and freedom

of expression will be translated into policies and programs.

It is far less certain how the sometimes uncertain visions of the past, which may have become distorted by the dominant society, might affect women in the movement toward self-government.

The various positions taken by Aboriginal women and women's groups are not significantly different in their basic assumptions. For the most part, the social values they seek to entrench are the same: sexual equality, freedom of speech, etc. The differences lie in the paths chosen to secure those values and in the speeds thought safest to achieve them.

At the present juncture, it is important to priorize the values themselves. This is an undertaking for all the Aboriginal Peoples and not just for Aboriginal women. The metaphor of the eagle flying should be kept in mind, not only for a vision of how Aboriginal men and women can work together, but also for a vision of how Aboriginal and non-Aboriginal peoples can work together. The eagle cannot fly with only one wing beating.

NOTES

1   The author wishes to acknowledge the assistance of Jennifer Stevens, First Nations Law Program at the University of British Columbia, for providing relevant materials for the chapter and an initial discussion of its vision. As well, I appreciated receiving comments on an earlier draft from John Ekstedt, Al Patenaude, and Hannele Janti.

2   Turpel (1989) makes a helpful distinction between self-government and self-determination. She feels that self-determination is the more hopeful concept. Quoting Deloria and Lytle (p. 38), she notes: "Self-government . . . implies a recognition by the superior political power that some measure of local decision-making is necessary but that this process must be monitored very carefully so that its products are compatible with the goals and policies of the larger political power. (I)t implies that . . . people . . . are now ready to assume some, but not all, of the responsibilities of a new municipality."

3   *Globe and Mail,* May 29, 1992.

4   The effects of the repeal have not, however, been positive in every respect. Arlene Guerin (1993), of the Musqueam Band in British Columbia, for example, argues the repeal has left a legacy of other difficulties that now result in "splits" between husbands and wives over matters of property.

5   Whatever the plight of the Aboriginal Peoples generally, the fate of Aboriginal women is even worse. In times of economic and social oppression, Aboriginal women rank among the most severely disadvantaged in Canada (Fleras and Elliott 1992). Their social problems are worse because of poor housing, substance abuse, inadequate child-rearing conditions, and, most especially, because of physical and sexual abuse. These conditions result in

"high rates of suicide, alcohol dependency and neglect of children" (Fleras and Elliott 1992, p. 19).

6   This perspective is substantiated with reference to how the Aboriginal Peoples have been treated until quite recent times. For example, numbers instead of names were assigned to Inuit involved in divorce cases (Crawford 1985).

7   See R. Noah Estate, (1961), 32 D.L.R. (2nd) 185, and R. Adoption of K., (1961), 32 D.L.R. (2nd) 686, Northwest Territorial Court.

8   *Saila v R.* (1984) C.N.L.R., Vol. 1, pp. 173–81.

9   Section 33 of the Charter allows federal and provincial governments to opt out of certain sections of the Charter if they deem it necessary.

10   However, the AFN did support the Charlottetown Accord, which provided that Aboriginal self-government would have to comply with the Charter of Rights and Freedoms. But, once established, these governments would have the right to opt out of the Charter, just as provinces and the federal government do, through the use of a "notwithstanding" clause. The Accord was subsequently rejected by the Canadian people in a national referendum.

11   In 1992, according to the *Montreal Gazette,* Saturday, March 28, 1992, there were 1,153,800 Natives in Canada, and 447,128 of these were women. Reserve populations totaled 155,989 men and 133,697 women. There were 603 bands and 60 female chiefs.

12   As Palys (1993, p. 6) observes, "(t)raditional forms of governance were undermined by a century of funding Band Councils, with the result that, in many communities, Band Councils and more traditional structures now conflict over funding and tribal policies."

13   In a similar vein, Monture-OKanee (1991) has pointed out that there is no word in Ojibwa for justice. Justice is a way of being that is learned from childhood and a process learned by example. She quotes Alex Denny: "Harmony, not justice is the idea." (p. 44)

14   Some authors have suggested that in the "pre–white man's era," there was equality between Aboriginal men and women (Greschner 1992; Monture-OKanee 1992). Others are more skeptical (see Van Kirk 1988). The latter position holds that the imposed European patriarchy cannot explain the observed disparities that seem to have existed prior to the white man's emergence as a controlling influence.

15   The present discussion does not intend to diminish the importance of balancing these concerns with the concerns that other Aboriginal women have expressed about the need for community, grass-roots development.

REFERENCES

Brockman, J., and D. Chunn, eds. 1993. *Investigating gender bias: Law, courts, and the legal profession.* Toronto: Thompson Educational Publishing.

Canadian Press. 1992. Indian negotiators say deal will protect native women. Toronto: *Globe and Mail,* September 24.

Clark, Donna. 1992. Interview with Lillian Head. *Aquelarre,* pp. 47–51.

Cooper, F. 1992. Fearful Native women plead for protection against ancient rituals. Vancouver: *Vancouver Sun,* Monday, March 16, p. A3.

Crawford, A. 1985. Outside law and traditional communities in the Northwest Territories. Paper presented to the Western Regional Science Association, San Diego, California, February 1985.

Ekstedt, J. W. 1991. Canadian crime policy. In *Canadian criminology: Perspectives on crime and criminality,* ed. M. Jackson and C. Griffiths. Toronto: Harcourt Brace Jovanovich.

Fine, S. 1992. Native women aim to block national referendum in court. Toronto: *Globe and Mail,* Tuesday, October 13.

First Nations Summit. 1992. Native women well represented at national constitutional talks. Sechelt, BC: *Kahtou News,* October 15.

Fleras, A., and J. L. Elliott. 1992. *The nations within.* Toronto: Oxford University Press.

Genaille, S. D. 1992. Metis women endorse agreement. Toronto: *Globe and Mail,* September 30.

Giesbrecht, Winnie. 1992. Vancouver: *Vancouver Sun,* February 12.

Greschner, D. 1992. Aboriginal women, the constitution and criminal justice. *University of British Columbia Law Review (Special edition)* 338–59.

Guerin, Arlene. 1993. Personal communication, March 24.

Hammersmith, B. 1992. Aboriginal women and self-government. Pp. 53–59 in *Nation to nation: Aboriginal sovereignty and the future of Canada,* ed. Diane Engelstad and John Bird. Concord, ON: Anansi Press.

Haveman, P. 1983. The indigenization of social control in Canada. Paper presented at a conference sponsored by the Commission on Folk Law and Legal Pluralism, Vancouver, August 19–23.

Jackson, M. A. 1985. Unequal justice and the law: Traditional versus customary law. Montreal: Proceedings from the Canadian Law and Society Annual Meeting.

Little Bear, Leroy, Menno Boldt, and J. Anthony Long, eds. 1984. *Pathways to self-determination: Canadian Indians and the Canadian state.* Toronto: University of Toronto Press.

Mahoney, Kathleen. 1993. Toronto: *Globe and Mail,* Tuesday, October 13, p. A10.

Marule, Marie Smallface. 1984. Traditional Indian government: Of the people, by the people, for the people. Pp. 36–45 in *Pathways to self-determination: Canadian Indians and the Canadian state,* ed. Leroy Little Bear, Menno Boldt, and J. Anthony Long. Toronto: University of Toronto Press.

Monture-OKanee, Patricia. 1992. Reclaiming justice: Aboriginal women and justice initiatives in the 1990's. Paper presented to the Royal Commission on

Aboriginal Peoples, Round Table on Justice Issues, Ottawa, November 25–27.

————. 1991. Reflecting on flint woman. In *First Nations issues*, ed. R. F. Devlin. Toronto: Emond Montgomery Publications Limited.

Monture-OKanee, Patricia, and Mary Ellen Turpel. 1992. Aboriginal peoples and Canadian criminal law: Rethinking justice. *University of British Columbia Law Review (Special Edition)* 239–77.

Moss, W. 1990. Indigenous self-government in Canada and sexual equality under the Indian Act. *Queen's Law Journal* 15:299–305.

Nahanee, T. 1992. Dancing with a gorilla: Aboriginal women and the charter. Paper presented to the Royal Commission on Aboriginal Peoples, Round Table on Justice Issues, Ottawa, November 25–27.

Native Women's Association of Canada. 1992. *Statement on the Canada package*. Ottawa: Native Women's Association of Canada.

Palys, T. 1993. Prospects for Aboriginal justice in Canada. Unpublished Manuscript.

Picard, A. 1992. Native women cling to charter: Won't trade rights for unity deal. Toronto: *Globe and Mail*, May 29.

Platiel, R. 1992. Aboriginal women divided on constitutional protection. Toronto: *Globe and Mail*, January 20.

Richstone, J. 1983. The Inuit and customary law: Constitutional perspectives. Paper presented at a conference sponsored by the Commission on Folk Law and Legal Pluralism, Vancouver, August 19–23.

Scott, S. 1992. The Native rights stuff. Montreal: *The Montreal Gazette*, Saturday, March 28, p. B5.

Turpel, Mary Ellen. 1989. Aboriginal peoples and the charter: Interpretative monopolies, cultural differences. *Canadian Human Rights Yearbook* 3.

Van Kirk, S. 1988. Women in between: Indian women in fur trade society in western Canada. Pp. 150–66 in *Out of the background: Readings on Canadian Native history,* ed. R. Fisher and K. Coates. Toronto: Copp Clark Pitman.

York, G. 1992. Support for deal growing among Native women. Toronto: *Globe and Mail*, October 9.

CHAPTER 11

ABORIGINAL SELF-GOVERNMENT
AND THE MÉTIS NATION

CLEM CHARTIER, MÉTIS SOCIETY OF SASKATCHEWAN
AND MÉTIS NATIONAL COUNCIL

When one hears the term *Aboriginal self-government,* images of Indians or Inuit usually come to mind. This is easy to understand, since over the past ten to fifteen years, the media has reported on treaty issues, the Indian Act, and land claims agreements involving the Indian Nations and Inuit Peoples. As well, most Canadians are aware of Indian reserves.

The concept of self-government or "Aboriginalness" is not as easily associated with the Métis. This is not surprising. With the exception of Alberta, there is no land base for Métis, and, except in the Northwest Territories, Métis are not included in the land claims process. Yet, as I will show in this chapter, self-government is as important for Métis as it is for other Aboriginal Peoples.

During the renewal of the Canadian Constitution in the 1980s and 1990s, Métis participated directly in negotiations for self-government. This helped to focus attention on Métis rights and aspirations. Internal reorganizing by Métis also fostered an understanding of what it means to be Métis, and a recognition that the Métis are one of the three Aboriginal Peoples within Canada. As a result, in recent years, Métis have been focusing increasing attention on self-government issues, and the Métis voice has become increasingly stronger.

There are, however, many obstacles. In the absence of a federal statute dealing with the Métis, Métis political structures have emerged primarily on the basis of provincial legislation and policy. Thus programs and services have depended upon the priorities and resources of provincial governments. Nevertheless, the Métis identify themselves as a nation and have established a national organization—the Métis National Council—to represent their interests. But, as I describe below, the path to self-determination has been a difficult one.

WHO ARE THE MÉTIS?

Since the birth of the Métis Nation, confusion has surrounded us, not just with respect to self-government or rights, but with respect to the very identity of the Métis. Because of the dispossession of Métis, and the subsequent outlawing of the Métis way of life, our lives were seriously disrupted. Many communities disintegrated, which led to severe social and economic problems. Although these problems had the effect of suppressing Métis nationhood for a time, our pride and dignity in being Métis was never destroyed.

Faced with impoverished living conditions for our people, and virtually no resources, Métis political organizations have always struggled to overcome hardships. The challenges have been continually increasing. Our people, however, were not the only ones who faced such adversity.

When hundreds of Indian people lost their Indian status and treaty rights—becoming "non-status Indians"—during the 1960s and 1970s, many of these Indian people joined Métis organizations. Perhaps they did so because both groups faced similar economic, social, and political conditions. Because of that relationship, the terms Métis and non-status Indian were used interchangeably for many years.

The Canadian Constitution was patriated in 1982.[1] As a result, the "existing aboriginal and treaty rights" of the "Indian, Inuit and Metis peoples of Canada" were recognized, and provisions required Canada to negotiate with the Aboriginal Peoples about Aboriginal rights. We were convinced that it was the time to assert our rights as a Métis Nation. Indeed, it became abundantly clear that the Métis Nation needed to regroup as a single entity to advance our position vis-à-vis Métis rights. The two cornerstones of these rights were, and remain, a Métis land base and self-government.

While it must be acknowledged that there are so-called mixed-blood people throughout Canada, and, in fact, throughout the whole of the Western hemisphere, the Métis are the only "mixed-blood" people who emerged as a separate and identifiable Aboriginal People or Nation. The emergence of Métis as a distinct Aboriginal People is an important element in addressing the inherent right of self-government. In the final analysis, it is a community of individuals, not isolated individuals, that possesses the right to be self-governing.

Support for the proposition that the Métis are indeed a Nation or People is found in an opinion of the International Court of Justice. It was stated (quoted in Green 1970/71) that:

A group of persons living in a given country or locality, having a race, religion, language and traditions of their own and united by this identity of race, religion, language and traditions in a sentiment of solidarity, with a view to preserving their traditions, maintaining their form of worship, ensuring the instruction and upbringing of their children in accordance with the spirit and traditions of their race and rendering mutual assistance to each other [and their] existence . . . is a question of fact; it is not a question of law.

Further support that our people fit the definition of "people" or "nation" is based on the following criteria advanced by the International Commission of Jurists (Indian Law Resource Center 1984, p. 14):

1. A common history;
2. Racial or ethnic ties;
3. Cultural or linguistic ties;
4. Religious or ideological ties;
5. A common territory or geographic location;
6. A common economic base; and
7. A sufficient number of people.

While it is not within the scope of this chapter to deal with the economic and social history of the Métis, respected authorities have concluded that the Métis satisfy the above criteria. More importantly, the Métis National Council (1983a), in its pamphlet entitled *The Métis: A Western Canadian Phenomenon,* states:

The essence of Métis existence can best be described as Métis national-ism which embodies the political consciousness of that newly emerged community of aboriginal people. This political consciousness, which also found expression in cultural activities and values, was confined to a specific geographic area of North America. This geographic area, commonly referred to as the Métis Nation or Homeland, encompasses the Prairie Provinces, north-eastern British Columbia, part of the North-west Territories, northwestern Ontario and a portion of the northern United States.

This was further elaborated upon by the Métis National Council (1983b) in a brief presented to the Standing Senate Committee on Legal and Constitutional Affairs:

Outside of this historic Métis homeland, a Métis identity did not emerge with the result that to this day people of mixed ancestry in the Maritimes or the Yukon, for example, generally identify either as Indians or Whites. The point we wish to make is that, contrary to the assumptions of many, being Métis is not just a matter of being mixed-blood: if that was the case, many if not most Indians, both Status and Non-Status and indeed many white people would be Métis. They are not because they do not share our nationality which has been moulded by a common history, culture and political will. The Métis Nation is a historic national minority conceived and developed on the soil of Western Canada.

As expressed above, the Métis Nation or homeland includes a specific geographic area of North America, with the majority of the homeland falling in what is now known as western Canada. Over the past decade, in part because of the constitutional debates, we have been successful in promoting an understanding of our people, our homeland, and an awareness of what it is to be Métis. Despite this progress, however, we have not yet determined the exact number of our people.[2]

In order to assist governments and others to understand who we are, the Métis National Council (1983a) set out the following criteria:

1. The Métis are:
    *   an Aboriginal people distinct from Indian and Inuit;
    *   descendants of the historic Métis who evolved in what is now western Canada as a people with a common political will;
    *   descendants of those Aboriginal Peoples who have been absorbed by the historic Métis.
2. The Métis community comprises members of the above who share a common cultural identity and political will.

While these have been the criteria used during the constitutional processes, and for other general purposes, the Métis National Council, in October 1992, negotiated a draft Métis Nation Accord with federal, provincial, and territorial governments that set out the following criteria:

a) "Métis" means an Aboriginal person who self-identifies as Métis, who is distinct from Indian and Inuit and is a descendant of those Métis who received or were entitled to receive land grants and/or scrip under the provisions of the Manitoba Act, 1870, or the Dominion Lands Acts, as enacted from time to time.

b) "Métis Nation" means the community of Métis persons in subsection (a) and persons of Aboriginal descent who are accepted by that community.

The latter criterion was employed because it reflected continuing discussions among Métis since 1983. This group would form the nucleus for an enumeration and registry system that has been proposed by Métis.

CONSTITUTIONAL NEGOTIATIONS

The major turning point for the Métis Nation in its quest to have its rights recognized was the patriation of the Canadian Constitution in 1982. Because of substantial opposition by eight of the ten provinces, the federal government sought direct support for patriation from the Canadian public. The government also sought support from the Aboriginal Peoples. The government felt that Aboriginal support was necessary to enhance their position because of the special political, legal, and constitutional relationships that had developed through the colonization process.

In January 1981, the federal government received support from the Aboriginal Peoples by agreeing to entrench the Aboriginal and treaty rights of the Aboriginal Peoples in the Constitution. In exchange for Métis support, the government agreed to include a definition of Aboriginal Peoples that included the Métis, along with the Inuit and Indian peoples. While this development was of tremendous significance to the Métis, its impact was considerably diminished by subsequent events.

On April 24, 1981, the then-minister of justice, Jean Chretien, wrote to the Métis leadership that the federal government had concluded that Métis rights to land had been extinguished. Furthermore, we were advised that grants to conduct research on this issue were terminated. A legal opinion accompanying the letter, dealing with the specific case of Saskatchewan, stated:

As a result of the scrip program, which was authorized by Parliament, whatever aboriginal rights or title that the Métis might have had were extinguished.

The minister further stated that the government remained "very concerned about the social and economic conditions experienced by many Métis," and that "those problems would remain a focus of the Government's attention." Not surprisingly, this was the approach used by the federal government in relation to the Métis at the 1983 First Ministers Conference on Aboriginal Constitutional Matters.

Early in November 1981, in an attempt to reach consensus, first ministers agreed to constitutional changes that did not recognize Aboriginal rights. Subsequently, in November 1981, after considerable pressure, first ministers agreed to include "existing aboriginal and treaty rights" of the Indian, Inuit, and Métis peoples in section 35 of the Constitution. In addition, a commitment was made in section 37 to engage in a constitutional conference with the Aboriginal Peoples. These developments, and pressure from Métis, resulted in the minister of justice clarifying the federal position on the issue of Aboriginal rights and the constitutional process. In a December 1981 letter to the Métis, the minister wrote:

> I have, furthermore, stressed to you that land title does not exhaust the list of aboriginal rights which you may claim. It is therefore mistaken to say that to deny the validity of land claims is to deny you any and all rights. . . . Our final stance on these issues will be negotiated around the conference table.

As mentioned above, the federal thrust at the 1983 conference for Métis dealt primarily with the need to address the social and economic conditions facing our people. It is, however, interesting to note that the Métis, as represented at the 1983 conference by the Métis National Council, were able at the opening of the conference to add to the agenda an item dealing with a "land base for the Métis." Self-government was already on the agenda.

While there was limited success in resolving Métis issues at the 1983 conference, the commitment to hold three further conferences (held in 1984, 1985, and 1987) was considered a major breakthrough. The subsequent conferences enabled us to educate governments, and Canadians generally, on the Métis Nation and People. As well, although those conferences did not result in any amendments to the Constitution, discussions on self-government began to take place on a more serious basis. Those discussions included public government, a contingent right of self-government, and the inherent right of self-government.

The 1985 conference ended in failure. Several premiers said they lacked an understanding of what self-government would mean and they were unwilling to make any commitments before the implications were spelled out. As a result, a parallel tripartite process involving the federal government, the provinces, and mainly Métis and non-status Indian organizations was established. The purpose was to develop models of self-government that could be presented to premiers for discussion. Unfortunately, the process did not achieve any great measure of success, and the 1987 conference also ended in failure. Perhaps the outcome might have been different had the Aboriginal Peoples been willing to accept the entrenchment of a contingent right of self-government. However, unlike 1985, all of the Aboriginal national organizations agreed to nothing less than the entrenchment of the inherent right of self-government, something that the government parties would not agree to.

Following the failure of the 1987 conference (the last constitutionally guaranteed conference dealing with Aboriginal issues), the national focus shifted to Quebec. It was not until March 1992 that the Aboriginal Peoples were once again able to substantially participate in the constitutional debate.[3]

The inclusion of the Aboriginal Peoples in the 1992 constitutional discussions was an important and welcome development because there was a major push to deal with Quebec. That province virtually gave Canada an ultimatum—either make them full partners in the Constitution (based on a number of conditions), or they would hold a referendum to determine if there was enough support to separate from Canada. The danger for Aboriginal Peoples was that if we were excluded while Quebec was accommodated, we would again be isolated and our rights would not be dealt with seriously.

As it turned out, the outcome of that round of negotiations was successful for Quebec, the Aboriginal Peoples, and other provinces that were promoting their own interests. It was a truly multilateral process that covered a wide range of issues and rights.

The result of the 1992 process was the Charlottetown Accord. Amongst other things, it contained provisions that addressed the entrenchment of the inherent right of Aboriginal self-government (as one of the three orders of government in Canada). It also contained a commitment to negotiate the implementation of the right of self-government (including issues of jurisdiction, land and resources, and economic and fiscal arrangements). In addition, the Accord would have made clear that section 91(24) of the Constitution covered all Aboriginal Peoples, including Métis.

In order to agree to deal with section 91(24) and the Métis, two basic understandings had to be in place. Firstly, the federal government insisted that the provinces provide land required for the Métis Nation. Secondly, the federal government agreed it would not reduce funding and services to Indian peoples, and both the federal and provincial governments agreed they would not reduce funding or services to Métis.

As referred to earlier, the Métis Nation Accord provided a definition of Métis for the purposes of the Accord. Based on that definition, the Accord provided for an enumeration of the Métis Nation, and a national registry to be administered and maintained by the Métis Nation. The Accord restated the commitment to negotiate the implementation of self-government, but with the objective of concluding tripartite agreements that would spell out the relationships between the Métis Nation, Canada, and the provinces.

That the Métis Nation Accord addressed land and resources was considered a major breakthrough for the Métis Nation. The Accord stated:

> Within the context of self-government negotiations,
>
> a)   Canada and the Provinces agree, where appropriate, to provide access to lands and resources to Métis self-governing institutions;
> b)   Where land is to be provided, Canada and the Provinces, except Alberta, agree to make available their fair share of Crown lands for transfer to Métis self-governing institutions;
> c)   The value of the transfers and access referred to in this section shall be taken into account in self-government negotiations; and
> d)   Canada and the Provinces agree to enter into discussions with representatives of the Métis Nation on the establishment of a land negotiation process.
>
> Consistent with the above, it is acknowledged that Alberta has negotiated and transferred the fee simple in 1.28 million acres of land to the Métis in Alberta and has committed to spending $310 million over 17 years, pursuant to the Alberta-Métis Settlements Accord.

Two other sections of the Accord were also of great significance to the enhancement of Métis self-government. These had to do with the areas of devolution and transfer payments:

> In self-government negotiations, Canada and the Provinces will negotiate the transfer to Métis self-governing institutions the portion of aboriginal programs and services currently available to Métis. . . . Within the context of self-government negotiations,
>
> a)   Canada and the Provinces agree to provide Métis self-governing institutions with transfer payments to enable them to establish and deliver programs and services to Métis.
> b)   These transfer payments shall assist Métis self-governing institutions to establish similar types of programs and services as those enjoyed by other Aboriginal peoples.

As can well be imagined, after finally convincing the political leaders of the federal and provincial governments to recognize and entrench our rights in the Constitution and address others in a legally binding, justiciable, and enforceable Métis Nation Accord, the rejection of the Charlottetown Accord in the October 1992 national referendum was devastating to the Métis Nation.

WHAT NOW?

To many, Métis self-government is inconceivable, perhaps because we have been without a land base for the past century. Moreover, many Métis now live in urban areas or small rural communities, while still others live in northern communities under municipal government structures established by provinces. All that has kept the Métis united over the past century are the various political and cultural movements and organizations that have continued to exist.

Yet, there is an exception to the landlessness of the Métis. Eight Métis settlements were set aside by the province of Alberta in 1938. These communities currently exercise a degree of self-government based on provincial legislation.[4]

Because of these differences in circumstances, it is now widely accepted that our people will be forging ahead with self-government and self-governing institutions both on and off a land base. It must be pointed out, however, that while self-government is possible off a land base, many members of the Métis Nation will not be satisfied with this approach. Many of our people want to acquire a land and resource base upon which they can continue to exist and flourish as a distinct people.

Métis self-government would not be without problems for our people and Canadians generally. To begin with, many of our people suffer the consequences of colonization; they have become dependent on the Canadian state.[5] It is clear that more education and community development will have to take place in order to continue working on the process of decolonization. Additionally, we need to continue to educate the general public about who we are—as a nation, a culture, and a people with rights. Therefore, it is critical that members of our nation contribute through various media, including writing, videos, art, and poetry. It is especially important that our people increase the volume of written material about our history, culture, way of life, aspirations, and rights.

In the absence of the constitutional negotiations process, and faced with the defeat of the Charlottetown Accord, there does not appear to be much immediate hope for Métis self-government. Yet, a number of avenues for pursuing self-government remain open. One of these is the tripartite self-government negotiations process. This was certainly the signal that was given our people by the federal government. In May 1993, the Prime Minister wrote:

> In spite of the outcome of the October 26 Referendum, which did not provide sufficient basis to proceed with constitutional reform as proposed, it remains that provincial and federal governments and Métis people must work cooperatively to achieve self-sufficiency and self-reliance for Métis. . . . To this end, the federal government is participating in tripartite self-government discussions with the Métis National Council's affiliates in four provinces—Manitoba, Alberta, Saskatchewan and Ontario. Exploratory discussions have also begun with Métis representatives in British Columbia which may lead to formal tripartite discussions. Where provinces are prepared to initiate and lead tripartite self-government discussions with the Métis, the federal government will be full partners at the table. . . . The federal government is prepared to discuss land in tripartite negotiations where it will contribute to economic development or cultural initiatives.

The Métis living in the Northwest Territories are not mentioned in the Prime Minister's letter. They are engaged in a comprehensive land claims process, along with the Dene Nation, although many are now pushing for a distinct and separate Métis land claims settlement. Assuming that the outcome of the negotiations results in an agreement or agreements, they would find constitutional protection in section 35(3), since it provides that land claims agreements are deemed to be treaties for the purposes of section 35(1). If the agreements contain self-government provisions, they become protected as treaty rights.

Métis who are members of the Métis settlements in Alberta are also not mentioned in the Prime Minister's statement. Both the Métis settlements' leaders and the provincial government have attempted to entrench the Métis settlements in the Alberta Act through section 43 of the Constitution Act 1982. In order to effect such a constitutional change (where it only affects one or more provinces but not all of them), the cooperation of the federal parliament is necessary. However, the federal government refuses to introduce the necessary resolution in the House of Commons, because it maintains that section 43 does not cover the Alberta Métis situation.[6] If there is a change of policy at the federal level, section 43 could be used to bring about constitutional changes that would recognize self-government.

If the section 43 approach is adopted for the Alberta situation, that same avenue could be used to address the rights of the Métis Nation as a whole (as reflected in the Métis Nation Accord) or, alternatively, constitutional changes could be introduced on a province-by-province basis. This represents a further avenue for the Métis People. For example, the Métis within Saskatchewan could have their rights accommodated through an amendment to the Saskatchewan Act, which, like the Alberta Act, is part of the Canadian Constitution.

Given the current reluctance on the part of the federal government to address constitutional issues, a further strategy involves the Métis National Council attempting to keep the Métis Nation Accord alive by converting it into a non-constitutionally based tripartite self-government agreement. Accordingly, all references to constitutional amendments would be deleted, while the substance of the Accord, such as the enumeration, land claims process, self-government provisions, transfer payments, and devolution of programs and services, would remain in place. This conversion enhances the tripartite processes already under way at the provincial level, while continuing to provide a nationally based, coordinated approach to Métis self-government.

As it now stands, each of the Métis organizations engaged in the tripartite process has a separate agreement and process. In the case of the Métis Society of Saskatchewan, for example, a five-year agreement was entered into on February 18, 1993 (after having been discontinued in 1987). The Métis Society identified the following priority agenda items for year one: Métis self-management structures; economic development and housing; land and resources; a Métis data base, enumeration and registry system; education, training, and employment; social services and justice issues; and health services.

Seven sub-committees have been established. They are responsible for identifying:

1. Program, service, and policy needs relevant to the Métis;
2. Fiscal and human resources dedicated to the respective agenda topics;
3. Required organizational structures (including where existing Métis structures can be used for implementation and the jurisdictional issues involved); and
4. Legislative adjustments required to devolve authority to Métis self-governing institutions.

Given the federal government's continuing position on Métis Aboriginal title and rights to land, another avenue open to Métis is to pursue our rights through the courts. The Manitoba Métis Federation, for example, is currently proceeding to trial seeking a judicial determination that their land rights are still in existence. Their action is based on the Manitoba Act, 1870, which is part of the Constitution of Canada. For the Métis in the rest of the homeland, any court action would have to be brought under the Dominion Lands Act. If actions under these provisions are successfully concluded, our people will possess "existing" Aboriginal rights to land under section 35(1) of the Constitution Act 1982. If that were to be the case, then access to the comprehensive claims process should be provided, and the potential for dealing with self-government under the claims process would be a distinct possibility.

Alternatively, the Métis Nation, or provincial affiliates of the Métis National Council, or a Métis community, could decide to unilaterally exercise the inherent right of self-government on the basis of section 35(1) of the Constitution, by passing Métis legislation. For example, a Métis Hunting Act could be adopted that provides for hunting seasons and a licensing/enforcement system. Hypothetically, when a Métis hunting law conflicted with provincial law, the Métis person exercising his or her right would be prosecuted by the province. The judicial system would then have to decide whether the Métis law is a valid exercise of self-government, thus overriding the provincial legislation.

This sort of legislative action by the Métis is not as remote as some may think. At the time of this writing, members of the Métis Nation are engaged in internal rebuilding and restructuring processes on the basis of Métis self-determination. In Saskatchewan, the Métis Society of Saskatchewan has embarked on a five-year self-government restructuring process, aimed at moving from a non-profit corporation to a duly mandated Métis government. This could occur either by virtue of provincial or federal enabling legislation or by self-declaration.

The current structure of the Métis Society has already adopted a skeletal framework for self-government. The leaders of the political arm of the Métis Society are elected on the basis of one person one vote, with ballot boxes in each of our community-based units. The elections take place every three years. Métis sixteen years of age and over, who want to participate, have the right to seek office and to cast ballots. Programs and services currently provided by the Métis Society are administered through semi-autonomous affiliated institutions that have their own boards of directors. Those affiliated institutions have to be expanded. This may be possible through the tripartite process, since that process is viewed as complementary to the internal developments.

While planning the implementation of Métis self-government within Saskatchewan is in its formative stages and extensive consultation with the Métis communities is currently under way, there have been indications that some form of Métis legislative assembly should be created. Once that occurs, it is conceivable that Métis legislation would be adopted, perhaps even where it conflicts with provincial and federal laws (as in the above situation concerning Métis hunting).

At the Métis Nation level, the Métis National Council, the sole and legitimate representative of the Métis People, has also begun a process of internal self-government implementation. At its Métis National Assembly in February 1993, a Constitution commission, composed of elders and senators of provincial/territorial member organizations was established. That action was taken in response to failed attempts since 1988 to restructure the Métis National Council. As well, since its creation in March 1983, there has not been a full-time elected leader of the Métis National Council. However, with the growing desire by our people to exercise the right of self-determination, the continuing frustrations and failures of the constitutional process, and exclusion from land claims and self-government processes at the federal level, the leadership of the Métis Nation decided it is time for action. Thus, the Constitution Commission will be presenting its report and recommendations to the Métis National Assembly in late 1994.

As an interim measure, the Métis National Council has moved ahead with a cabinet system. Within that system, each of the presidents of the member organizations, as well as the president of the Métis National Council of Women, are responsible for several portfolios. While not yet determined, one of the potential outcomes could be the establishment of a Métis parliament situated at Batoche, the site of the last armed conflict between the Métis and the government of Canada. If that does occur, the Métis parliament could begin enacting Métis legislation.

Finally, the February 1993 Métis National Assembly also decided to pursue Métis rights through more active involvement at the international level. One of the first orders of business is to formalize a relationship with those members of the Métis Nation who live south of the border between Canada and the United States. As a first step in becoming part of the international community of nations and peoples, the Métis Nation (International) will seek consultative status as a non-governmental organization with the Economic and Social Council of the United Nations. Further efforts will be taken at a later stage to enhance this relationship. To help pursue those developments, the Métis National Assembly has appointed an ambassador to deal with international matters.

A significant impediment to Métis self-government is the confusion over which level of government has the legislative jurisdiction to deal with the Métis Nation. By virtue of section 91(24) of the Constitution Act 1867, the federal government has jurisdiction with respect to "Indians, and lands reserved for the Indians." In 1939, the Supreme Court of Canada concluded that Inuit were Indians under section 91 (24).[7] The only remaining issue is whether Métis, as the third Aboriginal People of Canada, also fall within the generic meaning of the term Indian as used in 91(24).

"Indian" in the Constitution Act 1867 has a different meaning from "Indian" in the Indian Act and in section 35 of the Constitution Act 1982. While Inuit are Indians for the purposes of section 91(24), they are not Indians as defined by the Indian Act, nor are they Indians under section 35(2). In the same way, while Métis are not Indians as defined in the Indian Act, this does not mean that Métis are not included in the term Indian in section 91(24). This view is held by the Métis Nation, as well as the provinces within which the Métis homeland falls.

The federal government has taken the position that Métis are not included under section 91(24), and, therefore, are under provincial jurisdiction. This interpretation places the members of the Métis Nation at a disadvantage, because many federal services and programs are denied the Métis, as are the current federal/Aboriginal self-government negotiations that will subsequently be ratified and implemented through federal legislation.[8]

While the province of Alberta passed specific legislation dealing with the Métis in 1938, and has done so on other occasions, it is by no means certain that other provinces will do likewise. In the absence of either level of government passing legislation dealing with Métis self-government, our people will remain within a "jurisdictional limbo."

CONCLUSION

One of the major impediments to self-government for the Métis is the lack of a discrete land base, and lack of access to lands and resources. Unfortunately, much of the general public can only associate self-government with residence on land holdings—that is to say, reserves. For the public, if Aboriginals stay on their land, there is no objection to how the land is used or how affairs are conducted. On the other hand, if someone wants to live in a non-Aboriginal community, the public expects they will abide by the rules and customs of the so-called dominant society.

While most Métis want a land and resource base, there is a continuing denial of access to the land claims processes. The federal government maintains that Métis rights to land have been extinguished through the land grant and scrip processes implemented during the late 1800s and early 1900s. The Métis of the Northwest Territories are the exceptions to this, and they are involved in the land claims process with the Dene Nation.

Needless to say, the Métis do not agree that rights to land have been adequately dealt with. Although they have not been able to make progress to date in accessing the land claims processes, the Métis of Manitoba are engaged in the judicial process challenging the federal government's position that their land rights have been fully dealt with. In other parts of the Métis homeland, judicial action is also being considered as a necessary step to legitimate recognition of Aboriginal rights and title to land and resources.

When it comes to the Métis and self-government, there are many obstacles beyond those faced by the Indian nations and Inuit people. However, the Métis Nation has exhibited determination in the face of great odds over the past century, and the setbacks of the past two decades have not diminished our resolve to secure our rightful place within Canada. If anything, our resolve becomes greater and our determination to succeed grows stronger.

If we are to succeed, it is apparent that success will be determined by the distance we are prepared to go with our internal developments based on our right of self-determination.

NOTES

1　Enacted as Schedule B to the Canada Act 1982, (U.K.) 1982, c. 11. Section 35 entrenched Aboriginal rights and defined the Aboriginal Peoples, while section 37, since repealed, provided for constitutional conferences to further negotiate the rights of the Aboriginal Peoples.

2　Since 1983, Métis have been pushing for an enumeration and a registry so that accurate population figures could be established. Discussions are continuing.

3　At a meeting in Ottawa in March 1992, the province of Ontario insisted that Aboriginal representatives be included, as equals, in that particular round of constitutional negotiations. The federal and provincial governments agreed.

4　See Metis Settlements Act, Chapter M-14.3 1990.

5　For example, this was evident in the debate surrounding the referendum on the Charlottetown Accord. Because of the apprehensions and misrepresentations, many Métis were afraid to embrace self-government. They feared losing the various forms of social and financial assistance that were offered by provincial and federal governments.

6　It should be noted that an amendment entrenching bilingualism in New Brunswick was effected through section 43 in 1993.

7　See Re Eskimos, [1939] S.C.R. 104, 2 D.L.R. 417.

8　For further reading on this issue see Chartier (1978/79; 1988).

REFERENCES

Chartier, Clem. 1988. *In the best interest of the Métis child.* Saskatoon, SK: University of Saskatchewan, Native Law Centre.

————. 1978/79. "Indian": An analysis of the term as used in section 91(24) of the British North America Act, 1867. *Saskatchewan Law Review* 43:37.

Green, Leslie C. 1970/71. Canada's Indians: Federal policy, international and constitutional law. *Ottawa Law Review* 4:101.

Indian Law Resource Center. 1984. *Indian rights—human rights: Handbook for Indians on international human rights complaint procedures.* Washington, D.C.: Indian Law Resource Center.

Métis National Council. 1983a. *The Métis: A western Canadian phenomenon.* Ottawa: Métis National Council.

————. 1983b. *A brief to the standing senate committee on legal and constitutional affairs.* Ottawa: Métis National Council.

Métis National Council et al. 1992. *Métis Nation Accord.* Ottawa: Canadian Intergovernmental Conference Secretariat.

CHAPTER 12

ATTITUDES TOWARD ABORIGINAL PEOPLES AND ABORIGINAL SELF-GOVERNMENT IN CANADA

J. W. BERRY AND M. WELLS, QUEEN'S UNIVERSITY

Aboriginal Peoples in Canada are viewed by members of the larger society in a variety of ways, ranging from the classical image of "nobility," to the more contemporary associations with poverty and as "environmental stewards." This variability is important to understand. A number of observers of Aboriginal–non-Aboriginal relations in Canada have noted that the orientations of people in the larger society will be crucial to the realization of the goals of the Aboriginal Peoples (for example, Ponting and Gibbins 1981; Clark 1990).

The attitudes of the dominant society are important for several reasons, the main one being that political power (in terms of numbers, organization, funding, etc.) is not now completely in Aboriginal hands. Therefore, the successful attainment of the goals of the Aboriginal Peoples necessarily depends on the goodwill of the majority. To say this is not to deny the importance of other factors. Obviously, the motivation and ability of the Aboriginal Peoples will also play a role; however, these are already well developed. Therefore, the facilitating or inhibiting role of members of the larger society becomes centrally important.

A reading of Canadian history (for example, Patterson 1972; Jaenen 1976) could easily lead to despair about non-Aboriginal goodwill. The arrival of the Europeans, their assumption of superiority and control, the displacement of the Aboriginal Peoples, and, finally, the marginalization of Canada's First Peoples, all suggest that there can be little goodwill left. Nevertheless, research over the past decade (for example, Gibbins and Ponting 1978; CROP 1979; Berry 1981; Reid 1990) indicates that, at present, there is no substantial hostility toward the Aboriginal Peoples. Rather, there is a moderate degree of sympathy, accompanied by a moderate degree of apathy and ignorance.

The question naturally arises: Is the present level of non-Aboriginal goodwill sufficient to allow the Aboriginal Peoples to pursue their goals with support or, at least, without major hindrance or conflict? And if it is not, what can be done to enhance the level of goodwill so that Aboriginal goals might be attained? The purpose of this chapter is to outline some findings in the area of attitude research, and to assess their implications for the attainment of the goal of Aboriginal self-government.

THE NATURE OF ATTITUDES

In social psychology and sociology, the concept of "attitude" has a central place in understanding the social behavior of individuals and groups. Attitudes are orientations that we have toward any aspect of our lives—what we like to eat, the political parties we prefer, or the groups and individuals we bring into our social environment.

Attitudes incorporate three components:

1. COGNITIVE. This refers to what is believed or known about the object;
2. AFFECTIVE. This refers to what is felt, for or against, the object; and
3. BEHAVIORAL. This refers to what one does about, or to, the object.

Typically, attitude research assesses the evaluation of the object, that is, the "affective" component, or the extent to which a person likes or dislikes, accepts or rejects, the object. What is believed or known about the object is usually measured separately, often using the concept of "stereotype." What is done about the object can also be measured, using the concept of "discrimination." Of course, there is expected to be some consistency among the three components of attitudes, and this is usually the case. However, individuals do not always act out their beliefs and evaluations. For example, there may be constraints on action, such as laws, norms, and social obligations, that limit the consistency between behavior, belief, and evaluation.

There are three kinds of attitudes discussed in this chapter:

1. INTER-GROUP ATTITUDES. These attitudes are held by the larger society toward the Aboriginal Peoples. They provide an understanding of the extent to which the larger society evaluates the Aboriginal Peoples positively or negatively;
2. ACCULTURATION ATTITUDES. These indicate the way in which Aboriginal and non-Aboriginal groups would prefer to relate to each other, and the changes they are willing to accept as a result of contact; and
3. ATTITUDES TOWARD ABORIGINAL SELF-GOVERNMENT. These attitudes are more specific, since they relate to a particular policy option.

We will also examine the related issue of land claims.

INTER-GROUP ATTITUDES

What is known about non-Aboriginal attitudes toward Aboriginal Peoples? There are identifiable literatures in the fields of social psychology, sociology, anthropology, political science, and history. Our review of the literature, however, will be centered on the concepts of "attitude" and "stereotype," which are often considered to be at the core of inter-group relations. We may ask two questions that divide the general question posed earlier into more manageable units:

1. At the present time, in Canada, what is the level of tolerance for ethnic groups generally, and for the idea of cultural diversity? and
2. What are the specific stereotypes, attitudes, and prejudices held by non-Aboriginal peoples toward the Aboriginal Peoples?

1. GENERAL ETHNIC TOLERANCE IN CANADA

In an earlier national survey, Berry, Kalin, and Taylor (1977) concluded that the "climate for multiculturalism" was moderately good, there was reasonable tolerance for ethnic diversity, ethnocentrism was generally low, and respondents saw the consequences of multiculturalism to be an asset for Canada. This same conclusion can be drawn from a more recent survey conducted in 1991 (Berry and Kalin 1993).

These results do not indicate that Canadians have achieved a level of tolerance that is ideal. We have not. There are some groups of non-European origin, the Aboriginal Peoples among them, who receive low evaluations. Furthermore, among many Canadians, particularly those of low socio-economic status, those who are culturally isolated from the experience of diversity, and those who feel culturally or economically insecure, there are rather high levels of intolerance and prejudice. But the overall situation is encouraging and should provide a generally positive climate within which to foster improved relations between the Aboriginal Peoples and the larger society.

If the research had found a discouraging picture, then it would be hard to be optimistic about the successful pursuit of Aboriginal goals. Indeed, the danger of a backlash would have to be considered. However, the current situation is one in which general tolerance levels are sufficiently high to make the successful pursuit of Aboriginal aspirations possible.

2. ATTITUDES TOWARD ABORIGINAL PEOPLES—THE HISTORICAL
   CONTEXT

In this section, the literature pertaining to specific stereotypes and attitudes held by non-Aboriginal peoples toward Aboriginal Peoples, is surveyed.[1] However, it is only in the context of first contact that contemporary attitudes can be understood. The writings of Jaenen (1976), Bailey (1937), and Trigger (1976) are particularly important for describing this early context.

One famous dictum (Parkman 1899, p. 131) stated: "Spanish civilization crushed the Indian; English civilization scorned and neglected him; French civilization embraced and cherished him." In commenting on the validity of this dictum, Jaenen points out two facts. First, it was the Europeans who sailed to the Western Hemisphere, not the other way around. Moreover, Europeans assumed that Europe was the center of the world; the very claim of "discovery" is inherently ethnocentric. Secondly, if there were any real differences between the three groups of Europeans, it was not due to any absence of ethnocentrism, but to the specific nature of economic relations. As Jaenen (1976) argues, the agricultural English found it necessary to displace Aboriginal groups, while the French were dependent on the Aboriginal Peoples for safety, sustenance, and the pursuit of the fur trade. Relationships were largely symbiotic in Canada, where the French were trading, but involved subjugation in the United States, where the British were busy establishing colonial settlements (Trigger 1976).

Early French behavior was not free of ethnocentric values and discriminatory acts. Slavery was not uncommon. It was justified by the argument that "the imperfect must be subject to the perfect" (Jaenen 1976, p. 15), a view borrowed from the Spanish. In an analysis of this kind of rationale, Washburn (1959) has noted that there were numerous moral and legal justifications for acting toward the Aboriginal Peoples in a discriminatory fashion, including their supposed treachery and barbarism.

Other views held that the Aboriginal Peoples were "the living representation of ancient Europeans who were retarded in their development" (Jaenen 1976, p. 26). Views such as these implied that, with "tutelage" (Honigmann and Honigmann 1965) and care, the Aboriginal Peoples could realize their full potential. Contemporary descriptions portrayed the Aboriginal Peoples as "backward or less evolved, different in degree but not in kind . . . therefore capable with education and training to rise . . . to a status of equality with the ruling group" (Jaenen 1976, p. 153). In keeping with these attitudes, the French policy was based on the premise that the Aboriginal Peoples were capable of assimilation into French culture, and accordingly, they set up educational and religious programs for their inclusion. By 1685, "the missionaries had abandoned all hope of assimilating the Aboriginals and making French-men of them" (Jaenen 1976, p. 183).

The failure of the assimilation policy led to an opposite reaction—that of discrimination (Jaenen 1976). This approach, however, never became dominant, nor was it passed into official legislation. The net result appears to have been an attitude of tolerance, qualified by a degree of mystery about why the Aboriginal Peoples didn't adopt the "obviously" better way of the French.

Early British views are documented largely for the areas now within the United States. Contrary to Parkman's (1899) generalization, described earlier, attitudes toward the Iroquois Nations in the northern United States and southern Canada were generally positive. However, they must be examined in light of the military alliance that then existed between the British and the Iroquois.

The reciprocal attitudes (those held by Aboriginal Peoples toward the French and British), were far from positive. It may be surmised that the failure of the assimilation policy had to do, at least in part, with negative attitudes toward the French lifestyle, and possibly toward the French as a people. More specific statements of Aboriginal Peoples disapproving of intermarriage and the placing of Aboriginal children with French families can also be found (Jaenen 1976). Jaenen (1976, p. 19) notes that the Aboriginal Peoples of the seventeenth century:

> . . . seem to have stereotyped the Englishman as a farmer or town-dweller, whose activities gradually drove the original agriculturalists deeper into the hinterland, whereas the stereotype of the Frenchman was as a trader or soldier laden with baubles and brandy who asked only for furs and hospitality.

Yet, Aboriginal attitudes toward the French were not universally positive. Jaenen (1974) has documented Aboriginal views of the French as physically inferior, weak, soft, ugly, smelly, excessively hairy, frequently deformed, having low standards of morality, unappetizing food, inadequate clothing (especially for winter), poor social organization (evidenced by the existence of poverty and beggars), being inhospitable and parsimonious, and exhibiting rigidity, lack of flexibility, authoritarianism, and excessive concentration of power at the top of administrative pyramids.

Lurie (1959) and Trigger (1976) have both pointed out that Aboriginal responses to the presence of Europeans varied widely, depending upon the particular Aboriginal lifestyle, the particular European needs, and the interaction between them. Thus, general statements do not capture the nuances that characterized local contact situations.

3. CONTEMPORARY ATTITUDES TOWARD THE ABORIGINAL PEOPLES

With respect to contemporary views held by non-Aboriginal people, a first general point to be made is that a diverse object of attitude ("Aboriginal Peoples") is involved. This fact alone makes it difficult to say anything "in general" about the attitudes held by non-Aboriginal peoples, since attitudes vary as a function of specific subsets of the attitude object (Indian, Inuit, Métis; status, non-status; rural, reservation based, urban, etc.). Nevertheless, there appears to be some collectivity that is identifiable for most Canadians, which may serve as a generic attitude object. Colloquially, we speak of the Aboriginal People(s), Aboriginal rights, etc., suggesting the existence in the minds of Canadians of some general category of "Aboriginal Peoples."

A second general point is that there appears to be great diversity among the holders of attitudes. This fact also makes it difficult to say anything "in general" about non-Aboriginal attitudes. It is well documented that regional (Maritime, Quebec, southern Ontario, northern Ontario, Prairie, B.C., Yukon, NWT), ethnic (French, English), and socio-economic factors are associated with differences in attitudes. Nevertheless, it is possible to define, if only by the negative criterion of not being Aboriginal, a population of attitude holders.

As if to frustrate the first point, the literature says virtually nothing at all about attitudes toward Inuit or Métis peoples, as distinct from Indian peoples. This is a serious problem. The one study that did distinguish among the various groups (Berry et al. 1977), did so only at a cognitive level and not at an evaluative level. In this national study, Anglo-Celtic and French Canadians categorized various Aboriginal groups with themselves more often than they did "immigrant" ethnic groups. But Aboriginal groups were not categorized with themselves as often as members of their own "charter" groups (that is to say, Anglo-Celtic, or French Canadian).[2]

Even though there is some evidence that unique labels (Indian, Métis, "Eskimos") may sometimes be responded to distinctively, these findings suggest a collective view of ethnic categories that distinguishes minimally among Aboriginal groups, or, indeed, between Aboriginal and charter groups. The collective view does, however, distinguish between all peoples of long-standing residence in Canada and those whose presence has been felt only in the last century or so. If these results are accepted at face value, a generic group of "Aboriginal Peoples" can be identified.

There are contradictions in the research literature. On the one hand, there is now fairly consistent evidence of general sympathy, empathy, and goodwill toward the Aboriginal Peoples. This evidence comes from the Gibbins and Ponting survey (1976a; 1976b; 1978), the follow-up CROP survey (1979), the study by Frideres (1978), the Indian and Inuit Affairs overview (1980), and in national surveys reported by Reid (1990) and Berry and Kalin (1993). On the other hand, there is also evidence that the Aboriginal Peoples are being placed low in an affective hierarchy. This is suggested in the work of McDiarmid and Pratt (1971), Mackie (1974), Berry et al. (1977), Pineo (1977), and Price (1978).

In the Gibbins and Ponting national survey that examined "Indians" specifically, and in the partial replication conducted by CROP, general sympathy for Indians was high and general antagonism was largely absent. Concern for problems facing Indians was greater than, for example, concerns about the rights of women, but it was less than concern for inflation. The main problem facing Indians was considered to be "prejudice, discrimination, bigotry, racism" (39 percent), well above "poverty and unemployment" (26 percent), or "lack of education" (24 percent). Land claims were considered valid by 61 percent of respondents. Clearly this is a sympathetic, even empathetic, picture.

Similarly, Frideres (1978) found that prejudice toward Indians was relatively low in a survey in Alberta: 80 percent were considered to have low levels of prejudice toward Indians, 20 percent to have medium levels, and none to have high levels. The comparative figures were 65 percent, 34 percent, and 2 percent for attitudes toward French Canadians, and 21 percent, 77 percent, and 2 percent, for attitudes toward Asians.

In the more recent national survey by Reid (1990, p. 6), a generally positive view was presented:

> Canadians have positive feelings about this country's Aboriginal Peoples. They have a special respect for their culture and art, and even more importantly for Aboriginals' relationship with the land and the environment. Canadians feel a basic responsibility toward Aboriginal Canadians and would prefer their government's actions to reflect this feeling of responsibility more effectively. They believe that the approach Canadian governments have taken on Aboriginal affairs has done more harm than good insofar as they feel it has ghettoized Natives and made them too dependent on the government.

In contrast to this fairly positive view, the evidence from the work of Mackie (1974), conducted in Alberta, indicates that Indians are viewed as "lazy," "poor," "uneducated," "dirty," and that they "drink excessively" and are "oppressed." And out of twenty-four groups listed, the social distance of Aboriginal groups tended to be the greatest ("Eskimos"—twentieth, Métis—twenty-second, and Indians—twenty-third). Canadians were in first position, and the Hutterites were in twenty-fourth position. Similarly in the Berry et al. (1977) national survey, Canadian Indians were viewed as being low on scales of "hardworking," "clean," "similar to me," and "wealthy." And in a prestige ranking, Pineo (1977) found Canadian Indians to be ranked third from the bottom out of thirty-six groups. English Canadians were ranked in first place, and only "Coloureds" and "Negroes" were ranked lower than "Indians."

In a more recent survey (Berry and Kalin 1993), "Native Canadian Indians" were evaluated more highly than in these previous studies: of fourteen groups, they placed ninth, below all groups of European origin—such as British, French, Germans, Portuguese—and the Chinese, but above five groups of non-European origin, including, West Indian blacks and Indo-Pakistanis. Moreover, although ranked moderately low, their actual evaluations were positive and similar to those for Portuguese and Germans.

Finally, there is the evidence in the study by McDiarmid and Pratt (1971) of very negative stereotyping of Indians in school texts. Of the six groups examined, Indians were least favorably presented. They were described predominantly as "savage," "fierce," and "hostile," and seldom as "friendly" or "skilful." Happily, in a more recent analyses (Pratt 1983), Indians are presented far more positively: "massacre" and "savage" virtually disappeared from the texts.

What can be made of this apparently contradictory evidence? One interpretation might be that Canadians have unstable attitudes. There appears to be substantial goodwill, but also a large measure of uncertainty and ignorance (Bradford 1977).

Many observers have noted that the Aboriginal Peoples are not an integral part of Canadian society, rather, they are a people apart.[3] Thus, the possibility exists that being on the edge of Canadian society, Aboriginal Peoples are largely unknown and perhaps feared. Social psychological theory suggests that under conditions of ignorance and fear, negative attitudes predominate (Amir 1969; Berry et al. 1977).

Evidence for some relationship between familiarity and positive attitudes has been found by Berry et al. (1977) and Frideres (1978). In these studies, a significant positive correlation was found between self-rated familiarity with Indians and attitudes toward them. However, there are two sources of evidence that suggest knowledge, including contact or familiarity, may not be important in the distribution of attitudes toward Aboriginal people. Gibbins and Ponting (1978) found only a weak relationship between knowledge about Indians and attitudes toward them. Kalin and Berry (1982) found no relationship between the percentage of Indians in respondents' residential vicinity and attitudes toward them. These findings run counter to well-established trends in social psychology, where greater familiarity and contact are usually associated with more positive attitudes.

In terms of the fear factor, Berry et al. (1977) found no significant relationship between feelings of cultural and economic insecurity and attitudes toward Indians, although there was a relationship for some other groups. Frideres' (1978) study, found feelings of "actual competition" did not correlate with attitudes; however, "future competition" did correlate significantly and negatively. Thus, there is a possibility that it is uncertainty about the future, rather than any factor in the present situation, which may account for existing negative attitudes.

Another possibility is that there has been a real change over time toward more positive attitudes. The generally positive characterization by Reid (1990), and the substantial rise in relative acceptance between the 1974 and 1991 surveys (Berry et al. 1977; Berry and Kalin 1993), may signal a real improvement in the level of goodwill toward the Aboriginal Peoples by members of the larger society.

It is not known what accounts for the apparent moderate level of goodwill that presently exists. Contact and lack of fear do not seem to matter much, and level of education is generally not very important either.[4] Ethnicity appears to have some effect. Ponting and Gibbins (1981) suggest that French Canadians may be more positive in their attitudes toward Indians, but no difference between English and French Canadians was found by Berry et al. (1977) or by Berry and Kalin (1993). Moreover, the level of general prejudice is only minimally related to attitudes toward "Native Canadian Indians" in the Berry and Kalin (1993) study. This too is unusual in the social psychological literature. Thus, it appears there are gaps in our information about correlates and determinants of attitudes toward Aboriginal Peoples, gaps that only conjecture can fill until further research is conducted.

What may we conjecture? One possibility is that the existing goodwill is artifactual, that is, it is due to social desirability—to a current vogue to be in favor of Aboriginal Peoples and their aspirations. Another possibility is that the existing goodwill is real enough, and that it reflects the general tolerance for diversity noted earlier. Perhaps it is enhanced in the case of Aboriginal Peoples by a moral sense of the legitimacy of their aspirations or by a sense of commitment to them.

It is not possible to choose empirically between the two alternatives;

however, our hunch favors the latter. We have seen that in the perception of ethnic groups, Anglo-Celtic and French Canadians tended to include Aboriginal Peoples in their own cluster—this despite their saying negative ("dirty," "lazy," etc.) things about them. In addition, in the same survey (Berry et al. 1977), Indians were rated as high as English Canadians and French Canadians on the dimension "Canadian." Moreover, in a factor analysis of all the attitudinal data (Berry et al. 1977), of all the non-charter ethnic groups only Indians loaded on an attitude factor in the same (positive) direction as the two charter groups. These three indicators suggest that there is some bond, or some recognition of commonalty. While not clearly defined, much less proven, if it does exist, it might explain the general goodwill that is now evident.

ACCULTURATION ATTITUDES

Perhaps the most useful way to identify various orientations to acculturation is to note that two issues predominate in the daily life of most acculturating individuals in plural societies. One pertains to the maintenance and development of one's cultural distinctiveness—deciding whether or not one's cultural identity and customs are of value. The other involves the desirability of inter-group contact—deciding whether relations with other groups in the larger society are of value and ought to be sought out.

The two issues are essentially questions of values that can be responded to on a continuous scale, from positive to negative. However, for conceptual purposes, it is useful to see them as dichotomous ("yes" and "no") preferences. The model that results from this approach (Berry 1984) identifies four acculturation strategies:

1. Assimilation;
2. Integration;
3. Separation; and
4. Marginalization.

The assimilation option involves relinquishing one's cultural identity and moving into the larger society. This can take place by way of absorption of a non-dominant group into the larger society, or by way of the merging of many groups to form a new society, as in the "melting pot" concept.

The integration option involves the maintenance of the cultural integrity of the group, as well as movement by the group to become an integral part of a larger societal framework. In this model, many distinguishable cultural groups, all cooperating within a larger social system, result in a "mosaic" of the type that is officially promoted in Canada.

When there are no relations with the larger society, and this is accompanied by a maintenance of cultural identity and traditions, a further option is defined. Depending upon which group (the dominant or non-dominant) is in control, this option may take the form of segregation or separation. When the pattern is imposed by the dominant group, classic segregation, aimed at "keeping people in their place," appears. On the other hand, the maintenance of a traditional way of life, outside full participation in the larger society, may derive from a cultural group's desire to lead an independent existence, as in the case of separatist movements. Thus, segregation and separation differ primarily with respect to which group, or groups, has the power to determine the outcome.

Finally, there is the marginalization option. This is difficult to define precisely, because it is accompanied by a good deal of collective and individual confusion and anxiety. However, it is characterized by striking out against the larger society, and by feelings of alienation, loss of identity, and acculturative stress. The group loses cultural and psychological contact with traditions, but also with the larger society. When imposed by the larger society, it is tantamount to ethnocide. When stabilized in a non-dominant group, it constitutes the classical situation of marginality.

Attitudes toward these four alternative modes of acculturation have been assessed among many cultural groups in Canada (Berry et al. 1989), including a number of Aboriginal groups (Berry 1975). In all nine Aboriginal communities studied by Berry (1975) in the 1970s (James Bay Cree, Ojibway, Dene, and Tsimshian), the clear preference was to develop as Aboriginal Peoples while integrating with, and within, the larger Canadian society. This remained true for the three James Bay Cree communities, even after the construction of the James Bay hydroelectric project (Berry et al. 1982). For Cree and Ojibway communities, separation was the second preferred alternative, followed by assimilation. Marginalization was the least acceptable alternative. For the Dene and Tsimshan, however, assimilation and separation were reversed in order of preference.

In contrast, while there is evidence (Berry et al. 1977; Berry and Kalin 1993) that Canadians generally support integration, in that they have moderately high levels of acceptance of cultural diversity, when it comes to how they want the Aboriginal Peoples to relate to them, Euro-Canadians prefer assimilation over integration (Berry 1975). Thus, acculturation attitudes of Aboriginals and non-Aboriginals are not the same. The difference carries the message from the larger society that "we prefer you to give up being Aboriginal Peoples as the price of our acceptance of you." This negative message could create problems for the attainment of Aboriginal self-government.

ATTITUDES TOWARD ABORIGINAL SELF-GOVERNMENT

Earlier studies (for example, Gibbins and Ponting 1978) found a fairly high level of support for Aboriginal land claims and for various political tactics in their pursuit, such as lawsuits and protest marches. However, in the Reid (1990, pp. 6–7) survey, carried out shortly after the confrontation at Kanesatake, it is reported that:

> Canadians do not believe that aboriginals have any more inherent and natural right to self-government than any other group in Canada. However, they do recognize aboriginal Canadians' need for some control over their own destiny and express support for a significant degree of native self-government. At the same time, most Canadians feel that along with self-government comes self-responsibility and self-reliance; should native self-government become a reality, the public believes the federal government's financial obligations to aboriginal Canadians should diminish, if not disappear.

More specifically, with respect to land claims, Reid (1990, pp. 10–11) found that:

> The vast majority believe Canada has an obligation to honour treaties with aboriginals, even if these treaties were made 150 to 200 years ago. . . . Comprehensive land claims, wherein aboriginal groups want to reach settlements on land that was never turned over in a treaty, are much more controversial. . . . A bare majority of Canadians support the concept of comprehensive land claims while better than four in ten are opposed. . . . Only one in six Canadians believes that the total area natives historically occupied or used for hunting or fishing before white settlement, should be involved in land claim negotiations. Almost half of the general public would limit land claim negotiations to land reserves specified as part of treaty settlements. . . . Only about one in ten believe that none of the claims are legitimate and that there should be no new settlements. However, only one in four Canadians believes that aboriginal peoples should be fully compensated for all claims in land, money or both.

With respect to Aboriginal self-government, Reid (1990, pp. 12–13) found that:

> Almost all Canadians would grant at least some level of self-government to aboriginal peoples on reserve lands; however, very few would grant them complete sovereignty with Canadian federal and provincial governments having no authority on native lands. . . . Only in the area of environmental protection did a majority of Canadians surveyed prefer that aboriginal self-government be given significant powers, akin to those of a provincial government. . . . Four out of five Canadians believe that aboriginal self-government should be limited to reserves and aboriginal communities. . . . Almost all Canadians believe that aboriginals should have ownership of the natural resources—such as forestry, the fisheries and oil—on their lands.

With such large variations in attitudes toward Aboriginal self-government, it is important to know what might account for these variations and, using this knowledge, try to change attitudes to be more supportive of Aboriginal goals. Such a study was carried out by Wells and Berry (forthcoming).

In the Wells and Berry study, two factors were hypothesized to influence negative attitudes toward Aboriginal Peoples generally and toward Aboriginal self-government specifically:

1. A lack of knowledge about what is meant by, and included in, proposals for Aboriginal self-government; and
2. The sense of threat, fear, or insecurity generated by such a lack of knowledge.

Two groups of university students were presented with scales to assess their attitudes toward Aboriginals and their feelings of cultural security. In one group, a page of information about the meaning of Aboriginal self-government was presented between a pre-test and post-test of attitudes. This information was a "neutral" (neither positive nor negative) description of Aboriginal self-government. The other group was presented with information on an irrelevant topic.

Results showed that the two groups did not differ in their attitudes in the pre-test, but they did after the information was provided. The group given the information about self-government was significantly more positive than the group not given information. In both groups, feelings of cultural security were positively and significantly correlated with attitudes toward both Aboriginal Peoples generally and Aboriginal self-government. However, the correlations were larger in the informed group, as was the correlation between the two attitudes.

Wells and Berry concluded that by providing information about Aboriginal self-government, a more positive attitude toward self-government could be brought about. It was also concluded that feelings of cultural security play an important role in allowing individuals to accept self-government. Moreover, knowledge and security combine to contribute to even more positive attitudes.

It is apparent that the results of this study require replication in a more general sample of Canadians. If the same results were to be found, then there would be a sound rationale for engaging in a public education campaign to provide information about Aboriginal self-government. Such a campaign could reasonably be expected to increase acceptance of self-government in the larger society.

CONCLUSION

Aboriginal self-government is an important goal.[5] It is seen by many as an essential step in the Aboriginal Peoples taking control of institutions and social forces that have had a negative impact on their lives and communities (for example, Richardson 1989). "Owning" the problems, in the two senses of "owning up" (admitting to them) and "owning" (being responsible for) solutions to them, are more likely to come about with the attainment of self-government than with the continuation of present arrangements.

It follows that it is important to consider the factors that will influence the attainment of Aboriginal aspirations. In this regard, we have argued that the attitudes of Canadians toward the Aboriginal Peoples, and specific attitudes toward self-government, are of fundamental importance.

Despite an extensive literature, there is not a lot that we can claim to know about non-Aboriginal orientations toward Aboriginal Peoples in Canada. At a general level, there appears to be a moderately high level of acceptance of ethnic and cultural diversity, and a moderately high level of goodwill toward the Aboriginal Peoples. However, specific attitudes toward Indian, Métis, and Inuit peoples are not known at all well, and where there is information (almost entirely for Indians), few of the established variables in social psychology play a role. There is a good deal of uncertainty, ambivalence, and perhaps, even randomness in the existing information. Yet, there is some indication that Aboriginal Peoples occupy a "special status" in the attitudes of non-Aboriginal peoples.

The contrast (even conflict) in acculturation attitudes between the Aboriginal Peoples and the non-Aboriginal community is cause for some concern. While Aboriginal groups seek integration (participation in the larger society on their own cultural terms), non-Aboriginals around them indicate a preference for assimilation ("we can accept you, but only if you become like us"). This latter message denies cultural legitimacy.

While there is an obvious need to address the significant gaps in the current knowledge base, there is some evidence that the provision of information about the Aboriginal Peoples and about self-government can influence attitudes. While there are many factors to be considered in setting up self-government, the Aboriginal and non-Aboriginal leadership should not forget about the importance of informing the attitudes of the larger society.

NOTES

1   Readers are also referred to some of the most important reviews of the literature in this area (Indian and Inuit Affairs 1980; Valentine 1980; Berry 1981).

2   In a card-sorting task, Anglo-Celtic respondents (n = 661) placed the stimulus card "myself" with ethnic group stimulus cards with the following frequencies: English Canadian 75 percent of the time, French Canadian 48 percent, Québécois 37 percent, Canadian "Eskimo" 32 percent, and Metis 21 percent. Other ethnic groups included German (22 percent), Italian (19 percent), Ukrainian (17 percent), and Chinese (15 percent). A similar pattern emerged among French Canadian respondents (n = 398). When subjected to a multidimensional scaling procedure, a cluster around "myself" included the other charter groups and all three Aboriginal groups, but no other groups.

3   Berger (1977) has argued that Euro-Canadians have refused to take Aboriginal culture seriously. Stymeist (1975) has pointed out that the Aboriginal Peoples are regarded as outsiders—as a people who have no place in the community. Patterson (1972) has said that, from the point of view of the European, the Indian has become "irrelevant." Ponting and Gibbins (1980) have illustrated the way "out of irrelevance" in their overview of Indian affairs in Canada. Valentine (1980), too, has noted that Aboriginal societies, rather than being an integral part of Canadian society are a cluster of satellites, with the major issue between Aboriginal and non-Aboriginal peoples being at what level, and under what guarantees, their entry into the larger society might take place.

4   Berry et al. (1977), Gibbins and Ponting (1978), Fideres (1978), and Berry and Kalin (1993) all found no important relationships between education and attitudes toward Indians. This is also unusual in the social psychological literature.

5   Although it has not been the focus of the present discussion, attitudes also affect the establishment and maintenance of social and psychological health for Aboriginal Peoples (Berry and Hart Hansen 1985) and other acculturating groups (Beiser et al. 1989). When public attitudes are negative, the self-esteem of the acculturating group will be low and health problems will more likely arise (Berry 1992). When attitudes are positive, self-esteem will more likely be positive and well developed, and health problems will be less likely to appear.

REFERENCES

Amir, Y. 1969. Contact hypotheses in ethnic relations. *Psychological Bulletin* 71:319–41.

Bailey, A. G. 1937. *The conflict of European and eastern Algonkian cultures, Monograph Series No. 2*. St. John: New Brunswick Museum.

Beiser, M., C. Barwick, J. W. Berry, et al. 1989. *After the door has been opened: Mental health issues affecting immigrants and refugees*. Ottawa: Health and Welfare, and Multiculturalism and Citizenship.

Berger, T. 1977. *Northern frontier, northern homeland,* vol. 1. Ottawa: Supply and Services.

Berry, J. W. 1992. *Psychological and social health of Aboriginal peoples in Canada*. Ottawa: Royal Commission on Aboriginal Peoples.

———. 1984. Cultural relations in plural societies: Alternatives to segregation and their sociopsychological implications. In *Groups in contact,* ed. N. Miller and M. Brewer. New York: Academic Press.

———. 1981. Native peoples and the larger society. In *A Canadian social psychology of ethnic relations,* ed. R. C. Gardner and R. Kalin. Toronto: Methuen.

———. 1975. Amerindian attitudes toward assimilation: Multicultural policy and reality in Canada. *Journal of Institute of Social Research and Applied Anthropology* 1:47–58.

Berry, J. W., and J. P. Hart Hansen. 1985. Problems of family health in circumpolar regions. *Arctic Medical Research* 40:7–16.

Berry, J. W., and R. Kalin. 1993. Multicultural and ethnic attitudes in Canada: An overview of the 1991 national survey. Paper presented to the Canadian Psychological Association Annual Meetings. Montreal: unpublished.

Berry, J. W., R. Kalin, and D. Taylor. 1977. *Multiculturalism and ethnic attitudes in Canada*. Ottawa: Ministry of Supply and Services.

Berry, J. W., U. Kim, S. Power, M. Young, and M. Bujaki. 1989. Acculturation attitudes in plural societies. *Applied Psychology* 38:185–206.

Berry, J. W., R. M. Wintrob, P. S. Sindell, and T. Mawhinney. 1982. Psychological adaptation to culture change among the James Bay Cree. *Naturaliste Canadien* 109:965–75.

Bradford, J. 1977. *A preliminary survey of trends in non-Native attitudes toward*

Indian people. Ottawa: Department of Indian Affairs and Northern Development.

Clark, B. 1990. *Native liberty, crown sovereignty: The existing right of self-government in Canada.* Montreal & Kingston: McGill-Queen's University Press.

CROP. 1979. *A Study of attitudes toward Canadian Indians.* Ottawa: Department of Indian Affairs and Northern Development.

Frideres, J. 1978. British Canadian attitudes toward minority ethnic groups in Canada. *Ethnicity* 5:20–32.

Gibbins, R., and J. Rick Ponting. 1978. *Canadians' opinions and attitudes towards Indians and Indian issues: Findings of a national study.* Ottawa: Department of Indian Affairs and Northern Development.

———. 1976a. Public opinion and Canadian Indians: A preliminary probe. *Canadian Ethnic Studies* 8:1–17.

———. 1976b. Indians, and Indian issues: What do Canadians think? *Bulletin of the Canadian Association in Support of Native Peoples,* 38–43.

Honigmann, J. J., and I. Honigmann. 1965. *Eskimo townsmen.* Ottawa: Canadian Research Centre for Anthropology.

Indian Affairs and Northern Development. 1980. *An overview of some recent research on attitudes in Canada towards Indian people.* Ottawa: Department of Indian Affairs and Northern Development.

Indian and Inuit Affairs. 1980. *Recent trends in attitudes toward Indians.* Ottawa: Department of Indian Affairs and Northern Development.

Jaenen, C. 1976. *Friend and foe.* Toronto: McClelland and Stewart.

———. 1974. Amerindian views of French culture in the seventeenth century. *The Canadian Historical Review* 55:261–91.

Kalin, R., and J. W. Berry. 1982. Social ecology of ethnic attitudes in Canada. *Canadian Journal of Behaviourial Science* 14:97–109.

Lurie, N. 1959. Indian cultural adjustment to European civilization. In *Seventeenth century America,* ed. J. M. Smith. Chapel Hill: University of North Carolina Press.

McDiarmid, G., and D. Pratt. 1971. *Teaching prejudice.* Toronto: OISE.

Mackie, M. M. 1974. Ethnic stereotypes and prejudice: Alberta Indians, Hutterites and Ukrainians. *Canadian Ethnic Studies* 6:39–52.

Parkman, F. 1899. *The Jesuits in North America in the seventeenth century.* Toronto.

Patterson, E. P. 1972. *The Canadian Indian: A history since 1500.* Toronto: Collier-Macmillan.

Pineo, P. 1977. The social standing of ethnic and racial groupings. *Canadian Review of Sociology and Anthropology* 14:147–57.

Ponting, J. R., and R. Gibbins. 1981. English Canadians' and French Quebecers' reactions to contemporary Indian protest. *Canadian Review of Sociology and Anthropology* 18:222–38.

———. 1980. *Out of irrelevance: A socio-political introduction to Indian affairs in Canada.* Toronto: Butterworths.

Pratt, D. 1983. Prejudice, textbooks and multiculturalism: progress and problems. In *Multiculturalism in Canada,* ed. R. Samuda, J. W. Berry, and M. Laferrière. Toronto: Allyn & Bacon.

Price, J. A. 1978. Four degrees of current anti-Indian racism in Canada. Paper presented at the Canadian Ethnology Society Conference. London: unpublished.

Reid, A. 1990. *Canadians' views and attitudes regarding issues associated with Aboriginal peoples.* Vancouver: Angus Reid Group.

Richardson, B., ed. 1989. *Drumbeat: Anger and renewal in Indian country.* Toronto: Summerhill Press.

Stymeist, D. 1975. *Ethnics and Indians: Social relations in a northwestern Ontario town.* Toronto: Peter Martin.

Trigger, B. G. 1976. *The children of Aataentsic: A history of the Huron people to 1660.* Montreal and Kingston: McGill-Queen's University Press.

Valentine, V. F. 1980. Native peoples and Canadian society: A profile of issues and trends. In *Cultural boundaries and the cohesion of Canada,* R. Breton, J. Reitz, and V. Valentine. Montreal: The Institute for Research on Public Policy.

Washburn, W. E. 1959. The moral and legal justification for dispossessing the Indians. In *Seventeenth century America,* ed. J. M. Smith. Chapel Hill: University of North Carolina Press.

Wells, M., and J. W. Berry. Forthcoming. Attitudes toward Aboriginal self-government: The influence of knowledge, and cultural and economic security. *Canadian Journal of Native Studies,* in press.

PART IV

FUTURE PROSPECTS

CHAPTER 13

FUTURE PROSPECTS FOR
ABORIGINAL SELF-GOVERNMENT IN CANADA

JOHN H. HYLTON, HUMAN JUSTICE AND PUBLIC POLICY
ADVISOR AND CANADIAN MENTAL HEALTH ASSOCIATION

While the prospects for Aboriginal self-government in Canada are influenced by the long history of relations between the Canadian state and the Aboriginal Peoples, they are also influenced by a number of more contemporary developments. Since past relations, and the scars they have left, have been well documented in this volume and elsewhere, the focus of this concluding chapter is on these more recent developments, and, in particular, on what these developments can tell us about the future.

The picture that emerges from a canvassing of the Aboriginal policy terrain in Canada is by no means clear. While some recent events suggest that Canada may be on the verge of opening a new chapter in relations with the Aboriginal Peoples, others are a cause for grave concern. They suggest that change will not come quickly or without pain. How these conflicting trends will influence the course of future events remains to be seen; however, at the conclusion of the chapter, I provide some of my own predictions.

ON THE BRINK OF A NEW ERA?

A number of recent trends suggest that a new era in Canada's relations with the Aboriginal Peoples, based on self-government, may be on the horizon. Specifically, the following may be noted:

1. The Aboriginal Peoples in Canada are increasingly engaged in the practice of self-government in a wide variety of forms, and a number of Aboriginal Nations have already negotiated far-reaching self-government agreements;
2. There has been an expression of very considerable "political will" on the part of Canadian governments;
3. The current federal Liberal government appears more ready than the

previous administration to enter into new arrangements with the Aboriginal Peoples;

4. The final report of the Royal Commission on Aboriginal Peoples, expected within months of the publication of this volume, will almost certainly fuel the self-government momentum;

5. Public opinion appears supportive of a "new deal" for Canada's Aboriginal Peoples; and

6. The further implementation of self-governing arrangements would be consistent with practices that governments are adopting to cope with current political and fiscal realities in Canada and elsewhere.

These developments, which are discussed more fully below, suggest that major changes in Canada's approach to Aboriginal policy could well occur in the foreseeable future.

1. SELF-GOVERNMENT: A REALITY IN CANADA

It would be misleading to discuss self-government as something that could happen in the future when, in a number of important respects, it is already a reality in Canada. Today, in every province and territory of Canada, the Aboriginal Peoples are designing, implementing, and evaluating programs for their own communities. Moreover, they are developing democratic institutions and banding together to form local, regional, and national governments. While these activities are taking place within a context that could hardly be described as supportive, and while the pace of development is very uneven across the country, the fact remains that the Aboriginal Peoples in Canada are increasingly governing themselves.

Self-government finds many different expressions in Canada. As we have seen from the contributions to this volume, programs governed by the Aboriginal Peoples now cover virtually every conceivable field of human activity—justice services, education, community infrastructure, housing, health care, social services, sport and recreation, economic development, and many others. Moreover, no single approach to self-government can be observed. Rather, programs are proceeding under a wide variety of different administrative arrangements, ranging from initiatives undertaken independently by Aboriginal communities, to ones that are closely circumscribed by policies and administrative arrangements of Canadian governments.

Notably, new forms of self-governing arrangements have been emerging, particularly in the last decade. One such development has been the introduction of formal self-government agreements. These agreements, which involve Aboriginal Nations and Canadian governments, have been concluded with the James Bay Cree; with First Nations in the Yukon Territory; with the Aboriginal Peoples of the Northwest Territories in the context of the establishment of Nunavut; with the Sechelt Band; and elsewhere.

Self-government agreements are a particularly important development because they involve Canadian governments recognizing that the Aboriginal Peoples have the right to be self-governing. In referring to these agreements, and, in particular to the Cree-Naskapi (of Quebec) Act, and the Sechelt Indian Band Self-Government Act, the deputy minister of the federal Department of Justice has said:

> The bands concerned have been given a wide range of law-making powers, which permit them to exercise authority over numerous matters that directly affect them. The governing Acts take precedence over other federal laws in the case of conflict, and band laws similarly prevail over provincial laws that are inconsistent with them. These are extremely significant powers that extend beyond the range of most local governments in Canada. (Tait 1991, p. 45)

The direct involvement of the Aboriginal Peoples in a variety of self-governing arrangements has contributed significantly to the emergence of a strong Aboriginal leadership that was largely stifled under colonialist approaches to program design and delivery. While the general public has witnessed the more highly visible and vociferous Aboriginal political leadership at the provincial and federal levels, political leadership is only the tip of the iceberg. In addition, the Aboriginal leadership has been growing in the occupations and professions—bankers, lawyers, doctors, tradespeople, social workers, administrators, entrepreneurs, and the like.[1] While the numbers are nowhere near what they should be given the Aboriginal population in Canada, the fact of the matter is that the numbers have grown significantly.[2]

The pace of reforms, the growth in Aboriginal leadership, and increased communication and coordination among Aboriginal leaders from across the country has resulted in a significant momentum toward self-government. Moreover, the momentum is growing month by month, as new self-government programs continue to be put in place.

2. POLITICAL WILL[3]

Changes in political institutions are required to bring about self-government, and these changes depend on the exercise of political will. The political leadership in Canada has demonstrated considerably more political will on the question of self-government in recent years than it has in the past. A brief recounting of recent events will help to make this clear.

At the 1983 First Ministers Conference, little progress was made on the issue of Aboriginal rights. In 1987, during the Meech round of constitutional renewal, the Aboriginal Peoples were largely excluded from the process of constitutional renewal. In fact, it was largely because the Aboriginal Peoples were excluded, a fact vividly highlighted by Elijah Harper's actions in the Manitoba Legislature, that the Meech round failed. By 1992, however, all the premiers, the federal government, and the Aboriginal leadership of the country agreed that Aboriginal self-government should be entrenched in the Constitution.[4]

The 1992 agreement, embodied in the Charlottetown Accord, attested to unprecedented movement on the part of the political leadership of the country. Although the federal government under Kim Campbell showed signs of repudiating the agreement following the defeat of the Accord in a national referendum, provincial premiers have not only reiterated their support for Aboriginal self-government, they have agreed to lobby the federal government on the issue.[5]

While it is beyond the scope of this paper to analyze the reasons for the growing support of self-government among federal and provincial political leaders, several factors can be briefly mentioned here:

1. Landmark reports, such as the Penner report (Canada, House of Commons 1983), and the report of Manitoba's Aboriginal Justice Inquiry (Hamilton and Sinclair 1991), which were commissioned by federal and provincial governments, have strongly favored a new deal for the Aboriginal Peoples, based on self-government;

2. There have continued to be a litany of studies pointing out the desperate social and economic conditions faced by the Aboriginal Peoples in Canada, and many of these have resulted in the kind of front-page headlines that pressure political leaders to respond;[6]

3. There have been a number of landmark legal decisions that have supported Aboriginal treaty and self-government rights;[7]

4. Canada's treatment of the Aboriginal Peoples has increasingly come under international scrutiny, heightening pressure on the political leadership;[8]

5. The Aboriginal leadership has been increasingly effective in putting forward the case for Aboriginal self-government in the constitutional and other fora; and
6. As discussed more fully below, increasing public support for new political arrangements with the Aboriginal Peoples has been evident.

Spurred on by these developments, the politicians seem more prepared now than at any other time in our history to recognize Aboriginal self-government, and to enter into a new era of relations with the Aboriginal Peoples.

3. THE LIBERAL PLAN FOR CANADA[9]

In the months leading up to the federal election in October 1993, the Liberal party announced publicly that, if elected, it would recognize the inherent right of the Aboriginal Peoples to be self-governing.[10] This promise, and many others, were contained in the Liberal party's platform document (the "red book") that was released during the election campaign (Liberal Party of Canada 1993). In a separate chapter devoted to Aboriginal policy, the Liberal party promised:

1. To "act on the premise that the inherent right of self-government is an existing Aboriginal and treaty right" (p. 98);
2. That the Department of Indian Affairs would gradually be wound down;
3. Jurisdictional uncertainty with respect to the Métis and off-reserve Indians would be resolved with the provinces;
4. "A mutually acceptable process to interpret the treaties" would be developed (p. 98);
5. Social and economic conditions would be addressed;
6. Housing and infrastructure problems would be reviewed in a manner that emphasized "community control, local resources, and flexibility in design and labour requirements" (p. 100);
7. Education and training programs would be reformed to better equip the Aboriginal Peoples to participate in the Canadian labor force;
8. A comprehensive health policy would be developed and implemented;
9. Alternative justice systems for Aboriginal Peoples would be developed; and
10. An independent claims commission would be established to speed up resolution of land claims.

While these are clearly "election promises," and ambitious ones at that, it would be difficult to interpret them as hostile to the aspirations of the

Aboriginal Peoples. While circumstances may well intervene to interfere with the attainment of these goals, or at least their rapid attainment, the policy directions articulated in the Liberal platform certainly suggest that the current federal government is unlikely to be content with the status quo.

As this volume goes to press, the federal government announced a "pilot project" in Manitoba aimed at devolving responsibilities from the Department of Indian Affairs to the First Nations Peoples in that province. While details are not available, and may not become available for some time, the announcement confirms the Liberal party's intention to act on long-standing concerns about the role of the department. Unfortunately, as at this writing, it is not known whether the government's intention is to transfer only administrative responsibility for programs (as in the case of Pathways, health transfer agreements, and others), or real control over program design and allocation of funds.

4. THE ROYAL COMMISSION ON ABORIGINAL PEOPLES[11]

On April 23, 1991, in an address to an Aboriginal congress in Victoria, British Columbia, then-Prime Minister Brian Mulroney announced that the government would establish a Royal Commission on Aboriginal Peoples. The commission was given broad terms of reference. It was asked to delve into every aspect of Aboriginal life in Canada, to explore the relations between Aboriginal Peoples and the Canadian state, and to make recommendations about how the conditions faced by the Aboriginal Peoples could be improved.[12]

The establishment of a royal commission was, to some significant degree, a response to the Oka crisis and the failed Meech Lake Accord. It will be recalled that during the Meech round of constitutional discussions, national attention and sympathy was focused on the frustrations of Canada's Aboriginal Peoples when Elijah Harper withheld the unanimous consent that was required for the Manitoba Legislature to consider the resolution approving the Accord. This action symbolized for the country that major social, economic, and constitutional issues could not be effectively addressed without the full participation of the Aboriginal Peoples.

As at this writing, the royal commission is in the third year of its mandate. Its final report is expected later in 1994 or early in 1995. In advance of a final report, it may be premature to evaluate the impact the commission will have on Aboriginal policy in Canada. However, royal commission reports are notoriously "shelf documents," therefore, placing too much emphasis on the final product may not be warranted. Moreover, as was most vividly demonstrated in the case of the Berger inquiry into the

Mackenzie Valley pipeline (Indian Affairs and Northern Development 1976), commissions can and do achieve their objectives not only in their reports, but also in the processes they employ to complete their work. In this sense, a significant measure of what the royal commission can accomplish may already have been achieved.

The Royal Commission on Aboriginal Peoples has been a massive undertaking, even by Canadian standards. It is estimated that the price tag for the three and a half years or so of commission work will run to fifty million dollars or more (Roberts 1994). As a result, a plethora of activities have been undertaken that have served to raise the profile of Aboriginal policy issues with the country's leadership, as well as with the general public. Some of the most noteworthy accomplishments to date include the following:

1. Through four rounds of public hearings held in every part of the country, the commission provided an opportunity for hundreds of Aboriginal and non-Aboriginal leaders to present their views on current problems and future directions. Some one hundred thousand pages of written transcript have been amassed as a result;
2. An ambitious research program was initiated by the commission covering all aspects of Aboriginal affairs. This program has resulted in the preparation of literally hundreds of literature reviews and research documents;
3. A number of special consultations and round tables were convened by the commission to examine high-priority issues such as self-government; suicide; and health, justice, urban, and education issues;
4. An Intervenor Participation Program provided funds to assist interested Aboriginal and non-Aboriginal organizations to prepare briefs to the commission outlining their perspectives on key issues; and
5. The commission has issued numerous interim reports covering work in progress on a number of important subjects.

Together, these activities have raised expectations for change, and significantly improved the prospects that change will occur.

One commission report deserves special mention here because it deals directly with the question of self-government—*Partners in Confederation* (Royal Commission on Aboriginal Peoples 1993a). In a previous document (Royal Commission on Aboriginal Peoples 1992), the commission had outlined a number options for recognizing the right of Aboriginal Peoples to govern themselves in the Constitution; however, with the death of the Charlottetown Accord, it was evident that ways of recognizing this right that did not depend on constitutional reform also had to be considered.

In *Partners in Confederation*, the commission asserts that the Aboriginal Peoples have an inherent right to self-government, but that "it is open to question whether constitutional amendment is actually necessary to accommodate (this) . . . right" (p. v). Rather, the commission suggests that the right already exists in the Constitution by virtue of the fact that it is an existing right and therefore guaranteed by section 35(1) of the Constitution.[13] Although the historical and legal analysis provided by the commission focuses on Indian First Nations, the commission makes it clear that "a review of the history of Inuit and Metis as distinct Aboriginal peoples would lead to the same conclusions" (p. v).

Some Aboriginal leaders have expressed concerns that the commission's line of argument could be used as a justification for not amending the Constitution to recognize the inherent right to self-government. For present purposes, however, the significance of the commission's work lies in the fact that it does not dispute that there is an inherent right to self-government. On the contrary, it argues that this right does exist. It then proceeds to analyze various means for recognizing its existence. Such a position, taken by a royal commission, can only be seen as offering positive encouragement to the development of self-governing arrangements.

5. PUBLIC OPINION[14]

If there is any truth to the rumor that community leaders listen to their constituents, then public opinion presumably has some bearing on the positions of political leaders. This "theory" gains credibility when one remembers the inclination of all governments in Canada to commission public opinion polls on a regular basis. What, then, are these polls telling our leaders?

Although the Charlottetown Accord failed to win the support of the Canadian people, it appears this was not because of the provisions relating to Aboriginal policy. In fact, surveys conducted immediately following the referendum indicated that some 60 percent of Canadians supported the constitutional changes that had been proposed to deal with Aboriginal issues. Moreover, half of those questioned, notwithstanding the failure of the Accord, were in favor of the government giving a high priority to Aboriginal self-government (George 1992). The current level of public support for Aboriginal self-government is estimated to be between 65 percent and 85 percent (Roberts 1994).[15] These surveys confirm the findings of other studies that show the level of goodwill expressed by the public toward Aboriginal Peoples has improved.[16]

For those interested in shaping public opinion, studies also show that when information about self-government is provided, more positive attitudes result.[17]

6. PUBLIC POLICY AND COMMUNITY DEVELOPMENT[18]

In examining the prospects for Aboriginal self-government in Canada, it is also useful to review trends in government-community relations generally. In the last several decades, significant shifts have been occurring in the strategies adopted by governments to deal with community problems.[19] These broader trends will, I believe, influence future relations between Canadian governments and Aboriginal communities to a significant extent. In fact, these trends may have more bearing on future prospects for self-government than any decisions pertaining specifically to Aboriginal policy.

In the past, it was common for the public to look to professionals, experts, and government officials to "solve" their problems, and authorities believed that, in many instances, they had "the answers" to pressing community concerns. Governments declared wars on crime, wars on drugs, and wars on poverty. "Master plans" were developed for stimulating economic growth and creating jobs. Royal commissions told us how to "fix" what was ailing the country.

What these examples have in common is a centralist, "top-down" approach to addressing community concerns. In this model of planning, the experts in federal and provincial capitals not only defined the problems, but they told us how they should be resolved. In most instances, the community was not asked to participate in the development of solutions since, after all, that was the role of the experts. Rather, the community's role was to accept the solutions, and, of course, pay the bills.

While this traditional approach to governing is still widely employed, a lot has changed over the past several decades.[20] Increasingly, governments have had to face the fact that the best ideas, and the brightest experts, have not been able to solve many of the country's most daunting challenges. Moreover, the "top-down" approach has created many problems of its own. In particular, it has not been very effective in responding to the range of unique circumstances facing different regions of the country, and it has been very costly.

The Economic Council of Canada (ECC) has been one of a growing chorus of voices critical of the "top-down" approach to government policy development and service delivery. In an analysis of national economic development programs, the ECC has noted that community economic decline exists in all regions of Canada and in all industrialized countries.

Moreover, uneven patterns of unemployment and income have continued to exist, despite a long history of government policy measures designed to eliminate them. The ECC (1990, pp. 1–3) notes:

> Despite decades of intervention by government, these gaps in opportunity have not only persisted but, in many cases widened. . . . Top-down, bureaucracy driven plans for regional development have fallen into disrepute and policy makers know they need to consider new approaches.

In a similar vein, Wismer and Pell (1981) have referred to the growing pessimism about the effectiveness of centrally sponsored "solutions":

> At one time leaders told us that publicly sponsored economic development efforts were bringing us closer and closer to a national goal of full employment . . . these days we hear little about full employment. . . . The truth is that governments have no solutions for us.

While these examples deal with economic development, similar critiques have developed in relation to government social programs.

With respect to the cost of the "top-down" approach, the average taxpayer has come to question the value of many public expenditures. While most see an important role for government, it is a circumscribed role, in areas where the effectiveness of government programs can be clearly demonstrated. There is no appetite for growing deficits or for increased taxation to fund questionable government initiatives.

In part, the fiscal crisis faced by governments accounts for their interest in exploring new approaches to planning and service delivery. Continued expansion of government programs, or even the maintenance of key programs, has become increasingly difficult as government deficits have spiralled out of control. The difficulties encountered by governments in recessionary times are enormous. They often feel that their choices are not about whether to cut budgets, but about how much to cut and in what areas.

Public attitudes and expectations have also changed. In the face of economic de-industrialization, environmental degradation, loss of local control, social degradation, and the erosion of local identity, the public has a heightened interest in becoming involved in finding local solutions to local problems (Nozick 1992). Moreover, the community has become cynical about governments and about experts. They no longer believe that governments and experts will, or can, solve their problems. In fact, governments that claim to have "the solution" are no longer credible with the public.

In this environment, governments have become loathe to make independent decisions about new initiatives or program reductions. More and more, they have been asking communities to enter into a partnership, so that solutions can be developed on the basis of community input, or even community control. Governments recognize that the quality of decisions can be improved if there is community participation in the decision-making process. They have also seen the value of supporting communities to find their own unique solutions to pressing problems. And they have come to appreciate that they can distance themselves from unpopular decisions, if the community shares the responsibility for setting priorities and directions.

In the new approach, governments no longer see themselves as the only vehicle for the delivery of programs that are needed by the community. In fact, increasingly, powers and resources are being devolved to the community level, so that services can be designed and delivered by the communities themselves. Moreover, incentives are being created for communities to design more effective solutions and contain expenditures.

While the new approach implies significant new roles for communities, there are also far-reaching implications for governments. With communities taking increasing responsibility for services, governments are moving away from their traditional service delivery role. Instead, governments are concerning themselves with the challenge of facilitating and supporting community planning. In addition, they have recognized that there will continue to be an important need for central development of standards, auditing and evaluating of programs, and mechanisms for fair and equitable distribution of resources. In fact, these roles take on even greater importance in a decentralized service delivery structure.

As a result of the concerns about centralized approaches to addressing community problems, there has been increasing interest in revisiting community development strategies that were popular in the 1960s and 1970s. These approaches are based on a belief that new solutions will have to come from ordinary people in society. They involve the "empowerment of individuals and their communities to better meet their economic and social needs" (Benett 1992, p. 3). Originally, community organization and community development approaches were mostly employed to deal with social problems and social development issues at the community level. However, increasingly, it has been recognized that the same principles and approaches can be employed to address a variety of community economic concerns as well.

As Fairbairn et al. (1991, pp. 12–13) point out:

> Community development involves processes of education and empow-
> erment by which local people take control and responsibility for what
> used to be done to them . . . where other strategies of government and
> corporate business tend toward centralization, community development
> depends fundamentally on the greatest possible decentralization of
> power, knowledge, control, and wealth.

Similarly, Nozick (1992) has described the community development
process as involving three steps—self-awareness, community action, and
linking with others outside the community.

Whether the initiatives relate to social or economic concerns, or a
combination of the two, community development requires a measure of
community control. Nozick (1992, p. 99) has described what this community control means:

> Community control means that the decision-making process and organi-
> zational structures within a community are especially designed to give
> all members of the community the power and means to manage their own
> affairs. Since society is primarily organized on a top-down basis,
> community control will necessarily require a transformation from
> hierarchical to non-hierarchical structures so as to allow the maximum
> participation by community members in the decision making and
> development process.

I believe the implications of these trends for self-government are quite
clear. The principles underlying self-government and the principles of
community development are remarkably similar—devolving power from
central authorities, community involvement and control, bottom-up planning and priorization, etc. Therefore, it is highly likely that the trends in
government-community relations that I have referred to will offer positive
encouragement and support to self-governing arrangements.

BARRIERS TO CHANGE

While this discussion suggests there is reason for optimism about the future
of self-government in Canada, there is certainly no guarantee that progress
will be rapid or that change will come easily. On the contrary, there are a
number of significant barriers standing in the way of improved self-
governing arrangements. Among them:

1. Constitutional renewal is on the back burner and likely will remain there for the foreseeable future;
2. The country has not yet emerged from a deep recession, and budget deficits have created a mood that is hardly conducive to the establishment of new arrangements with the Aboriginal Peoples;
3. Many Aboriginal communities remain in the grip of desperate social problems wrought by a century of colonialism, and, as a result, they are ill-equipped to forge ahead quickly with any new arrangements that would place an increased burden of responsibility on already overtaxed community leaders;
4. In many respects "self-government" remains an illusive concept, subject to varying, sometimes contradictory, interpretations. Moreover, there are many "first order" questions about self-government that have not yet been satisfactorily resolved; and
5. There are still many leaders in the non-Aboriginal community who remain skeptical about self-government. They remain convinced that "tinkering" with Aboriginal policy will do just fine and that fundamental changes are not required.

These obstacles, which are discussed more fully below, will have to be overcome in order to make significant progress on self-government in the years ahead.

1. CONSTITUTIONAL RENEWAL[21]

What for a decade seemed to be a never-ending process of renewing the Constitution of Canada is now at a standstill. Moreover, the federal government has indicated that the Constitution will remain a low priority, at least during its current term (which expires in 1998).

Although it has been suggested that much progress can be made on self-government within the existing constitutional framework (Royal Commission 1993a), Aboriginal leaders have generally taken the view that self-government and other Aboriginal and treaty rights should be explicitly guaranteed in the supreme law of the land. Beyond the legal significance of entrenching rights, the process of coming to grips with a nation's constitution has important byproducts: it is a way of defining the national will, of reaching consensus, of compelling action, and of achieving closure. In the absence of the constitutional process, it is not immediately apparent how these important byproducts can be attained. Other options have been proposed, such as non-constitutional agreements, but these options have not yet been clearly defined, nor has there been an indication that all the key stakeholders will agree to participate in these alternative approaches.

Public opinion polls in Quebec suggest that the separatist forces are gaining in popularity. It appears likely that there will be a further referendum on the question of separation, and the Constitution may well have to be reopened to address national unity concerns that were left over after the demise of the Charlottetown Accord. Even if this occurs, however, it is by no means clear that there would be an opportunity to resolve pressing Aboriginal concerns.

2. THE PROBLEM OF RESTRAINT

So much has been written about deficits and public debt in Canada that the figures do not need to be repeated here. Regular updates are furnished by the media, and the news, it seems, is never good. Suffice it to say that Canadian governments have accumulated large debts, and despite a good deal of rhetoric on the subject, most Canadian governments are unable to reduce annual shortfalls, much less address their accumulated debt problem.

As a consequence of the public debt, and a recession from which the country has yet to emerge, the public policy agenda in Canada has been largely dominated by talk of jobs, free trade, monetary policy, interest rates, and the economy. Discussions of social programs, even in provinces with social democratic governments, are mostly concerned with "refining," "streamlining," "reforming," and "coordinating" programs so that they cost less. To say that this has led to public concern, particularly in the area of health reform, would be an understatement.

I have often mused that there is a direct, negative correlation between the depth of a government's financial woes and its creativity in overcoming its fiscal challenges. Perhaps this is because deficits and restraint become a too easy reason to dispense with new ideas. Perhaps it is because finance ministers and their officials often hold more sway in times of restraint, even though they may not be the best equipped to come up with creative alternatives. Or perhaps it is because the idea of cutting back something that is already in place becomes so ingrained in the psyche of the public and public administrators that there is no time or energy left over to think about building something new and better. Whatever the reasons, times of restraint do not generally give rise to creative new institutional arrangements.

There can be little doubt that proposals for new Aboriginal initiatives will not easily succeed in the current environment. Governments, and the public, may automatically assume that self-government requires more resources. Political leaders may have other, "more pressing," priorities. In other words, the very political will and public support discussed earlier may be jeopardized by fiscal realities and by those who claim that cutbacks are the way to the promised land.

Social activists have long argued that budget deficits are used as an excuse to downplay social programs by those who do not support these programs in the first instance. It is not at all difficult to envision similar dynamics coming into play in relation to self-governing arrangements.

3. THE NEED FOR HEALING[22]

Many Aboriginal communities in Canada, particularly those close to major population centers in Quebec, Ontario, Alberta, and British Columbia, are highly sophisticated and integrated social, economic, and political organizations that meet the needs of their members as well as or better than any communities in Canada. For a long time, they have been ready to take a more active role in determining their own future, but they have been frustrated by the slow pace of reform.

Many other communities, however, particularly those in the rural and northern regions of Canada, are isolated communities with economies based on welfare and too many desperate social problems to list. In some instances, these communities have lost the will to survive. In others, there is no hope. And too few leaders struggle to overcome the legacy of Canada's Aboriginal policies. In these communities, there is a diminished capacity to be self-governing.

Leaders of these communities often speak about the need for "healing." The Royal Commission (1993b, p. 51) has summed up the sentiment of many Aboriginal leaders in this way:

> Health is the core of the well-being that must lie at the centre of each healthy person and the vitality that must animate healthy communities and cultures. Where there is good health in this sense, it reverberates through every strand of life.

There is no one approach to healing,[23] but there are a number of principles that are widely accepted. These include:

1. Holistic approaches to problems and solutions;
2. Recognition of the interconnectedness of mind, body, spirit, and emotions;
3. Recognition of the interconnectedness of the individual, the family, the community, and the earth;
4. Valuing of traditional practices, medicines, and healers; and

5. Local control over "what counts" as health, wellness, and well-being.

Healing is vigorously debated among Aboriginal leaders. Must healing come before self-government? Will self-government lead to healing? Should healing and self-government proceed on "parallel tracks"? The answers to these questions often depend on the circumstances of particular communities. What is clear, however, is that healing is a priority for many Aboriginal communities, and without healing some communities cannot meaningfully determine their own futures. Even for those Aboriginal leaders who accord the pursuit of self-government the highest priority—and there are many—there is a recognition that self-governing arrangements are a beginning, not an end.

In the absence of healing on a community level, it will be difficult for many communities to carefully assess options for self-government and choose the option that is in the community's best long-term interests. Communities may feel the pressure to move ahead before they are ready, and they may agree to approaches that have not been carefully analyzed or tested. In these circumstances, there is a very real danger that Aboriginal communities will simply adopt the ineffective approaches to policy development and program delivery that characterize the existing system.[24] Since traditional Aboriginal approaches in health care, justice, child care, education, and many other areas have often proved to be more effective than the approaches of the dominant society (Hylton 1993b), this outcome would be most regrettable.

4. SELF-GOVERNMENT: MANY MEANINGS

In 1983, during the first ministers' meetings on the Constitution, a number of premiers refused to recognize the right to self-government until the concept was clearly defined. While this problem did not re-emerge as a stumbling block during the Canada round of constitutional discussions resulting in the Charlottetown Accord, the fact of the matter is that there remains considerable confusion about the term. Even among Aboriginal communities, the concept has a variety of meanings.

There is not one "Aboriginal people" in Canada, but some six hundred Aboriginal communities, many with distinct cultures, traditions, and languages. Each has different needs, different wants, different capacities, and different priorities. As a consequence, there are many different ideas about what self-government should accomplish in practice. The Royal Commission (1993a, p. 41) describes these variations in this way:

Self-government means different things to different Aboriginal groups. For some, it may mean reviving traditional governmental structures or adapting them for modern purposes. For others, it may mean creating entirely new structures or participating more actively in new or existing institutions of public government at the federal, provincial, regional or territorial levels. For certain groups, it may involve developing structures of public government that would include all the residents of a particular region or territory. For still other groups, it may mean greater control over the provision of governmental services such as education and health care. In discussing the implementation of self-government, it is important to remember that there is more than one way for the Aboriginal peoples to achieve the goal of greater autonomy and control over their lives. No single pattern or model can be adequate, given the great variety of aspirations and circumstances among Aboriginal peoples.

Thus, a singular approach to self-government involving the all-too-familiar centrally defined, top-down techniques of government institutions will not be very effective in achieving self-government, and this approach would almost certainly have destructive consequences in some communities. A more community-oriented, bottom-up approach will be required, but this represents a different way of doing business for most of the government agencies that will have a role in self-government arrangements.

Many questions about the implementation of self-government have yet to be resolved, and some of these are highly controversial. Many of these issues have been discussed in earlier chapters—financing arrangements, the Métis, institutional arrangements in urban communities, protection of the rights of women, off-reserve Indians, reconciling individual and collective rights, and sorting out jurisdictional disputes involving federal, provincial, and local governments. There are many others.

The further development of self-governing arrangements, therefore, will require continuing dialogue on the meaning of self-government, new approaches to government-community relations, and a concerted effort to resolve many outstanding issues related to the practical aspects of self-government implementation.

5. RESISTANCE TO CHANGE

Resistance to change manifests itself in many ways and for many different reasons. There are winners and losers whenever policy choices are made, and however dysfunctional the current institutional arrangements, there are many who benefit from them. These people will resist change, particularly change that has the potential to affect their personal security or status. These concerns are real, they are legitimate, and they must be addressed.

Whether personally affected or not, there are those who resist change for any reason. It is said that "we do not deal with change well"! Furthermore, there are those with racist beliefs who may resist any reforms they believe will benefit the Aboriginal Peoples. Still others may earnestly believe that the status quo, or some variation of it, can be made to work.

Attempts to avoid fundamental structural changes by "tinkering" with existing policies and programs have taken many forms over the years, but there are a few common types of initiatives that remain very much in vogue:

1. The adoption of affirmative-action hiring policies;
2. The establishment of specialized Aboriginal units, staffed by Aboriginal employees, within larger non-Aboriginal programs and agencies. (Perhaps the best known example of this approach is the Indian Special Constable Program established by the RCMP);
3. Promoting greater awareness among non-Aboriginal staff about Aboriginal "clients" through programs of cross-cultural awareness and training;
4. Allowing Aboriginal input into decision-making in non-Aboriginal programs. (For example, elders are consulted about the sentencing of offenders, the band council is consulted about the apprehension of a child, committees are established to provide community input into the work of non-Aboriginal agencies); and
5. Introducing traditional Aboriginal practices into non-Aboriginal programs. (Correctional institutions, for example, sometimes permit sweat lodges, sweet grass ceremonies, and the attendance of elders and spiritual leaders).

While an analysis of these types of initiatives is beyond the scope of this chapter, extensive evaluative research has been carried out.[25] Although some exceptions do exist, these types of approaches have generally met with very limited success. In isolated instances, some improvements in effectiveness and acceptance have been noted; however, on the whole, the gains have been modest. Furthermore, even with these types of initiatives, non-Aboriginal programs do not generally achieve the level of effectiveness or acceptance that these same programs enjoy in non-Aboriginal communities.

There have been remarkably few efforts reported in the literature to significantly modify the social programs or policies of the dominant society to better meet the needs of the Aboriginal Peoples. Rather, the programs and policies developed by the non-Aboriginal authorities are usually taken as a given. They are typically viewed by the dominant system as the best possible approach for both Aboriginal and non-Aboriginal clients. Various reform efforts, such as those described above, are then instituted to assist the Aboriginal Peoples to fit in with, accept, and adjust to the non-Aboriginal system. Ours is a history of attempts to tinker with the policies and programs of the dominant society, in the vain hopes that these systems could be made to work for the Aboriginal Peoples.

Even with an ambitious program of self-government, many Aboriginal people will continue to rely on the programs and services of the dominant society, at least in some instances. This may occur, for example, in providing services to Aboriginal people living in urban centers. It may be required in instances where specialized medical care, educational programs, or other specialized services are required. Similarly, Aboriginal governments and Aboriginal entrepreneurs will need to access capital through the financial institutions of the dominant society. There may be instances were the Canadian legal and court systems would be accessed. These are just a few examples. Therefore, if the Aboriginal Peoples are to be treated fairly and effectively, and if they are to enjoy the basic rights afforded to other Canadians, there will need to be continuing efforts to sensitize the programs and systems of the dominant society to their needs and aspirations.

These initiatives to sensitize dominant systems, however, ought not to be seen as a substitute for significant structural changes involving self-government. When they are proposed as the "solutions" to the economic and social problems facing the Aboriginal Peoples, or as an alternative to structural change, then these initiatives ought to be seen for what they all too often have been—a manifestation of resistance to change.

CONCLUSION

While there is no way of predicting the future with exactitude, it is evident from the foregoing discussion that there are many sound reasons to believe that the prospects for Aboriginal self-government are quite good in Canada. Self-government is already being practised, new self-governing arrangements are being implemented on a more or less continuous basis, there appears to be political will, the new federal government has indicated its support, court decisions are paving the way, public opinion is favorable, and the final report of the Royal Commission will add a positive boost.

Given the considerable momentum that has been building over the last decade and the high expectations that have been created among the Aboriginal Peoples, lack of meaningful progress on self-government poses real dangers for the country. The frustrations of the Aboriginal Peoples, which have built up over many years, have been held in check largely because of the promise of a better tomorrow. Therefore, if governments place roadblocks in the way of self-government, they do so at their peril. The results could well be a rejection of the political process by Aboriginal people, a breaking down of trust between Aboriginal and Canadian political leaders and organizations, and a resorting to other means, including civil disobedience, to bring about social change.[26]

Yet, even if governments do move forward, a long and winding road lies ahead. There are many questions about self-government that have to be addressed. Not all Aboriginal communities are well equipped to proceed with self-government; current systems, and those who run them, resist change; and the country remains in a desperate financial predicament that is stifling creative new solutions to the problems facing the nation.

That the constitutional renewal process is at a standstill will also have significant consequences for the manner in which self-government proceeds. In the absence of a national framework, one that is supported by all the key stakeholders, there is the very real likelihood that self-governing arrangements will evolve through numerous bilateral, tripartite, and multilateral agreements, each with a limited scope. Although progress can be made in this way, this is a cumbersome approach that will have a heavy cost in terms of complicated, time-consuming, and costly negotiations and subsequent administrative arrangements. Of greater concern, however, is the likelihood that the absence of a national framework will be used by some to justify maintaining existing policies that are manifestly inadequate.

It would be comforting to think that governments act out of a sense of moral obligation, because they are interested in justice or fairness, because they recognize the need to address historical wrongs, or even because there is a right way of doing things. While governments no doubt do act on the basis of this high moral ground from time to time, experience indicates they are more likely to act on the basis of pragmatic considerations.

In the case of self-government, governments could have acted on the basis of treaty and Aboriginal rights a long time ago. Regrettably, however, they did not. And, if the past is any indication, "rights" are unlikely to carry the day in government decision-making in the future, unless, of course, action on rights is forced upon governments by the courts. In this case, governments are always ready to put a magnanimous face on the actions they are forced to take.

Self-government may well be supported by governments for pragmatic reasons, however, and not only because it is the right, just, or fair policy for Canada. It is more likely that government support will be based on the realization that self-government represents the adoption of a community development approach to the problems experienced by Aboriginal communities. As such, relative to the "top-down" approaches of the past, self-government may be seen by governments as a more efficient and effective way to "do business" with Aboriginal communities. This approach would be consistent with larger trends in government-community relations— trends that have emerged because they assist governments to respond to the political and fiscal challenges they now face, and will continue to face, in the 1990s and beyond. It would not be the first time governments did the "right" thing for the "wrong" reasons.

Whether adopted for pragmatic purposes, or for other reasons, all the available evidence indicates that self-government will prove to be a public policy that is good, not only for the Aboriginal Peoples, but for all of Canada.

NOTES

1   In health care, for example, Longboat (1993) has reported that there were 16 Aboriginal physicians in Canada in 1983 and 51 in 1993, with an additional 21 in training. The Department of Indian Affairs and Northern Development (1992) recently reported that there were 21,442 registered Indians involved in post-secondary education in Canada in 1991–92, up from 60 in 1960.

2   The chapter in this volume by Hampton and Wolfson describes a post-secondary educational institution controlled by the Aboriginal Peoples. This type of facility is making an extraordinary contribution to the growth of Aboriginal leadership. There are many other examples.

3   Parts of this section are based on Hylton (1994).

4   Chartier's contribution to this volume provides a more detailed account of these events.

5   See Cox (1993).

6   A recent example is the series of tragic suicides and attempted suicides in Davis Inlet.

7   There are many examples. In the Sparrow case, for instance, the Royal Commission (1993a, p. 31) notes that the Supreme Court gives "constitutional protection to a range of special rights enjoyed by the Aboriginal peoples, shielding these rights from the adverse effects of legislation and other governmental acts, except where a rigorous standard of justice can be met."

8   One tangible example of the effects of this international scrutiny was the

federal government's decision to end discrimination against Aboriginal women under Bill C-31. See Jackson's chapter in this volume for further discussion.

9   This title is taken from the Liberal party's infamous red book—the platform document tabled during the federal election campaign. See Liberal Party of Canada (1993).

10 The July 28, 1993, *Ottawa Citizen,* for example, proclaimed "Liberals to recognize self-government right."

11 Parts of this discussion are adapted from Hylton (in press).

12 For a detailed presentation of the commission's terms of reference, see Royal Commission on Aboriginal Peoples (n.d.).

13 Section 35(1) reads: "The existing aboriginal and treaty rights of the aboriginal peoples of Canada are hereby recognized and affirmed."

14 Parts of this section are drawn from Hylton (1994).

15 Similarly, the Medical Services Division of Health and Welfare Canada (n.d.) reported that recent polls showed 53 percent of Canadians disapproved of budget cuts to Aboriginal programs, 49 percent supported full or significant Aboriginal control over health care, and 62 percent think that health care is an area where the Aboriginal Peoples should have full control or powers equal to provinces on their own lands.

16 I will not repeat the extensive review of many of these studies that has been provided by Berry and Wells in their contribution to this volume. While I have not conducted a systematic study, I believe that the treatment of Aboriginal issues by the popular press has also become significantly more sympathetic over the past decade. It is now commonplace, for example, for the media to discuss solutions as well as problems, and this often involves calls for changes to the current institutional arrangements. Whether the media's treatment has been influenced by changes in public opinion, or whether the media is helping to bring about changes in public attitudes is a matter for speculation. Perhaps the influences are running both ways. A systematic study of these trends would, I believe, be both interesting and worthwhile.

17 For example, see the chapter by Berry and Wells in this volume.

18 This discussion is a brief summary of a more detailed analysis of these trends published elsewhere (Hylton 1993b).

19 These trends have been the subject of extensive analysis. See for example Osborne and Gaebler (1993).

20 That old traditions die hard is evident in the recent example of the Liberal party's proposal to stimulate the economy through a national infrastructure program (Liberal Party of Canada 1993). During the federal election campaign, Preston Manning, the Reform party leader, likened the proposal to trying to start a 747 with a pen light battery.

21 See also Hylton (1993b).

22 Much of this section has been drawn from my experience in working with the

Northern Village of La Loche in northern Saskatchewan (Hylton 1993a).
23 For a further discussion of "healing" see Bopp (1985) and Hollow Water First Nation (1989; n.d.).
24 See La Prairie's and O'Neil and Postl's contributions to this volume for a discussion of these dangers in the justice and health systems respectively.
25 See, for example, VanDyke and Jamont (1980), Hamilton and Sinclair (1991), and Hylton (1992; 1994).
26 There is no useful purpose served by being alarmist about the potential for conflict; however, the fact of the matter is that incidents like Oka indicate what can happen when the process of meaningful dialogue breaks down. Moreover, Oka is only the best known recent example of bitter struggles over self-government issues. There have been many others—James Bay, Nass River, Lubicon Lake, Anishinabe Park, Old Man River, Restigouche, and Goose Bay, to name a few.

REFERENCES

Benett, Edward. 1992. Community-based economic development: A strategy for primary prevention, *Canadian Journal of Community Mental Health* 11(2):11–33.

Bopp, Michael. 1985. *Developing healthy communities: Fundamental strategies for health promotion*. Lethbridge: Four Worlds Development Project, University of Lethbridge.

Canada, House of Commons. 1983. *Indian self-government in Canada*. Ottawa: Supply and Services.

Cox, Kevin. 1993. Premiers agree on bid to restart Native-rule talks. Toronto: *Globe and Mail*, August 28.

Department of Indian Affairs and Northern Development. 1992. *Basic departmental data 1992*. Ottawa: Government of Canada.

———. 1976. *Mackenzie Valley pipeline inquiry*. Ottawa: Indian and Northern Affairs.

Economic Council of Canada. 1990. *From the bottom up: The community economic development approach*. Ottawa: Economic Council of Canada.

Fairbairn, Brett, June Bold, Murray Fulton, Lou Hammond Ketilson, Daniel Ish. 1991. *Co-operatives and community development: Economics in social perspective*. Saskatoon: University of Saskatchewan.

George, Ron. 1992. Poll says majority favour native rights. Regina: *Leader-Post*, December 1.

Hamilton, A. C., and M. Sinclair. 1991. *Report of the Aboriginal justice inquiry of Manitoba*. Winnipeg: Government of Manitoba.

Hollow Water First Nation. 1989. *Community holistic circle healing centre: History*. Hollow Water, MB: Hollow Water First Nation.

———. n.d. *Community holistic circle healing: 13 steps*. Hollow Water, MB: Hollow Water First Nation.

Hylton, John H. In press. Social policy and Canada's aboriginal peoples: The need for fundamental reforms. In *Justice and reform,* ed. Kayleen M. Hazelhurst. Queensland, Australia: University of Queensland Press.

―――. 1994. Financing Aboriginal justice systems. Pp. 150–70 in *Continuing Poundmaker & Riel's quest,* ed. Richard Gosse, James Youngblood Henderson, and Roger Carter. Saskatoon, SK: Purich.

―――. 1993a. *The La Loche report.* Regina: Saskatchewan Municipal Government.

―――. 1993b. Social policy and Aboriginal self-government. *Policy Options* 14(3):24–27.

―――. 1992. *Social problems, social programs, and the human services: Towards the development of a research program for the Royal Commission on Aboriginal Peoples.* Ottawa: Royal Commission.

Liberal Party of Canada. 1993. *Creating opportunity: The Liberal plan for Canada.* Ottawa: Liberal Party of Canada.

Longboat, Dianne. 1993. Pathways to a dream: Professional education in the health sciences. Pp. 171–213 in *The path to healing,* Royal Commission on Aboriginal Peoples. Ottawa: Royal Commission on Aboriginal Peoples.

Medical Services Division, Health and Welfare Canada. n.d.. *Business line review.* Ottawa: Medical Services Division, Health and Welfare Canada.

Nozick, Marcia. 1992. *No place like home: Building sustainable communities.* Ottawa: Canadian Council on Social Development.

Osborne, David, and Ted Gaebler. 1993. *Reinventing government: How the entreprenurial spirit is transforming the public sector.* New York: Plume.

Roberts, David. 1994. Listening for ways to heal old wounds. Toronto: *Globe and Mail*, January 7, p. 4.

Royal Commission on Aboriginal Peoples. 1993a. *Partners in confederation: Aboriginal peoples, self-government, and the constitution.* Ottawa: Royal Commission on Aboriginal Peoples.

―――. 1993b. *Focusing the dialogue.* Ottawa: Royal Commission on Aboriginal Peoples.

―――. 1992. *The right of Aboriginal self-government and the Constitution.* Ottawa: Royal Commission on Aboriginal Peoples.

―――. n.d.. *Royal Commission on Aboriginal Peoples: Terms of reference.* Ottawa: Royal Commission on Aboriginal Peoples.

Tait, John. 1991. The constitutional dilemma and the two-track strategy. Pp. 41–45 in *Aboriginal self-determination,* ed. Frank Cassidy. Victoria: Oolichan Books and The Institute for Research on Public Policy.

VanDyke, Edward, and K. C. Jamont. 1980. *Through Indian eyes: Perspectives of Indian constables on the 3b Program in "F" Division.* Regina: Royal Canadian Mounted Police.

Wismer, Susan, and David Pell. 1981. *Community profit: Community-based economic development in Canada.* Toronto: Is Five Press.

CONTRIBUTORS

JOHN W. BERRY is a professor of psychology at Queen's University. His research interests include the psychological study of human diversity and the application of research findings to multiculturalism policy. He has also studied cross-cultural psychology and parallel culturalism in Canada.

CLEM CHARTIER is a Métis lawyer, writer, lecturer, and activist from Buffalo Narrows, Saskatchewan. He has served as an elected official in provincial, national, and international Indigenous organizations.

CAROLYN DITTBURNER is a graduate and former research associate of the School of Public Administration at Carleton University. She has written on Aboriginal public policy issues for the Royal Commission on Aboriginal Peoples and is currently working in the area of community-based self-government with Ian B. Cowie & Associates.

TINA EBERTS studied sociology and psychology at the University of Ottawa. She has worked in the field of Aboriginal training and employment for the past fifteen years. She is currently a senior policy analyst with Human Resources Development Canada.

JOHN W. EKSTEDT is a professor at Simon Fraser University's School of Criminology and co-director of the Institute for Studies in Criminal Justice Policy. He is a member of the National Committee on Aboriginal Justice (Canada). Between 1986 and 1989, he was director of the Canada/Australia Aboriginal Justice Project.

EBER HAMPTON is president of the Saskatchewan Indian Federated College at the University of Regina. A member of the Chickasaw Nation of Oklahoma, he previously served as director of the American Indian Program at Harvard University and as chairman of the Department of Education at the University of Alaska. Dr. Hampton is a graduate of the Harvard Graduate School of Education.

ELIJAH HARPER represented the Rupertsland Constituency in the Manitoba Legislature from 1981 until 1992. He served as minister without portfolio responsible for Native Affairs, and minister of Northern Affairs. He has been an outspoken advocate for Aboriginal rights and, in 1990, was instrumental in blocking passage of the Meech Lake Constitutional Accord. In 1993, he was elected as a Liberal member of Parliament for Churchill.

JOHN H. HYLTON is executive director of the Canadian Mental Health Association in Saskatchewan. His previous publications include books on young offenders, impaired driving, community corrections, and Aboriginal human services. He has been a senior advisor to a number of commissions, including the Manitoba Aboriginal Justice Inquiry and the Royal Commission on Aboriginal Peoples. Dr. Hylton holds graduate degrees from Carleton University and the University of California, Berkeley.

259

MARGARET A. JACKSON is an Associate Professor in the School of Criminology at Simon Fraser University, and co-director of the Institute for Studies in Criminal Justice Policy. Her research interests include Aboriginal justice, clinical criminology, corrections, violence against women, sentencing, and criminal justice policy and planning. Dr. Jackson is a member of the National Committee on Aboriginal Justice (Canada), and co-director of the International Aboriginal Justice Network.

CAROL LA PRAIRIE holds a Ph.D. in sociology from the University of British Columbia. She has been active in research and writing on Aboriginal justice issues for over fifteen years. Dr. LaPrairie is employed with the federal Department of Justice's Aboriginal Justice Directorate.

ALLAN M. MASLOVE is a professor in the School of Public Administration at Carleton University. A economist specializing in public finance, he has written extensively on financing and fiscal arrangements for Aboriginal governments. He has served as an advisor to Aboriginal communities and to the Royal Commission on Aboriginal Peoples. Dr. Maslove is a graduate of the Universities of Manitoba and Minnesota.

JOHN D. O'NEIL is an associate professor and National Health research scholar in the Department of Community Health Sciences at the University of Manitoba, where he also directs the Northern Health Research Unit. For the past eighteen years, he has investigated cultural factors affecting the delivery of health services to Aboriginal communities in Canada, Australia, and Siberia. Dr. O'Neil received his Ph.D. in medical anthropology from the University of California (San Francisco-Berkeley).

EVELYN J. PETERS is an associate professor with the Geography Department at Queen's University. Her area of specialization is social geography. Dr. Peters has a long-standing research interest in Aboriginal self-government.

BRIAN O. POSTL is professor and head of the Department of Community Health Sciences at the University of Manitoba, and professor in the Department of Paediatrics and Child Health. A physician and member of the Royal College of Physicians, he has an extensive record of research and publications pertaining to Aboriginal health issues. Dr. Postl is currently co-chair of the Manitoba Provincial Task Force on Child Health.

MURRAY SINCLAIR is associate chief judge of the Manitoba Provincial Court. An Ojibwa from the Selkirk area of Manitoba, he was Manitoba's first, and Canada's second, Aboriginal judge. In 1991, together with Justice A.C. Hamilton of the Manitoba Court of Queen's Bench, he co-authored the widely acclaimed report of the Manitoba Aboriginal Justice Inquiry.

MARLENE WELLS is an honors graduate in psychology from Queen's University. Her research interests focus on attitudes toward Aboriginal self-government and land rights.

STEVEN WOLFSON holds a dental degree from the University of Pennsylvania and a master's degree in public health from the University of Minnesota. As well as writing and producing films, he is a health and education consultant, and sessional instructor at the Saskatchewan Indian Federated College.

INDEX